Science and social science

Is social science really a science at all, and if so in what sense? This is the first question that any course on the philosophy of the social sciences must tackle. In this brief introduction, Malcolm Williams gives students the grounding that will enable them to discuss the issues involved with confidence. He looks at:

- The historical development of natural science and its distinctive methodology
- The case in favour of an objective 'science of the social' which follows the same rules
- The arguments of social constructionists, interpretative sociologists and others against objectivity and even science itself
- Recent developments in natural science – for instance the rise of complexity theory and the increased questioning of positivism – which bring it closer to some of the key arguments of social science

Throughout, the book is illustrated with short, clear examples taken from the actual practice of social science research and from popular works of natural science which will illuminate the debate for all students whatever their background.

Malcolm Williams is a Senior Lecturer in sociology at the University of Plymouth.

Science and Social Science
An introduction

Malcolm Williams

London and New York

First published 2000 by Routledge
11 New Fetter Lane, London EC4P 4EE

Routledge is an imprint of Taylor & Francis Group

Simultaneously published in the USA and Canada
by Routledge
29 West 35th Street, New York, NY 10001

© 2000 Malcolm Williams

Typeset in Sabon by Routledge
Printed and bound in Great Britain by TJ International Ltd, Padstow,
Cornwall

British Library Cataloguing in Publication Data
A catalogue record for this book is available from the British Library

Library of Congress Cataloging in Publication Data
Williams, Malcolm, 1953–
Science and social science: an introduction / Malcolm Williams.
p. cm.
Includes bibliographical references and index.
1. Social sciences–Methodology. 2. Science–Methodology.
3. Social sciences–Philosophy. 4. Science–Philosophy. I. Title.
H61.W5576 1999
300'.1–dc21   99–33225
                                                 CIP

ISBN 0–415–19484–9 (hbk)
ISBN 0–415–19485–7 (pbk)

I do not know what I may appear to the world, but to myself I seem to have been only like a boy playing on the sea shore and diverting myself in now and then finding a smoother pebble or a prettier shell than ordinary, whilst the great ocean of truth lay all undiscovered before me.

Isaac Newton (cited in R.L. Weber, *A Random Walk in Science*, 1973)

Contents

Acknowledgements

Many people wittingly or unwittingly helped me in the writing of this book. For conversations, ideas, suggestions and material support I would like to thank Dave Byrne, Joan Chandler, Ken Connolly, Neil Cooper, Steve Fuller and Matt Treadwell. Dave Byrne, Elizabeth Ettorre, Robin Hendry, Liz Hodgkinson, Tim May and two anonymous referees read various chapters and made many helpful recommendations. Especial thanks to Tim for his encouragement, to Robin who saved me from too many scientific *faux pas* (though of course the responsibility for particular interpretations, or remaining errors, is mine alone) and to Liz, John and Laura for their love and support. Finally I would like to express my gratitude to Mari Shullaw, Ruth Graham, Shankari Sanmuganathan and the production team at Routledge for guiding this book from idea to actuality.

Introduction

Science and social science have been uneasy bedfellows. Investigators of the social world are divided between those who are convinced that what they do is science, those who are convinced it is not (and do not call themselves scientists) and those who are uncertain. My own position is sympathetic to the first group in that I believe that scientific social science is both possible and desirable. But that does not make me uncritical of science generally, or of social science that claims such credentials. The orientation of this book is, then, critically pro-science.

This book is an *introduction* to science and social science and is such in two senses:

It is an introduction to some of the key issues that divide advocates of science in social science from those who oppose it. Mainly, however, it is an introduction to science for those concerned with investigating the social world as students or professionals, as theorists or researchers. This does, however, beg the question of why such people would want to know about science?

My answer to this is twofold. First, it is because the status of social science is so contested it is important to know what science is in the first place. Only then can an informed view be taken. Historically I do not think this has been the case for most students of social science. Their experience has so often been an exposure to science and scientific method in the form of an uncomfortable mix of critical reflection on philosophical issues in science and science taken neat in the form of statistics. The two rarely connect and mixed messages and confusion ensue. Moreover, for many, the social sciences have been a haven from (in George Steiner's words) 'the murderous gadgetry of the age' (Steiner 1989: 49), or at least from the machismo of mathematics and the laboratory. So many enter social science because they are critical of the social order and part of that social order is science and its emergent technology. This may, or may not, be combined with a distaste for the supposed intellectual certainties purveyed by science. In other words so many social scientists begin as ideological or intellectual rebels. Science, as understood in this way, is not an obvious destination. In this book I want to present an opposite view:

that social scientists should reclaim science as being as much theirs as it is the physicist's or biologist's. But to do this it is important to know something of science.

Second, by excluding social science from science it becomes possible for natural scientists, particularly biologists, to lay claim to authority in providing explanations of social life. In the late 1990s popularisers of biological determinism have been more successful in getting their message across (at least in the sense that they sell more books) than those in the social sciences who oppose biological determinism (see for example Dawkins 1988, 1989; Herrnstein and Murray 1994; Ridley 1997). But of course the opposition from social science is so often a knee-jerk reaction rather than an engagement with the arguments presented. Maybe human behaviour is driven in some sense by the genes we have, maybe it is not, but to assume either position prior to understanding at least something of the arguments of the other is foolish and arrogant. This of course is true for both social and natural scientists. It is not beyond the bounds of possibility that there is some middle way which we are yet to discover – after all there has to be some kind of bridge between the social and biological world. As Peter Dickens remarks of sociology: 'pulling up the proverbial drawbridge around sociology is no substitute for relaxing disciplinary boundaries and recognising that neighbouring disciplines may well have much to offer' (Dickens 1998: 32).

There is, I believe, an even stronger reason for relaxing the boundaries between the social and natural sciences and it lies in a shift in the *weltanschaung* of natural science itself. This shift has been taking place for much of the century and is not yet complete, but has gained momentum in many of the sciences, particularly in the last few years. It can be characterised first as the embracing of probabilistic (as opposed to deterministic) ways of knowing the world. Probabilistic in two senses: that the laws that govern the way the world is, are themselves probabilistic and that scientific knowledge itself is probable and not certain.

Second, it is the acceptance that new characteristics can emerge from systems and these characteristics cannot necessarily be anticipated from descriptions of the systems from which they emerged. Third, 'atomistic' views of nature as divisible into discrete and identifiable bits have been largely discredited, and lastly, the view of science as being outside and beyond a wider value system in the social world has been exposed as myth.

The implication of this change is the possibility of a new wider conception of science as embracing studies of the physical and social world in which the latter can be seen as an emergent, but non-reducible property of the former or indeed in some cases vice versa. That is, the social world is connected to the physical world, but there is no one-to-one *necessary* connection between a physical characteristic and a social property. The source of the past divide and rejection of science by many social scientists was the belief that the only model of science available was deterministic, atomistic and dependent upon a credo of 'value freedom'. A science of the social world allegedly based upon these principles had been tried and found wanting (Philips 1987: chapter 4). However, a probabilistic, holistic, socially aware science may be a different matter and may eventually lead to an interdisciplinary approach to knowing the world (as opposed to knowing its separate physical and social manifestations).

Nevertheless there are many who seek to know the social world that do not start from the view that such a merger is a good thing, nor would they accept that an understanding of science would help at all in their task of knowing the social world. For someone who takes this view science is as irrelevant to them as it would be to a sculptor, or a composer. I am not wholly unsympathetic to this view. As a consumer of travel writing I look more for literary skills and a sense of place than I do for pin sharp and accurate description. But of course attempts to know the social world in this way are not social science, nor much of the time do they pretend to be such, preferring instead the description of cultural studies, or social appreciation. This is art and must be appreciated as such.

Social science becomes science (or potentially so) only when it has pretensions to produce descriptions and explanations of the social world that are meant to carry authority beyond the specific instances in which they take place. When Van Gogh painted his evocative scenes of Provence his only statement was a personal one of what that landscape meant to him at that moment. I do not believe he was saying 'this is what Provence is like', simply this is what it is like for me. This is quite different to even the most modest claim in social investigation. Leaving aside those 'studies' of the social world that make no more than aesthetic claims, it is the case that most activity of professional engagement with the social world is labelled 'research', or 'investigation', and at least implicitly seeks to make a statement that the social world (or part of it) is like this, or like that. The descriptions and explanations are intended to indicate that the investigator has learnt something tangible that is more than art or fiction. That this is going on is quite often denied and the investigations are termed 'thick description' (Geertz 1979), or 'interpretive interactionism' (Denzin 1983) and are intended to establish an intellectual authority, yet one that is not science.

A peculiarity of the denial of science in social science is that those who make such denials are so certain about the character of what it is they deny. Few philosophers or historians of science share this certainty and in this book I want to suggest that a rigid ahistorical model of science is neither tenable, nor desirable. Nevertheless I will suggest that despite historical contingency it is possible to define science as an activity which can provide objective knowledge of the world.

What to expect from this book

This book is about science in two respects. Firstly it is about science in the abstract, its history, its method and indeed the philosophical problems that are associated with method in science. It is also concrete in that it is about how history, society and philosophy embodied in method are made manifest in the activity of empirical science, both natural and social. Sometimes in this book the focus will be soft in order to make illustrative points. Other times the arguments will be more specific. The hope and intention is that the reader will emerge with at least some understanding of science in both its natural and social form and will be stimulated to enquire further.

This book is not a detailed exposition of the history of science, nor its method. Neither is it meant to be a meticulous and rigorous argument for science in social science. Others have done each of these tasks much more adequately than I am capable of doing. For this reason my illustrations from the history and practice of both sciences are not detailed and my examples from the natural sciences are mostly culled from works of popular science. First, this is because if this book is to arouse an interest amongst social scientists in what natural scientists do, then it must be accessible. Part of that accessibility is that the reader should be able to refer, in the first instance, to non-technical sources for more detailed information. Second, because I believe that if a general grasp of science (and here I include social science) cannot be gained by the educated lay person, then public understanding of science is not achievable. I believe in the value of the public understanding of science in both its natural and social forms, because I believe as an enterprise which impacts upon the lives of many more than are engaged in it, it should be accountable and accessible. This, however, does not mean I advocate or believe that a lay person should be *au fait* with the mathematics of the Planck Constant, or be able to work out a correlation co-efficient. Fortunately you do not need to do either to understand what is important in science. In this spirit, throughout the book, I have tried to keep technical language to a minimum, and for the most part offer only brief descriptions of natural and social science examples. For readers who require more I have made some suggestions for further reading at the end of each chapter, and at the end of the book have provided a glossary of natural science, or philosophical terms I use, but have not defined further in the text.

Though this book is concerned with science and *social* science, much of it is concerned with describing the origins, methods and controversies of natural science. This is for the very good reason that if one wishes to claim that the social sciences are science, then one must turn to the history and practice of science to explore generic features and problems. The exploration of these problems has, for the most part, been in the history, philosophy and sociology of natural science. It is perhaps telling that few methodological or philosophical questions in social science have been exported the other way. Briefly then, the plan of the book is as follows:

In Chapter 1 I focus on a few episodes in the history of science in order to demonstrate how it emerged as a social practice as the result of a dynamic encounter between its internal character, as a discipline, and external factors in the social world. However, my concern is that if we see science as wholly historically contingent then it could be characterised as simply what scientists do, which does not explain the growth of scientific knowledge. In the past few decades philosophers of science have attempted to characterise science through its method. Yet, as I suggest in Chapter 2, this is not without its difficulties. In Chapter 1 I suggest science arises out of human curiosity, but although science follows the same cognitive pattern of discovery as in everyday life, its cumulative knowledge distances it from the commonplace often making its findings or method counter-intuitive. But what gives science its intellectual authority, if it is historically contingent? Whilst I argue that attempts such as Karl Popper's to produce a logical demarcation criterion between science and non-science is unworkable, I conclude that scientific method must be seen as a heteroge-neous system of checks and balances involving theory choice, testing and inference, but because science is a human enterprise the final court of appeal for scientific findings is human consciousness.

Many of the philosophical problems about method exist in social science too, but a longstanding question has been what is it that makes, or can make, studies of the social world scientific? In Chapter 3 I explore 'naturalist' arguments for a 'science' of the social, maintaining that although the social sciences can rarely aspire to the levels of certainty achieved in physical laws, these even in natural science are not common-place and for the most part the natural sciences and the social sciences must depend on probabilistic explanation. This and the previous chapter represent the affirmative case for science in its natural and social forms, but there are opponents, of science in general and more specifically opponents of social science as science. In Chapter 4 I examine some arguments against science. The first of these I characterise as 'rejectionist' and the second 'social constructionist'. Rejectionism opposes science on moral or political grounds, but here I argue that whilst it is quite reasonable to demand that science abandons those things its detractors oppose, we cannot abandon science itself – such an option is not open to us. Social constructionism, I concede, has a case, in so far as science is a social practice, but if we view science as *only* a social practice then it becomes difficult to explain the huge predictive success and consistency of explanations through the history of science.

Opposition to science in social science can be part of a generalised opposition, or scepticism about science, but it also takes a specific form. 'Anti-naturalism' in social 'science' has found its most successful articula-tion in interpretivism. In Chapter 5 I examine anti-naturalist views through the methodological strategy of interpretivism. Here I show that through the use of interpretive methods, anti-naturalists wish to have it 'both ways'; that is, they claim as much for their approach in understanding the social as social scientists do through prediction and explanation, yet they deny the latter is possible. Their denial rests in an ontological claim of variability in the social world, arising from the reflective nature of consciousness. Whilst conceding that such variability exists, I argue that it is not as 'variable' as is claimed, nor does it rule out prediction and explanation. I nevertheless conclude that the case for interpretive methods is a strong one, but this can take place within a naturalistic social science.

Chapter 6 returns to a question arising from the social character of science. If one accepts that science is indeed social, then positivistic notions of value freedom are hard to defend. Instead I argue that what is seen as value neutral in science, in particular measurement, has social antecedents. Yet whilst this is undoubtedly true, there remains a need in science for an objective stance. A number of thinkers have attempted to square these two apparent contradictions and I illustrate these attempts with reference to the work of Max Weber and Helen Longino. The latter, in particular, has produced a subtle redefinition of objectivity as 'transformative interrogation' in the scientific community. Whilst this attempt is to be applauded I conclude that it simply replaces objectivity with intersubjectivity. I propose instead that objectivity be treated as a value, but one necessary to science, if it is to transcend the contingent nature of history represented as one ethical imperative or another. Indeed I argue that the scientist, though inevitably a citizen with views about the purpose and nature of scientific research, is defined only as the former through an objective stance.

In Chapter 7 I look at the possibilities not only of social science as science, but of the possibility of an integration of science. In particular I point to recent developments in complexity and emergence in both the natural and social sciences. This, I suggest, should be viewed optimistically, though cautiously. During this century natural science has gradually abandoned determinism, substituting in its place probability. Now whilst the latter has, in practice at least, been the way social science has known macro level phenomena, it has only been in recent years that developments in complexity theory have shown the way towards a more unified way of seeing the world. I conclude that though a synthesis does offer the promise of an eventual unity of science, it is not one that is a unity of disciplines, but instead an interdisciplinary approach to knowing the world.

Though the intention has not been to produce a meticulous and detailed analysis of the issues I raise, there is nevertheless much detail that is left out from this book that I would like to have included. In particular the status of psychology as the bridge between the social and the natural world is all but ignored. For the most part I would include psychology under the rubric of 'social' science in that it cannot ignore the existence and development of individual consciousness in isolation of other agents. But of course at the 'other end' of psychology the focus is firmly biological and here it would be more appropriate to consider psychology as a natural science. The difficulty I have here is symptomatic of a more general difficulty inherent in making a divide between the natural and the social sciences. For the most part I find this divide artificial and constricting and find myself supporting the philosopher Karl Popper's dictum that we are students of a problem not a discipline.

Note on terminology

I have used the terms natural science and social science in their orthodox, one might say normative, form here, though I have used the term physical world to refer to what philosophers called 'extended matter', that is things that have a physical as opposed to a mental or social existence. I use the term social science to refer to all of those disciplines, or parts thereof, that purport to describe or explain social life.

1   Where did science come from?

In the Introduction I tried to give some flavour of the controversies surrounding science, both as an activity in its own right, but also in its role in investigations of the social world. Before we can confront these matters we need to get some clearer views of what science is. This is the task of the next two chapters. In this chapter I want to look at a few episodes of what counted as science (particularly natural science) in past times in order to identify what kind of factors have been important in defining such practices as 'scientific'. Second, I want to show, again with some brevity, how it was that studies of the social world came to be called science.

The dynamic of science

Science is not miraculous, nor is its contemporary manifestation the result of miraculous birth. As a social activity it is of human parentage and like all offspring it has evolved characteristics of its own, though it has retained many of those of its parents. If we stand in awe of science, we stand in awe of ourselves. The history of science is not simply a dialectical development of a relationship of human beings with nature, but also of scientists with their theories, and scientists with society. Society here is shorthand for religion, philosophy, ideology and politics. By this I mean that the romantic idea of the lone scientist pitted against nature is just one small part of the picture. Nature, as the scientist imagines it, is the product of scientific theories, themselves rooted in a philosophical world view. This in turn may have been shaped by politics or religion. Moreover world views may themselves have been shaped by the discoveries of earlier scientists.

We can summarise three interrelated characteristics:

1   *The relationship between metaphysics and science*. Early science was mystical and bound up with religious beliefs about nature and the universe. What we might see as recognisably scientific content was small. Yet

throughout the history of science a desire to know the meaning of the universe was a key motivation. Post-Renaissance science is 'anti-mystical', but must still depend on some metaphysical assumptions.

2 *The social position of science.* This comprises a number of characteristics. The first is the separation of scientific activity and everyday activity. The second is the relationship between science and society, in which the character or power of one has been a formative influence upon the other. The way in which society shapes science can itself arise directly, or indirectly (perhaps through moral prescription) from metaphysical belief. The third characteristic is power: the power of science can be utilised or challenged from society. The most famous early example of this was the trial of Socrates (*c.*470–395 BC), who was sentenced to death by the Athenian Assembly for impiety and corrupting youth through his ideas (Russell 1979: 103–7). This was the persecution of science, but perhaps more important has been what Tolstoy refers to as 'the knowledge–power feedback loop' (Tolstoy 1990: ix), as science became more effective, so it became more desirable as a tool of economic prosperity, or war, and this in turn led to further scientific development.

3 *The cognitive development of human beings.* The learning capacity and reasoning ability of scientists has developed and increased incrementally (with some setbacks) through the history of science. The cognitive abilities of scientists at each stage of science have been an important characteristic and sometimes limiting feature. The insights of one age become the methodological tools of another. Some of these developments (described below), such as 'Thales' leap', Aristotle's development of deductive logic or Galileo's use of experimental method, are documented events, but like most discoveries about the world, these can mostly be seen as markers of the cognitive development of science at that time.

The emergence of unnatural thinking

In the beginning there was curiosity and a need to resolve problems, mostly those of survival. Humans learnt to hunt with primitive axes, which in turn gave way to arrows and once the effectiveness of hunting with arrows was established they were improved by using different materials, first iron and later bronze. But bronze required smelting and smelting required fire. The copper and tin themselves needed extracting and this, along with the smelting, required co-operation. Thus in early society we see evidence of technological success achieved through increasing cognitive abilities and social co-operation, some of the hallmarks of what was to become science.

As societies became more complex the role of ritual and metaphysical belief became more important. These beliefs informed and were informed by a desire and ability to measure and explain. The Babylonians,

Egyptians, Greeks and Romans set great store in predicting the future, which can perhaps be seen as evidence of a desire to know beyond the material, but crucially for the development of science it led to the emergence of a cognitive élite. The 'scientific' development of early society served the pragmatic needs of survival, but perhaps the emergence of a metaphysical curiosity was a necessary precursor to a scientific one?

An abstract metaphysical curiosity was the hallmark of growing social complexity and of urbanisation. This in turn went hand in hand with commerce and required a reliable system of measurement; one which, as Tolstoy notes, provided 'a continuous running check on the validity of methods' (Tolstoy 1990: 58). This was also the point where a segregation occurred between the 'superior' activities of mind and the 'inferior' activities of manufacturing (*ibid.*). The cognitive élite in many early societies may have been a priesthood; certainly in societies such as Babylon, where astrological abilities were prized, those with such skills would have been an élite. Of course, the precise evidence from these societies is fragmented and disputed, but it remains that by the time such endeavours were recorded by the Greeks a division of labour between the material and the intellectual was well established.

From our vantage point in the twentieth century we have to understand that there was no separation in intellectual activities between the meta-physical and the development of the technological (though of course there was between these and the employment of technology). For example, the development of the Egyptian calendar allowed accurate prediction of the flooding of the Nile, thus allowing a more successful prosecution of agriculture. Yet although this was achieved as a result of astronomical observation, the constellations themselves were identified with the deities. Science and religion were one and the same. If the 'scientists' could predict the flooding of the Nile, then presumably the view that 'The sky was a flat or vaulted ceiling supported by four columns or mountain peaks, and the stars were lamps hung from the sky by cables' (Dampier 1966: 6–7) would have been taken equally seriously. Of course much of the science was wrong, though it did often lead to accurate prediction and is therefore better described as right for the wrong reasons. It did, however, demonstrate the ability for social co-operation in the pursuit of knowledge and the means to employ this knowledge practically, but also it was the desire to find meaning in the world. Finally, it was an activity that was conducted by a sub-group of society.

For Lewis Wolpert (1992) the foregoing, though evidence of advanced technological thinking, does not amount to science. He maintains that science emerged only when there was a separation between what he calls 'natural' and 'unnatural' thinking. This separation, he believes, first took place in ancient Greece (Wolpert 1992: xii) and amounts to a cognitive disjuncture between common sense curiosity and scientific curiosity. Wolpert presents us with a number of simple scientific propositions which he believes to be counter-intuitive to the non-scientist. For example, the common sense view is that the natural state of any object is that it is at rest, but post-Newton scientists know that the natural state is for an object to move at a constant speed until stopped (Wolpert 1992: 3). Likewise few are aware that white light is composed of the colours of the spectrum. We can, he maintains, point to particular departures from unnatural thinking in classical civilisation and he accords the honour of being the first scientist to Thales of Miletos, who lived around 600 BC (Wolpert 1992: 35). The latter's contribution was to question the prevailing metaphysical ideas of the day to ask, 'What is the world made of?' His answer was 'water' – and of course wrong – but according to Wolpert, the fact that he could propose something that was so counter-intuitive prefigured such later successful propositions. Perhaps as importantly Thales provided a number of important mathematical insights, such as the observation that if two straight lines cut each other, the opposite angles are equal. As Wolpert remarks:

> Here, for the first time, were general statements about lines and circles – statements of a kind never made before. They were general statements that applied to *all* circles and lines everywhere ...
>
> (Wolpert 1992: 37)

Though generalisation was not new (Egyptian cosmology generalised), those that had a longevity beyond their historical setting were. Thales' contribution was, therefore, not simply lateral thinking, but some foundational mathematics, an essential tool for later science.

Wolpert's distinction is a useful one and offers a continuity with modern science: though still deriving from curiosity, science, however motivated, is rarely common sense. However, as Wolpert himself notes there is a circularity in the argument that science is 'unnatural'. If it were 'natural' and just a matter of common sense observation, then there would be no science to explain anyway. (I shall return to the question of curiosity in Chapter 2.) Moreover, what is known as 'Thales' leap' cannot be wholly attributed to one man's ability to think laterally, but also to the existence of a 'scientific', or at least proto-scientific culture and metaphysical foundation that allowed such a leap to be made.

Indeed it was not just Thales who leapt. Greek philosophical ideas were of immense importance to both science and to Western civilisation generally (see Russell 1979: parts 1 and 2). Perhaps the greatest contribution to science came from Aristotle (384–322 BC), though, like Thales, much of his science was 'wrong'; he too gave science an important tool, that of the syllogism. A syllogistic argument has two premises from which a conclusion is entailed. The conclusion can be deduced from the premises, as in the example below.

Premises:
   All mammals are warm blooded animals
   No lizards are warm blooded animals

Conclusion:
   Therefore no lizards are mammals

Science, as we shall see, depends on deduction – on this kind of argument – though we must be careful here, for a conclusion following from premises does not entail the truth of the premises, but what deduction gives us is a rational structure to argument (see Weston 1992). With the formulation of this way of thinking we also have the beginning of rationality, that is, to deny conclusions once we have accepted the premises from which they are derived would be an irrational act.

Deductive logic is a *formalisation* of patterns of inference (people inferred before formal logic) and provided a framework for science. It is often said that post-Renaissance science produced the culture of rationality that is the hallmark of modern science, but of course to a great extent the opposite had to be true. For rational science to gain legitimacy at least some semblance of a wider culture of rationality had to exist in society (Tarnas 1991: 224–32). The relationship between science and rationality might be seen as a symbiotic one.

In the name of God

With the decline of Classical Greek civilisation and the rise of the Roman Empire scientific endeavour declined, at least in Europe. It continued to flourish in the Muslim world, however, and important advances were made, particularly in mathematics and specifically through the invention of algebra, but from the beginning of the Christian era to the late Middle Ages scientific discovery, as opposed to its utilisation, did not flourish in the West. The cognitive development of science was hampered by the metaphysical basis of science in early Christian civilisation and by the social structure that arose from the Christian hegemony. Nevertheless, because there was little scientific advance on the achievements of the Greeks did not mean that the period was intellectually barren. The medieval period was one of enormous accomplishment, but this was in many ways spiritual. The great architecture of the cathedrals, though displaying enormous technical skill, were dedications to a spiritual faith. Curiosity was not absent but found its expression in Christian endeavours to attain divine knowledge. The metaphysical centre of gravity, as it were, was the Holy Spirit (Tarnas 1991: 156).

The Christian Church's power – spiritual, ideological and political – extended to all aspects of life. Within its embrace was contained much of that which was progressive, innovatory, barbaric and conservative. Although the power of the Church in society was enormous, alongside it a new economic order was taking shape, one that grew out of the success of agriculture and widespread commerce and was centred on the towns. With urbanisation came important advances in technological ability, which in turn improved commercial efficiency, prompting more investment in technology (Tolstoy 1990: 100). The Church itself was, of course, a major participant in medieval commerce and the source of much of the technological innovation. Indeed much of the learning of medieval Europe was either monastic, or under the auspices of the Church. Philosophers such as St Thomas Aquinas, William of Ockham and Roger Bacon were all churchmen. The Church, then, both set metaphysical limits on science as well as being the repository of knowledge – including scientific knowledge.

What were the metaphysical limits and how was this different to Classical Greece? In terms of scientific development the end of Classical Greek civilisation was also its apex. A product of this early scientific world view, or indeed possibly contributing to such a view, was a growing philosophical secularism, a shift from astrology and theism, first to the pantheism of the Stoics, but eventually in Epicurus to a philosophy which denied the existence of gods as the creators of nature. Epicurus' view was that gods were simply part of nature as humans are and that there is a finality in death (Dampier 1966: 39). Such views as this were not to be expressed again widely in the West until the Renaissance; the medieval world view was militantly anti-secular and this extended to learning. All sanctioned learning was in the service, or at least context, of theistic knowledge, whereby philosophical ideas – often the inspiration to scientific activity in Greece – were in the service of theology. Yet the very early Christian Church made a conscious effort to fuse together Christianity with Greek philosophy. The result was successful in terms of the ideological longevity of Christianity, yet, rather like Chinese whispers, what survived of the philosophy in medieval Europe was a faint echo. Aristotle's work survived, though in imperfect form and mainly expressed through his logical principles, themselves the basis of attempts to 'prove' the existence of God (Russell 1979: chapter 13), or through his physics of the direct perception of substance, essence, matter, form, quality and quantity. This, in Wolpert's term, was a 'natural' physics, which accorded with experience, but was wrong.

The doldrums into which science had sunk were dominated by mysticism sanctioned by ideology, limiting the cognitive development of science to the bounds of theology. Indeed, as we shall see in the case of Galileo, to enquire too much into the nature of reality was impiety, even heresy, not just because it challenged the hegemony of the Church, or a Church-dominated intellectual and political élite, but also because it undermined the spiritual security of the afterlife (Dampier 1966: chapter 2).

Galileo and the birth of modern science

Galileo (1564–1642) has often been called the 'father of modern science'. His work in dynamics and astronomy was certainly foundational for the version of science as we know it, but just as importantly for our purposes, he personifies the clash between secularism and mysticism, Enlightenment and medievalism and specifically between science and the Christian Church. Before considering Galileo and his ideas it is necessary to briefly say how the transition from the theistic medieval world came to pass.

Tolstoy (1990) calls the period between the fall of the Roman Empire and the Renaissance a period of transition between the science of the classical world and the modern one. The social and technological bases of modern science were laid down in this period of transition, and even though theology set limits to philosophy, ideas of great importance to later science evolved. One particular example is Ockham's Razor (named after a Franciscan monk, William of Ockham, *c.*1285–1349), the principle of parsimony, usually expressed as 'entities should not be multiplied beyond necessity', a principle important in choosing between scientific theories and a matter I will return to in Chapter 2.

The head on clash between science and religion came with the challenging of theological *a priori* truths with observation *and* reasoning – Wolpert's 'unnatural thinking'. Galileo's difficulties with the Inquisition are perhaps the most celebrated example of this. Two things are of importance here: first, what it was Galileo was challenging and what that challenge was, and second this as an exemplar, not of the formal defeat of Galileo (for that is what happened at his trial), but as the beginning of the end for Christian theology as a ruling ideology in the West.

I have noted above the importation of Aristotelian thought into Christian philosophy and science. With some modifications Aristotle's mechanics and cosmology had become the Christian world view. Galileo challenged both. Aristotle's physics appealed to common sense. The world, it was said, was made up of four elements: earth, fire, air and water. Fire moves upwards and earth moves downwards, thus the natural place of rocks is the centre of the earth, of water resting on the earth and of fire between the air and the surface of a sphere separating the earth from the heavens. It follows from this that motion will continue until the object moves to rest as close as it can to its natural place. The heavier a solid object, the more quickly it will fall to its natural place of rest – the centre of the earth. Galileo demonstrated that objects of different weights (assuming the same air resistance) will fall to the earth at the same speed. These experiments in dynamics and the claims that followed from them were not the focus of the dispute with the Church, but instead cosmological claims were. Aristotle's four earthly elements (he added a fifth heavenly one of the aether) were characterised by rectilinear and discontinuous motion, whereas the moon, the sun, the planets and stars were continuous and circular, a fact which was observationally demonstrable, as was their motion around the earth. These bodies were 'perfect and incorruptible' (Dampier 1966: 30) and thus evidence of a final mover – that of God.

Aristotelian cosmology was, like the medieval mysticism it served, of an *a priori* kind, that is, observations had to fit the existing metaphysical schema, and to challenge that schema was to challenge God. Perhaps it was because even prior to Galileo's published work the ideas of Copernicus and Galileo's contemporary Kepler were gaining ground and even finding wider intellectual acceptance, that the church took such exception to Galileo's views. Nicolaus Copernicus (1473–1543), in his *Commentariolus*, had first publicly proposed a heliocentric view of the universe, and this view was developed through the observations of Tycho Brahe (1546–1601) and later energetically championed by Johannes Kepler (1571–1630), but although each reasoned mathematically from observation and, in the course of so doing, abandoned an Aristotelian or Ptolemaic *a priori* anthropocentric cosmology, their views were simply regarded as 'hypotheses' and attempts to save the philosophical status quo. Galileo's contribution was not then seminal, but it was crucial in so far as his observations utilised a new and powerful technology – that of the telescope. He showed that the moon was mountainous and not a perfect sphere, he demonstrated the existence of the moons of Jupiter. The cosmos he showed to be vast, not just spheres in a relatively near aether. What is crucial, however, is that his reasoning began from observation and did not depend on immutable philosophical principles. His trial then was not an argument about the truth or falsity of particular premises, but was a clash between two metaphysical standpoints. Alfred North Whitehead put it rather well when he noted that 'Galileo keeps harping on how things happen, whereas his adversaries had a complete theory as to why things happen' (Whitehead 1997: 59).

In Galileo's trial we seen dramatically how science, metaphysics and the social world, here represented by the Church, come dramatically into conflict. In his use of deduction and induction we see the cognitive advances of earlier science becoming the technical ability of a later one, and in his willingness to publish we see the use of science to shape thought. However, perhaps the most important departure arose through the deployment of experimental method. I mean this both in the technical importance of this way of doing science, but also in the way it helped the scientist to regard the world as comprising objects to be manipulated, as separate to the scientist and the everyday. Actually scientific objectivity was born of Galileo in two ways, both in his view of the world as objects to be known by the scientist, and in his refusal to allow the ideological orthodoxy to determine the interpretation of his findings. Though these have since become conflated in science, it remains that they marked an important departure from a common sense 'ought' view of nature to a scientific 'is' one. Whether we can strictly delimit these is another matter and one I will return to in Chapter 6. This way of looking at the world has become an important part of the scientific attitude, but also it lies at the basis of claims that science is 'other', divorced from the humanity which created it.

Newton and the 'clockwork' universe

If Galileo's fame is at least partially iconic, the same is not true of Isaac Newton (1642–1727). Indeed such has been the impact of Newton on science and Western thought in general that many have seen the era of science that his discoveries heralded as being *the* scientific era, or at least a paradigm, as Kuhn ([1962] 1970) termed it, within which all other science, or thinking about science operated. The scientific world view was largely that which came in to being as a result of how Newton described and explained the physical world.

Newton's description and explanation of movement has been frequently likened to a clockwork model of the universe. A clock is dependable, predictable in its movement and obeys a straightforward everyday notion of cause and effect. Newton's work spanned gravitation, mechanics, optics and mathematics, though his three laws of motion are perhaps the ones which most influentially shaped the scientific world view. His first law states that bodies not subject to a force will continue to travel in straight lines. His second states that if a force is applied to a body, its momentum will increase in the direction of the application of the force; for a body whose mass does not change, the resulting rate of increasing speed is equal to the force divided by the mass. His third law states that for every action there corresponds an equal and opposite reaction.

Perhaps the law that led most directly to the appellation 'clockwork' being given to the explanation of movement is his law of gravitation. This states that two spheres, for example the sun and the earth, exert upon each other forces of attraction varying inversely with the square of the distance between their centres. This law, though independent of his laws of motion, can be said to provide a force function, which in conjunction with the latter provides an explanation of how gravitational force is expressed in the motion of objects. These relatively simple axioms gave rise to a model of the solar system that was dependable and predictable (Tolstoy 1990: 168) and until this century lay at the basis of our understanding of the cosmos, but just as importantly they provided both an exemplar of how science should be done and a model of what the world is really like.

I do not wish to create the impression that certainty was born of Newton, but rather that Newton's discoveries were taken by many as a demonstration of the possibility of certainty in science. They ushered in an age of great optimism in philosophy and confidence in science. Indeed, that science and philosophy remained substantially a unified venture, i.e. that many 'scientists' were 'philosophers' and vice versa, meant that the advances in science directly influenced those of thought, which in turn fed back into science. Though the scope and success of Newton's work was unrivalled in its time and perhaps until that of Einstein in the twentieth century, the world he inhabited was not intellectually lonely and there was an important cross-fertilisation of ideas. He corresponded with Leibniz and Bernoulli, he knew Locke and Pepys and had an enormous influence on the US President Thomas Jefferson, himself first a scientist and second a politician (Holton 1993: 110).

Newton's success and much of his fame undoubtedly arose from the predictive and explanatory success of his methods. Though there was nothing really new about his approach – it was one advocated by Aristotle and Roger Bacon (Losee 1980: 55) – it was nevertheless superior to theirs in that it depended on the experimental confirmation of consequences deduced from axioms. For example Newton's third law stated that for every action there is an equal and opposite reaction. If these axioms hold true we can deduce the effect of one body on another; if our deductions are correct the bodies should be observed to behave accordingly. A consequence of this apparently foolproof way to knowledge was a reification of this approach to science and eventually a reification of science itself. The popular view of Newton is that his method amounted to a claim to certain knowledge, i.e. that the deduction of key axioms and their confirmation, through experiment, would allow a calculation of every possible state the universe could be in. As well as 'clockwork', the phrase 'mechanistic' is often used to describe the Newtonian universe. The doctrine of metaphysical determinism (that is, everything that happens in the universe is determined by prior conditions and that it could be no other way), though not new, was given empirical authority because of the success of Newton's predictions. Thus the French mathematician and physicist Pierre Laplace (1749–1827) believed the entire universe was composed of 'different arrangements of atoms moving in accordance with Newton's laws of motion' (Tallis 1995: 12). It follows from this that if all such arrangements as exist now can be known with certainty, then all possible future arrangements can be determined.

Newton himself had been more circumspect, claiming only that we can establish the relations between phenomena using his methods and we cannot prove that the relation could not have been otherwise (Losee 1980: 94). This view was held by empiricist philosopher David Hume (1711–1776), who maintained that although we can observe that relationships between things or events are regular, that *A* appears to 'cause' *B*, there is nothing in *A* or *B* themselves to suggest that relationship is a necessary one. That

> ... even if our faculties were fitted to penetrate into the internal fabric of bodies we could gain no knowledge of a necessary connectedness among phenomena. The most we could hope to learn is that certain configurations and motions of atoms have been constantly conjoined with macroscopic effects.
>
> (Losee 1980: 101)

Hume's philosophical scepticism, though enormously influential since in the work of empiricists such as Mill, Russell, Mach and Hempel, has done little to dent the external view of science as a mechanistic enterprise implying 'the belief that everything was fixed. The future was contained in the present which was pre-destined by the past' (Appleyard 1992: 64).

The rise of social science

Had it not been for the success of the science and its resulting technology, inspired by Newton and his followers, studies of the social world might have taken on a very different character, at least initially. Thinkers from the seventeenth century (in particular) such as Thomas Hobbes and Giambattista Vico had emphasised the 'voluntaristic' nature of human beings (Manicas 1987: 29). Conscious, self-reflecting and creative, they required a different approach to being studied than did the objects of the inanimate world, one based on understanding and interpretation rather than explanation and prediction. Of course we cannot know whether under different historical circumstances this approach might have caught on, but it is nevertheless clear that a 'scientific ' approach to the study of the social world arose not because of its efficacy in its own right, but because science was in fashion and manifestly successful. The alternative hermeneutic approach, begun by Vico and continued by Schleirmacher and Dilthey (May 1996: 32–7), took on the role of the opposition with only Max Weber succeeding in any kind of compromise (Weber 1949; 1978b).

There was, however, an important, though not always stated, difference between the natural and social sciences in the nineteenth-century – even at their most avowedly scientific. The latter were not just about how the world 'is' but how it 'ought' to be. Indeed John Stuart Mill referred to the 'social' sciences as the 'moral sciences' (Mill 1987), implying their prescriptive character, though in this Mill was not advocating subjectivity. The success of science post-Newton convinced those (such as Mill) concerned with the conduct of human affairs that they could be known scientifically, and indeed that 'scientific' programmes could be devised to make social life more equitable and efficient. Mill believed that all of the sciences, including the 'moral sciences', were 'progressing towards the abstract and deductive character of classical physics' (Thomas 1985: 52). The natural sciences derived from physical laws, but the social sciences, he held, derived from the laws of mind, where the latter are in the final analysis dependent upon the former (Thomas 1985: 65–7). It was believed, then, that knowledge acquired through experience could lead to deductions and accurate predictions and was a principle that could be successfully translated from the physical to the social world. As Voltaire put it:

it would be very singular that all nature, all the planets, should obey eternal laws, and there should be a little animal, five feet high, who in contempt of these laws, could act as he pleased, solely according to his caprice.

(cited in Dampier 1966: 197)

Thus the 'scientific world view' (and in France particularly the Laplacian version of this) not only influenced a model of social science, but also a model of society which in its turn also influenced the infant social sciences.

This mixture of explanation and prescription was epitomised in the work of Auguste Comte, whose project R.A. Nisbet describes as replacing Catholicism with positivism (Nisbet 1970: 15), an attempt to fuse moral prescription with the rationality of science. However, despite his fame as the founder of 'positivism' there was more prescription than science in his world view. Though it is a matter of emphasis. In this, the history of the social sciences is even more genealogical than the natural sciences in that one can trace ideas back in more than one way. For example Comte is variously seen as emphasising science, or a kind of hankering for a pre-scientific conservatism (Nisbet 1970: 17–19). Though usually referred to as the father of positivism, his 'positivism' was an important, though partial determinant of the Durkheimian kind (Lukes 1981) and had little to do with the logical positivism of the Vienna Circle (Kolakowski 1972).

Max Weber similarly sought to put the social sciences on a 'scientific' basis, though his starting point was that of individual agency and the need to interpret actions so arising before making causal inferences (Weber [1922] 1947). However, in holding to methodological separation between the moral commitment of social policy and the value freedom required in its sociological operationalisation (Weber 1974) he was closer to science than interpretation. Nevertheless in a re-description of the work of any of these thinkers, and more especially those more 'politically' active thinkers in the Marxist tradition, one could emphasise ideological considerations and historical contingency as much as a desire to be 'scientific'. Indeed despite Weber's injunction that sociology should be 'value free', value laden language, such as 'grand figures' and 'perfection that is nowhere surpassed', permeates most of his work (Strauss 1963: 433). I shall return to this question of value freedom and objectivity in Chapter 6, but for the present I want to look at the apotheosis of science in social science, the era of positivism.

Positivism in natural and social science

There is much confusion about positivism in social science, or rather there is much confusion amongst social scientists about positivism. For many it is simply a term of abuse to indicate quantification, or the importation of 'scientific' method into social science (see for example Denzin 1983; Guba and Lincoln 1982), but of course if positivism was just science in social science then this would not explain why it was that for much of the twentieth century there has been a vigorous debate about positivism in the philosophy of the natural sciences (Losee 1980: chapter 11).

Though Comte coined the term 'positivism', *logical* positivism, unlike the Comtean kind, emphasised the methodological aspect of science, rather than the philosophical. In fact natural science was much more influenced by the empiricism of Hume (Gillies 1993: chapter 1) and Mill than the continental variants in Comte and Durkheim. Logical positivism was associated principally with the Vienna Circle, a group of philosophers and scientists including Moritz Schlick, Rudolph Carnap and Hans Reichenbach, and with the English philosophers G.E. Moore and A.J. Ayer (Kolakowski 1972: chapter 5). Much influenced by Hume, an important doctrine, especially early on, was that of verification expressed in the formula 'the meaning of a statement is the method of its verification' (Kolakowski 1972: 213). That is, unless we can state how it is a proposition can be verified it is meaningless. Verification of hypotheses can occur only through observations, and the means by which the verification can take place is through observation statements. If something is not observable then it is not verifiable, and if it is not verifiable then we are not entitled to make claims about it (Carnap 1969: 108–9). A problem with this, recognised by the logical positivists, was that an improvement in experimental technique could render a meaningless statement meaningful overnight. This doctrine was then relaxed somewhat to mean that a statement could in principle, if not actuality, be verified (Kolakowski 1972: 213). Apart from observation statements only analytic statements in logic and mathematics had a part to play in science, but of course these are tautological, can give only structure to propositions and can reveal nothing new about the world. Statements other than analytic or verifiable ones were not seen to be scientific; they were instead metaphysical and meaningless. This, of course, would include a great deal of theory, yet to be verified, or shown to be untrue. Only reluctantly were they admitted to play any part in science and then only as conventions adopted by scientists that constrain and structure scientific enquiry. The job of observation statements was to propose how theoretical statements could be tested. If verified they were admitted as meaningful, if not they were considered meaningless.

Like Caesar, logical positivism was killed, or at least mortally wounded, by one of its close associates, Karl Popper (Popper 1986: 87–90). Popper's objection was mainly that whilst the observation statements might refute a theory, they could never confirm it. Instead he developed his alternative of falsification, which I will discuss in the next chapter. A second related objection was directed towards the empiricism itself and the insistence of the logical positivists that observation statements and theory statements must be separated in order that the former can confirm or refute the latter.

Popper's objection was that observations are never made except in the context of one theory or another (Popper 1989: 24–30). Though not confined to Popper, this criticism has been the principal one levelled at logical positivism ever since.

It is hard to gauge the influence of positivism on natural science; really the relationship was more symbiotic. Ernest Mach and Hans Reichenbach, for instance, were physicists and philosophers; both were advocates of positivism (Losee 1980: 159–88). Yet it was the physics of the late nineteenth and early twentieth centuries that so influenced the philosophy. Perhaps then, historically, it was the last and most fawning celebration of science, believing, as did Comte, that the clarity and objectivity of the scientific method were the tools of a wider societal salvation. Though the influence on social science is even harder to gauge, it is possible that logical positivism was more influential on method than the positivism of Durkheim and certainly that of Comte.

Comte's importance was more that of an historical figure than in any lasting substantial contribution (Craib 1997: 25–6). Durkheim's influence on the explanation of social structure and on the use of official statistics in *Suicide* (1952) is tangible and important, but it was the mood of positivism in the natural sciences, especially its empiricist character, that was most influential. Comte and Durkheim asserted the possibility of the scientific nature of the study of the social world and the latter demonstrated its feasibility in *Suicide*, but it was the importation of empiricism into method, both implicitly and explicitly, that characterised the positivist influence. The influence of positivism on social science is perhaps more readily explained by the importation of logical positivism into American social science at a time of its great expansion, in the 1930s. Of course one could perhaps claim the opposite, that it was the importation of logical positivism that led to the success of social science. Either way the age of positivism in social science coincided with the growth of American dominance, particularly of sociology, itself motivated by the tremendous advances in science and engineering in the first quarter of the century in that country. There were criticisms, notably from R.S. Lynd and C. Wright Mills, but these fell on deaf ears in a profession 'trained in statistical methods, with mutually reinforcing motivations to win promotion and produce the "facts" needed by mayors, presidents and corporations' (Manicas 1987: 226).

Indeed positivism, or more specifically a commitment to methodological empiricism, was to dominate American social science for a generation and by extension that in the rest of the English-speaking world also. As a philosophical underpinning to science, social or natural, it is discredited and lives on only as a demon, and one suspects a convenient one, in the minds of certain interpretivist social 'scientists' (Philips 1987: 36–7). Nevertheless, it has left a threefold legacy. First, and I believe beneficially, as Michael Scriven noted, it was a knife that cut away much of the constricting metaphysics in philosophy, 'performing a tracheotomy that made it possible for philosophy to breathe again' (cited in Phillips 1987: 39). The ensuing rigour was hugely influential on 'scientific' social science and is one that remains. Second, less beneficially, it bequeathed a naïve empiricism to social science. This was Popper's complaint and is even more forceful when stated in relation to observations in the social world. Such observations depend on the derivation of categories, themselves a product of earlier experience. The measurement of class, for example, arises out of a theory that classes exist and have properties. As we know their existence in particular forms is postulated and often disputed (for a discussion of the 'reality' of class see Pawson 1989). Thus the measurement of class is in no sense a neutral observation. Nevertheless the assumption often remains in much of survey research, particularly that carried out by government agencies, or sponsored by them, that only what is observable can be measured and the measurement itself is an objective one of a real phenomenon in the world. A view that manages to be both naïvely empiricist and realist at the same time (Williams 1998: 12–13).

The objections of Popper and others aside, it was not the case that logical positivism was an unsophisticated doctrine – its exponents were very aware of developments in the physics and mathematics of the time. For instance in stressing the importance of observation in physics, Albert Einstein and Werner Heisenberg both qualified as 'positivists' (Popper 1985: part 1, section 12), as did the mathematician, often credited with prefiguring complexity theory (see Chapter 7), Henri Poincaré. However, like Chinese whispers the sophistication of the methodological debate in science became rather changed by the time it reached social science. The result was that whilst 'frontier' science was shifting the methodological (and indeed metaphysical) ground towards probability (in both senses that the laws that govern the way the world is are themselves probabilistic and that scientific knowledge itself is probable and not certain) and contingency, the social sciences seemed content to retain a deterministic model of causality more influenced by Laplace than Poincaré.

Science in the twentieth century

It is commonplace nowadays for scientists and science writers to complain about the lack of the public understanding of science (Sagan and Druyan 1996: 318–33). But perhaps it has always been thus – the peasantry of the Middle Ages was just as unenlightened about the workings of the universe as middle America is today. The difference is that our culture is now a 'scientific' one, that is we materially rely on science and its emergent technology, but also that the promise and threat of this lead more people than ever to have a view on science. What I described as the 'clockwork' view of the universe promoted by Laplace took seed in the public mind and, as I have suggested, was influential in social science. The view can be summed up by saying that science was the objective study of natural phenomena and depended on scientific method, which if applied rigorously would lead to certain knowledge. Alongside this a crude metaphysical view of the universe was reproduced through generations of school physics classes. It was vast, predictable and fixed, relative to us as observers, and was composed of planets orbiting stars, each possessed of gravitational properties which kept them in fixed unvarying relation to each other. This was the universal realm, but at the realm of the very small a similar behaviour was replicated with billiard ball atoms all behaving predictably in the miniature solar systems of molecules. Although a gross oversimplification of the Newtonian model of the universe, there is at least a common sense spirit of the original that in the intelligent lay person this understanding could be fairly easily converted into a more detailed and correct one. The point is simple: Newton's model was one that could be made intelligible through common sense imagery and this may be the secret of its longevity as a popular metaphysics.

The culture of science in the nineteenth century and the public culture that developed from it depended on successful prediction, which implied, if not determinism, then regularity. This in turn depended on a fixed time–space relationship of the observer to the rest of the universe. Space is an extended entity which contains all objects and events and time is a process which encompasses all other processes. This common sense metaphysical view began to break down within science during the nineteenth century, though there had long been some, such as the philosopher Leibniz, who disputed this 'mechanical' model (Gower 1997: 84–5). In the early years of this century Albert Einstein published two papers with consequences for science equal to those of Newton's work. Einstein, more than any, has perhaps come to symbolise the archetypal genius, but his science and its implications have not translated even into a common sense understanding in the same way as that of Newton did. There is an obvious reason for this, that his physics is completely counter-intuitive to our everyday experience. If every other period of science was, or could be made intelligible to an articulate citizen of the times, it is doubtful whether anything more than a 'hand waving' understanding of relativity theory, or his (and subsequent) work in quantum physics would be available to most of us. The physicist (and one of the originators of the first atomic bomb) Robert Oppenheimer, was pessimistic about the public's ability to understand the new science.

> Our knowledge today can no longer constitute, as knowledge did in Athens or 15th century Europe, an enrichment of genial culture. It will continue to be the privilege of small highly specialised groups, which will no longer be able to render it accessible to humanity at large as Newton's knowledge was rendered accessible.
>
> (Oppenheimer cited in Rouzé 1965: 33)

In the Newtonian or 'common sense' view time and space are fixed and discrete entities with bodies, such as the earth, moving through the 'aether'. This idea, as I noted above, is traceable to Aristotle. Experiments in the nineteenth century, particularly by Michelson and Morley with light waves, showed that the speed of light remains constant whatever the velocity of the observer. If the speed of light was constant for all observers whatever their velocity through space an aether could not exist. Einstein's Special Theory of Relativity, published in 1905 (see Einstein 1956), contains four important ideas: (1) time and space are actually closely linked dimensions; (2) the speed of light in empty space is the same for all observers, regardless of their own speed; (3) the speed of light itself cannot be exceeded; and (4) there is an equivalence of mass and energy (famously expressed as $E = mc^2$). The reasoning for each of these propositions is enormously complex and the result unsettling for one accustomed to a 'Newtonian' universe. It is that our motion is simply relative to the time frame we occupy. Imagine two spacecraft travelling in the same direction, one travelling 1,000 kph faster than the other. Provided there was no other immediate observable frame of reference (such as a planet or a star) to those in the slower spacecraft, the observed effect of the faster spacecraft passing by is no different than if that spacecraft had been stationary and the other spacecraft had passed at 1,000 kph. More mundanely a similar effect can be obtained if one is sitting on a train next to another in a station. Unless one can see beyond the second train to a 'fixed' object it is not possible to tell which train has pulled away. Thus what we see as our fixed position in the universe is not – it is a position simply relative to others.

The 'Special Theory' was an incomplete one, for it referred only to the 'special' circumstances of objects moving at constant speeds in straight lines. The 'General Theory' published in 1915 'generalises' the former to deal with gravity and acceleration, proposing that gravity is a property of space itself, not of bodies (such as stars and planets), and space itself becomes 'curved' as a result of the existence of bodies (Russell 1991: 194–203). Gravity is a consequence of space curved by matter. Finally, space, or more properly space–time, is expanding and can be likened somewhat to a balloon being inflated.

The above is simply a brief description and just tells us minimally what 'relativity' is; it doesn't explain how Einstein reached such conclusions. A successful understanding requires a working knowledge of Galilean and Newtonian mechanics and Euclidean geometry. Euclidean geometry applies to flat surfaces in flat space–time, but the General Theory proposes that since space–time is curved, it therefore depends on a non-Euclidean geometry. It replaces the three dimensions of space with a fourth dimension of space–time. For most of us, even if we had understood Galilean and Newtonian mechanics, it is still hard to hold a mental picture of what this implies. And this is only part of the story. The early years of the century were marked by a new understanding of the composition of matter. The new science of quantum physics arose out of the work of Max Planck, who theorised that energy is absorbed or emitted not as a continuum, or continuously variable entity, but instead in discrete units; what he termed 'quanta' (Hoffman 1963: 31–7). Relativity theory showed that matter and energy were interchangeable, and the outcome of these findings was a new understanding of matter as composed of discrete quanta of energy. In 1913 Niels Bohr went on to propose a model of the atom which showed a limited number of possible orbits for its constituent electrons. The new view of the atom, emerging over the next years, was of a number of subatomic particles behaving in distinct ways, depending on the type of atom. But later there came a twist in this story. In 1935 Werner Heisenberg proposed his 'uncertainty principle'. That is, the 'fundamental' particles, of which atoms are composed, behave with uncertainty. What is meant by this is that it is impossible to measure both the position and velocity of such particles simultaneously. Such measurement can be obtained only probabilistically. Indeed, attempts to measure one appear to have an 'effect' upon the other. This, it is claimed, is not the result of our inability to measure, but a property of the world itself (Rae 1986).

Relativity theory and quantum physics were not just fanciful ideas, but led to predictions which could be empirically verified. They changed the face of physics fundamentally. Knowledge of the energy–matter relationship led to the development of the atomic bomb, the General Theory of Relativity revolutionised cosmology and in turn led to the 'big bang' theory, whilst quantum physics became domesticated into quantum mechanics (Ikenberry 1962). Though science in other ages had the resources to describe the universe, the science of the twentieth century was the most ambitious science ever. In presenting theories of the history and composition of the universe from its origins to now and from fundamental particles to large scale structures spanning millions of light years (Sagan 1980), it embodied greater empirically confirmed detail than ever before. Physics, of course, is not all of science and any account of twentieth-century science would probably have to include the discovery of the structure of DNA by Watson and Crick in 1951 (Watson 1968) or the development of 'chaos' theory in mathematics (Gleick 1987), but it is mostly physics, since relativity and quantum theory, that has captured the public mind, either in fear of its consequences or in awe of its possibilities. Stephen Hawking's *Brief History of Time* (1988) was one of the best-selling non-fiction hardback books ever and it is a brave attempt to make the counter-intuitive science I spoke of intelligible (though of course the purchase of a book does not imply that it is always read, let alone understood!).

Paradoxically the interest in popular science is probably greater than ever at a time when science has reached a level of conceptual and mathematical complexity, such as to put it out of reach of most citizens without at least some knowledge of basic science and mathematics. Whilst the names of Einstein and Hawking are known far beyond their discipline, the everyday mundane world of the laboratory is mysterious and often misunderstood. The science of the twentieth century is truly unnatural.

So what is science?

In this chapter I have tried to show how throughout its history, science (or what has been called science) has been the product of a dynamic interrelationship of metaphysical, social and cognitive factors, not wholly determined by nature, society or prevailing philosophical beliefs. Some characteristics, such as a desire to explain and predict, have always been present, but of course these are present in other areas of life than science. We can point to certain periods in science, for example, the development of experimental method, or the mathematics of the calculus, as being crucial to the nature of modern science, but an encompassing historical definition of science escapes us because in each period what counts as science is different. Of course we could argue that the ensemble of beliefs, knowledge and methods that is science today is what science is. But there are three problems with this. First, it is actually very hard to produce an ensemble that would fit all sciences (and for the moment let us exclude social science). Even if we took the view of Ernest Rutherford that physics was *the* only science and the rest were 'stamp collecting' (Blackett 1973: 159) we would still have to invent a name to encompass the activities that have led to discoveries such as the structure of DNA, the existence of continental drift or the destructive effects of chlorofluorocarbons (CFCs). Second, we would have to explain how it was that past discoveries, that remain part of the current knowledge base of science, could have been discovered in a pre-scientific culture. Third, we would have to show that what counts as science now will continue to do so. If we are inductivists (that is we believe future experiences are likely to resemble past ones in important ways) then we have no grounds for assuming this, since science has changed and dramatically so even in this century. If we are anti-inductivists (see Chapter 2) we would say that we have no grounds to know if this will be the case anyway.

Is the corollary of this that science is anything you want it to be? That Christian science or astrological science are just as much science as physics? Clearly on that basis social science could be admitted to the club. I think the appellations science in the first two examples are simply instances of a desire to claim the authority of science, and I do not think science is whatever is called science. Yet there is more to it than this. In my view science is the ensemble of knowledge and practices that best reflect and operationalise a critical attitude to the discovery of the world at that moment in time. Under this rubric the very worst natural 'science' would not be science, but much of the better social science would be. However, much turns on what counts as the critical attitude to discovery and at any point in the history of science this will be embodied in its methods. It is to these I now turn.

Suggested further reading

Fuller, S. (1997) *Science*, Buckingham: Open University Press.
Horgan, J. (1996) *The End of Science*, London: Little, Brown.
Losee, J. (1980) *A Historical Introduction to the Philosophy of Science*, Oxford: Oxford University Press.
Tarnas, R. (1991) *The Passion of the Western Mind: Understanding the Ideas that Have Shaped our World View*, London: Pimlico.

2   Science and its method

In the last chapter I chose a few episodes in the history of science to illustrate the complex interrelationship between science, society and philosophical world views. The nature, role and influence of science changed historically and this had implications not just for what was regarded as science, but also how science was done, i.e. the method of science. In this chapter I will focus on how science is done, or how it is said it is done, through its method.

When scientists talk of scientific method they are usually referring to an ensemble of practices and understandings which differ from discipline to discipline. For example a physicist will often stress the role of experiments and a geologist the importance of meticulous observation, but there are few 'experiments' in geology and increasingly observation in physics is through the proxy of instruments. From this it would seem that there is no single algorithm for obtaining scientific knowledge but simply an ensemble of practices and knowledge that make up 'method'. So what is it that makes it scientific? Let me be more specific. Is the ensemble to which I refer an approved list of things that are 'scientific', or is it the case that if scientists do it, it is 'scientific'? The latter is indeed a charge that has been levelled against science: that science is simply a social construction. In Chapter 4 I will consider this charge in some depth, but for the moment I want to concentrate on the question of what method is supposed to be.

If the method of science is the route to knowledge which can be called 'scientific' then this has implications for investigations of the social world. Specifically if it is held that the social world arises from the natural world, or is continuous with it, then a reliable scientific 'method' would appear to be the best way to reliable knowledge of the social world. On the other hand if there is no dependable methodological route to knowledge of the natural world, but it is still held that the relationship between the natural and social world is emergent, or continuous, then the social and natural sciences may share methodological problems and solutions. There are two other possibilities. That is the social world is not emergent from, or continuous with the natural world, and there is no methodological common interest, or that even if it is, its manifest properties are so different that they cannot be known in the same way. This last is a view commonly advanced in social science and I will return to it in Chapter 5.

The question of method in science is often regarded as one of a demarcation between what is and isn't science, and raises issues not just of technique but of contested philosophical assumptions about knowledge and the nature of things that exist. A consideration of scientific method is not simply a technical exercise, but must also be a philosophical one. The measurement of X implies agreement not just on what is a good and accurate measurement, but also on what counts as X in the first place. Science is underwritten by agreements about what is knowledge and the means to it, and by agreement about the nature of existence – epistemology and ontology respectively. In turn these matters of knowledge and existence can be shaped by the discoveries of science. As Paul Davies notes: 'True revolutions in science involve more than spectacular discoveries and rapid advances in understanding. They also change the concepts on which science is based' (Davies 1989: 1).

A change in concepts will result in a change in methods. The Davies quote above is from the introduction to a book written by one of the pioneers of quantum physics, Werner Heisenberg, and the concepts in this case concern the nature of matter itself. As I observed in Chapter 1, prior to the emergence of quantum physics, the building blocks of all matter were considered to be atoms, discrete entities occupying a particular physical space and behaving as miniature versions of objects we see in the world around us. However, the atom turned out to have constituent 'parts' that did not behave in this way. Indeed, to describe fundamental particles as constituent parts at all is misleading. Heisenberg showed that though these particles had properties, such as velocity or position, they could not be observed simultaneously and furthermore the very act of observing itself seemed to have an effect on what could be measured (Heisenberg 1989: 32–3). The upshot of this is that the quantum world can only be known probabilistically. The realisation that material existence has a probabilistic and not deterministic basis had direct methodological consequences for measurement (Rae 1986: 53–62), but also philosophical consequences. Specifically, if the world is 'probable' and not 'determined' (though nevertheless probabilistically predictable) at the quantum level, to what extent and in which ways can it be 'determined' at the non-quantum level?

The acceptance of Heisenberg's 'uncertainty principle' by the scientific community is an excellent example of how scientific discovery changes the philosophical principles of science and in turn these principles influence the methodological choices of science (for a discussion of theories of scientific change see Richards 1997). Discovery in science (and everyday life), then, does not take place in a vacuum, but is shaped by theories, themselves the product of earlier discoveries. To get some feel for what science is it is useful to look at this process of discovery, a task I will undertake in the next section of this chapter. But, as I will suggest, discovery in science is paralleled by discovery in everyday life and though a necessary condition for science, it is not a sufficient one. Often what is known as the hypo-thetico-deductive model, which specifies the relationship between observation and inference, has been cited as a necessary condition in science. In the following section I will take a brief critical look at the inductive and deductive assumptions arising from different versions of this. Finally I will attempt to show that the process of science, and the relationships between scientists, and between scientists and nature, is a heterogeneous one and that what we call scientific method will reflect that heterogeneity.

Science as discovery

In science, as in everyday life, things are discovered by accident as well as design and quite often accidental discoveries come about when we are looking for something else. In the case of both discovery by design and by accident there is nevertheless a pre-existing body of knowledge that allows us to make sense of our discovery. Even accidental discoveries that occur when we are not even looking for something else still presuppose a body of knowledge that makes them sensible. As Louis Pasteur is reputed to have said, 'accidents favour the prepared mind' (Langley *et al.* 1987: 305). Perhaps there is something of a tautology here? X would not be known to be a discovery if we were unable to describe and place it within an existing body of knowledge.

The discovery and utilisation of penicillin neatly illustrates the process of discovery. In 1929 a bacteriologist, Alexander Fleming, found that a culture plate seeded with the micro-organism *staphylococci* had become contaminated with a mould. On the culture plate the *staphylococci* had grown except in the immediate vicinity of the mould, suggesting that there was something about the mould (itself a micro-organism) that could inhibit the growth of other micro-organisms. Through further tests Fleming found that this was the case. However, after publishing a paper of his results, Fleming did nothing further and it was another nine years before Ernst Chain and Howard Florey isolated pure penicillin and demonstrated that it could kill lethal streptococci in mice (Macfarlane 1979). The popular myth is that Fleming accidentally discovered penicillin and this was the birth of effective antibiotics. Yes it is true that Fleming had grown the mould accidentally as a result of leaving culture plates lying around, but he was nevertheless seeking a solution to the problem of infections in wounds. Medical orthodoxy held that antiseptics killed bacteria and wounds were treated accordingly. However during the First World War it had been noticed that such treatments led to the festering of wounds, despite the fact that the same antiseptic would kill bacteria in test tubes. Prior to his 'accidental' discovery of penicillin Fleming had already identified the bacteria responsible for the wound infections and discovered that antiseptics killed both these and the white blood cells the body manufactures as its own defence, but left behind a small quantity of a harmful bacterium that could then reproduce.

Fleming had been searching for a solution to this problem, but the solution was unanticipated and of a different kind to that sought. The later work of Chain and Florey led to an intended discovery – that penicillin could be produced and could cure lethal bacteriological infections.

The lesson of this story might be that to find anything we must be looking for something and that a lot of the time we are. This is as true of everyday life as it is in science. Science, as I suggested in the last chapter, is in this sense curiosity, but curiosity is also problem-solving. Perhaps, as Karl Popper argued, all organisms are constantly engaged in problem-solving and moreover must do so in order to survive (Popper 1979: 242). The patterns of discovery do, however, suggest a history to the problem. The history of the problem may be simple or complex, it may be personal or social, it may be well documented or just folk knowledge. The history of any problem will be that of past resolved problems. For example, I have a problem of book storage space in my office, but this arises out of the resolution of previous problems such as getting the books, an office, or a job, in the first place! In other words the solution of past problems makes the proposition of new problems possible. Even the most trivial problem arises out of a mass of accumulated knowledge, even in everyday life. In this sense discovery in science follows a pattern similar to that in everyday life (Langley *et al.* 1987: 7). Despite this, what we call scientific knowledge comes to be codified in particular ways. I will say something briefly about these.

Laws, theories, observation and hypotheses

1 *Laws and theories.* Scientific knowledge is embodied in laws, theories and hypotheses. The first thing to say is that there is no sharp distinction between a law and a theory. We talk of Newton's laws and Einstein's theories as important and reliable scientific knowledge, although it is often held that a law is derived from axioms and holds for all times and places, whereas a theory is a more speculative statement. We speak of the 'laws of nature', but post-Einstein we know that Newton's laws offered only a partial explanation of the workings of the universe. Conversely Einstein's 'Special' and 'General' theories can account for those things explained by Newton's laws and other phenomena besides, and they seem to be just as well founded as the former. Nevertheless laws might be regarded as 'facts' that are indisputable, and theories as generalisations from what we know, to what we believe to be the case. Laws also express regularities in the universe. Despite the complexity and apparent randomness of much of nature, there is also much that is regular. Although in any drop of water there are billions of hydrogen and oxygen atoms, their ordering is entirely

regular and determined. Of course this determined character breaks down at subatomic level and is not present in many large scale structures. Thus science aims to extend laws, possibly themselves necessarily of greater and greater complexity, so as to seek the existence of ordered arrangements where none may have been formerly perceived. Of course it may be the case that deterministic laws of the kind under which we can describe molecular structure cannot in principle be found to explain some parts of nature. In which case the search may be for statistical laws that can explain and predict aggregate behaviour, but not that of the components of the aggregate. Thus any particular scientific theory will be built on an edifice of laws and other theories, with the latter consisting of a number of propositions about the world, some of which are more well founded than others. This is an important point and I will return to it later.

2   *Observation and perception.* The process of discovery has a number of components. First, there is the thing in the world which is to be discovered, but there is nothing in the thing itself that will commend its discovery. Subatomic particles, gravity and penicillin do not say 'Hi, I'm here'; something else is needed. That something has both a psychological and a social aspect. First the psychological.

I have suggested above that the process of discovery is that of human problem-solving (with perhaps science as a special case). Cognitive psychologists account for this by seeing the human brain as an information processing system able to hold interrelated symbolic structures. This ability arises from our biology, the result of an evolutionary process. In thinking we copy, re-organise symbols in memory and resolve problems by creating symbolic representations that allow us to conduct a search for solutions along the most promising paths (Langley *et al.* 1987: 8). All of this cognitive equipment requires data and these data come from the apprehension of the world via our senses. Some of this apprehension is of physical characteristics and processes and some is of all already processed information. The apprehension of physical characteristics such as quantity, shape, size, colour etc. must come either from an innate capacity to know these things, what Kant referred to as the 'synthetic *a priori*' (Körner 1955: chapter 4), or it must come from previously acquired knowledge of the world – or, of course, both. However, even if we are genetically predisposed to know number, shape etc., much of the knowledge we need for discovery is social knowledge. That is, knowledge that is held in common. In science, as in any discipline with a recorded history, much of this knowledge will be held in artefacts such as books, papers etc. – what Popper called the 'Third World of knowledge' (or World 3). World 1 is physical objects, and World 2, conscious experiences (Popper 1994: chapter 3).

The difference between discovery in science and in everyday life lies in the nature of the social knowledge and of observation. The social knowledge of science is taken to be justified knowledge – that is facts – and these facts derive from structured and accurate observation. A rather good comparison between explanations deriving from non-scientific and scientific social knowledge lies in the perennially popular issue of life on Mars. In 1996 a meteorite of Martian origin was found in Antarctica. The meteorite contained, or appeared to contain, some primitive fossils, indicating that life may have, or may still exist on Mars (see *Nature*, 15 August 1997). This 'discovery' was taken seriously for it did not offend any of the 'facts' we already know about Mars, in that its chemical composition was recognisably Martian, and this we know this from probes which have been able to perform analyses on rocks *in situ* (see Ash *et al.* 1997). Conversely supermarket tabloid headlines like 'New NASA Photo Proves Humans Lived on Mars' do not have the same scientific status. Often at the centre of such a 'report' lies a grain of observational truth, but the 'knowledge' in which it is located has no empirical basis. Are the formations we can observe on Mars 'towers, columned temples, monumental statuary, immense frescoes? Or just rocks?' (Sagan 1996: 57). The scientist concludes the latter, for all her *experience*, both observational and that deriving from the social knowledge of science indicates this. This experience rests on a raft of other experiences, ultimately traceable to observational data – though observational data that accord with earlier experience.

Though of course anyone familiar with any refereed game such as football or baseball knows that what the referee sees, what the players see and what the crowd sees are often quite different. Thus it is in science. Russell Hanson asks us to consider two scientists observing the simple amoeba:

> One sees a one-celled animal, the other a non-celled animal. The first sees *Amoeba* in all its analogies with different types of single cells: liver cells, nerve cells, epithelium cells. ... The other, however, sees *Amoeba's* homology not with single cells, but with whole animals. Like all animals *Amoeba* ingests its food, digests and assimilates it. It excretes, reproduces and is mobile – more like a complete animal than an individual tissue cell.
>
> (Hanson 1965: 4)

Both scientists have seen the same thing, both can call upon the same 'Third World' of knowledge, yet they have interpreted what they have seen differently. Of course they may have actually *seen* something different, as in the celebrated 'duck–rabbit' picture (see for example Couvalis 1997: 12). Look at a picture one way, it's a duck, look at it another and it's a rabbit. But let us assume that their visual description is the same. Their explanation is, however, different because their description is 'theory laden', that is they depend on concepts the meaning of which is already known. For example, in cosmology the concept of 'redshift' describes the spectrum of a star moving away from an observer. This only makes sense if the scientist already knows that red light has a longer wavelength than blue light. A star moving away from an observer effectively 'stretches' the light emitted from it, rather like the sound from a police siren is 'stretched' as it moves away from the listener. Redshift itself was implicitly predicted by Einstein's General Theory of Relativity (Gribben 1996: 343), namely that the universe had to be in motion (expanding, or contracting). In 1929 the astronomer, Edwin Hubble, established the relationship between redshift and the position of galaxies, showing that certain galaxies were moving away from us and concluding that the universe was expanding. But of course to do this Hubble had to both know about the characteristics of the light spectrum and be familiar with the predictions of the General Theory in order for his observations to make sense.

Observations are neither passive, nor neutral. They are directed and dependent on an existing conceptual framework of beliefs. The directedness of observation will often take place with the context of an experiment and might be seen as an attempt to isolate and interrogate one part of nature. It is a socially contrived form of observation which is carried out under artificially produced conditions, which are deliberately controlled and therefore capable of being reproduced. By holding other conditions constant it is possible to observe the effects of one variable on another. In doing this the scientist is often mimicking an unexplained sequence of events already observed in nature. It is then an articulation of a problem of what causes X. The crisis of bovine spongiform encephalopathy (BSE) in Britain, during the late 1980s and 1990s, illustrates such a scenario well. The first observations by vets and farmers were 'passive'; though they had a knowledge of animal health and husbandry they were not looking for BSE. However, a large number of cattle had begun to develop symptoms of the disease in sheep known as scrapie (Lacey 1994). The development of BSE in British cattle coincided with the deregulation of animal feedstuffs by the Thatcher government, and permitted the feeding of preparations containing the processed remains of other animals, such as sheep. This much was strong circumstantial evidence, but the job of the scientists was to identify the transmission process. Evidence that contaminated feedstuffs were the agent of transmission from sheep to cattle was fairly readily established, but in order that the disease could be brought under control it was important to establish whether vertical transmission from cow to calf could take place. In 1988–9 the Ministry of Agriculture conducted an experiment in which 316 calves of BSE infected mothers were isolated as a control group and given foodstuffs that were screened for any BSE contamination. Any development of BSE in the calves would most likely be as a result of vertical transmission. Of the control group 19 succumbed to BSE showing that vertical transmission could take place (K. Taylor 1994). Nineteen cases in 316 was considered good evidence that vertical transmission could take place, but had this not been so it would have been possible to conduct a further experiment with a different control group comprising calves born of non-BSE mothers and protected from contaminated food. If a similar proportion (very unlikely) had developed BSE then doubt could be cast upon the hypothesis of a simple vertical transmission mechanism.

3   *Hypotheses*. Hypotheses are specific conjectures about the world that can be tested and are rather similar to the kind of 'low level' theories we have in everyday life. Often it will specify the mechanism by which an effect will be realised, such as in the BSE example above. In science hypotheses may not specify a particular effect in isolation, but instead will specify a measurement, or range of measurements. For example it may be hypothesised that interactions in a particular experiment will produce a temperature, or range of temperatures between n and n. Finally hypotheses can also be multiple. Any given theory may generate a number of hypotheses and some of these might be mutually exclusive of others.

Induction and falsification

The picture of scientific discovery I have tried to portray is one where the social-psychological processes of discovery in science parallel those in everyday life, but the form they take is specific to the practice of science. Scientific theories are built on an edifice of other theories and laws, which themselves are held to be 'true', but how do we know this is the case? Is it enough, for example, to say that observational experience can corroborate a theory? As we have seen observations are themselves theory laden, yet the scientist has only theories and observations (and the relationships between these) at her disposal as a means to know the world. Stripped of the language of science this seems to be pretty much the case in everyday life, so what is it that separates science from non-science? For many it is the hypothetico-deductive (HD) model, said to be the golden thread running through science.

The hypothetico-deductive model

The HD model is not the only model of science, but in its various forms it is seen by most scientists as offering the most rigorous route to knowledge. The model traces the path of discovery and justification and can be said to have its starting point in any of its phases. First it is an acceptance that hypotheses cannot be simply derived from observation (because observation is, as I noted above, contextual to begin with) and must arise out of an existing theory. Second, the hypothesis must be conjoined with the initial conditions that exist at the time. By this is meant all of those things in the environment that may have an effect on the hypothesis, or subsequent observations. Third, from the hypothesis and initial conditions a prediction is made which can be tested by observation. Our hypotheses become a clash with reality (Popper 1989: 117–18). In 'traditional' accounts if the observations are successful then the theory from which the hypotheses were derived is confirmed. A simple example would be that we hypothesise that water boils at 100° centigrade and an initial condition would be that this is at sea level. The prediction is that any given samples of water, if heated at sea level under normal atmospheric pressure, will boil at 100°. We then test the prediction by doing just that. The water boiling at 100° can be said to have been deduced from the hypothesis.

This sounds straightforward so far. Meticulous attention to the formulation of a hypothesis, derived from an existing body of theory, with due attention to initial conditions and rigorous experiment seem like an infallible recipe for success. There is, however, a major problem with the HD model, and although Karl Popper maintained he had resolved this, his resolution raised other serious problems.

The problem of induction

The problem is a logical one, that the confirmation of the hypothesis relies on the principle of induction, that is, from the observation of particular phenomena we can come to generalise about wider phenomena. To continue the simple example, if we heat many samples of water at sea level and they all boil at 100° it would seem that we can claim that all water boils at 100° at sea level. The problem is how many kettles of water would we need to boil to make such a claim? Certainly more than one. Five, maybe? Fifty? This problem has a long history in philosophy, but in the twentieth century its articulation became most famously associated with Popper (1959: 27–48). He too illustrated the problem with a simple example. For centuries Europeans believed that swans were white, and this knowledge was just about as firm as knowledge could be, but in the fullness of time (after Europeans first voyaged to Australia), black swans were discovered (Popper 1986: 43). It took only one black swan to 'falsify' such a long held theory. Popper goes on to propose a solution to this which keeps intact the HD model, but his solution raises as many problems as it solves.

Popper's 'demarcation' criterion

Because of the logical problem of induction theories can never be shown to be true, never finally confirmed, but they can be shown to be false. Popper's views on this matter derived from when he was a young man in Vienna. At this time Marxism and the psychoanalysis of Freud and Adler were highly regarded and claimed to be 'scientific'. Yet as Popper recalls:

These theories appeared to be able to explain practically everything that happened within the fields to which they referred ... [there were] confirming instances everywhere: the world was full of *verifications* of the theory. Whatever happened always confirmed it.

(Popper 1989: 34–5; emphasis in original)

How could these theories ever be shown to be wrong? He contrasts these with Einstein's predictions from the General Theory of Relativity. This, he claims, led to predictions which were risky – they predicted something novel (in this case the bending of light by the gravitational effects of large bodies, such as the sun). This conjecture could be experimentally tested and risked being wrong (Popper 1989: 36). However, if theories and their derived hypotheses can never be finally confirmed, what counts as a good theory? First, it is easy to find confirmations if we look for them. What Popper proposes is that we set out with a different spirit, that of trying to show that we are wrong by proposing the most rigorous tests possible of our theories. If the theories stand up to such tests, they can for the time anyway be accepted. Second, a theory should forbid certain things to happen and the more it forbids, the better it is. Third, theories which do not have criteria of falsifiability are not scientific (Popper 1989: 36).

Popper's views have been controversial since they first appeared in English in 1959. The case against 'falsifiability' has been rehearsed from a number of angles (Lakatos 1970; Jeffrey 1975; Reichenbach 1978; Gemes 1989). Two principle objections can be picked out. First that his falsification (at least in its early guise) is 'naïve' (Lakatos 1970: 95–113), that if it was upheld through the history of science then theories which were initially 'falsified' would have been abandoned. As Alan Chalmers notes:

An embarrassing historical fact for falsificationists is that if their methodology had been strictly adhered to by scientists then these theories generally regarded as being amongst the best examples of scientific theories would never have been developed because they would have been rejected in their infancy.

(Chalmers 1982: 66–75)

Chalmers cites examples to illustrate this, one of which concerns the fact that Newton's gravitational theory was falsified by observations of the moon's orbit, just a few years after the theory's inception. It took nearly fifty years to show that the causes for this had nothing to do with the theory itself.

A second problem often cited concerns probability. Falsification requires a conjecture to be set out in terms of precise observations anticipated. Einstein's General Theory, for example, predicted the bending of the sun's rays during a solar eclipse. Thus had the rays not been bent, the conjecture would have been falsified. But in much of science results are probabilistic – in social science this is almost universally the case. Much of the justification for induction has traditionally rested on an enumerative principle expressed as the probability of a hypothesis being right (Gower 1997: 189–207), but Popper's falsification principle must lead him to reject this on the grounds that however much evidence is gathered the probability of any *universal* statement is zero. The reasoning for this is that in a closed system of possible outcomes (say the tossing of a coin) we can predict that the probability of heads coming up is 50 per cent, but in expressing the probability of an event where the number of possibilities is potentially infinite we must assume a principle of the uniformity of nature, i.e. that the phenomenon of which we make the inference in general is and will remain approximately the same as the specific phenomena we measured. According to Popper, probability (at least in its usual frequency form) requires justification through a principle of induction (Popper 1959: 29–30). However, apart from rendering a great deal of science unjustified, a rejection of probability seems to be counter-intuitive in everyday life. Bookmakers, as we know, do very nicely out of a reliance on probability – they at least have no problem with inductive inference! Actually, because it seems hard to deny that science uses probability successfully, Popper had to modify his theory in order to show how scientists adopt methodological rules in order to treat probability estimates as falsifiable (O'Hear 1980: 124–32).

A third and very important problem is what counts as a falsification anyway? This brings us back to the social-psychological status of theories. Popper's view was that a theory is a 'bold conjecture' and it actually didn't matter where it came from; what mattered was what you did with it when you had it. It could derive from painstaking years in the laboratory, or could have been dreamt up after an evening's over-indulgence (Williams and May 1996: 31), but once stated it possesses logical properties. On the face of it this seems okay, but in allowing that there may be a social-psychological element in the derivation of theories it is hard to resist the charge that the means of falsification itself may also be prone to social or psychological subjectivity. How can we be sure that these means are more valid than the theory itself? We cannot, of course. Popper's defence is that the observation statements that might falsify a theory are themselves intersubjectively testable within the scientific community, thus in principle also falsifiable (Popper 1959: 95–106). However, we shall see later in Chapter 6, intersubjectivity in science is not without its difficulties.

The aim of Popper's approach was primarily to produce a demarcation between science and non-science (or pseudo-science) (Popper 1959: 42). The unintended consequence of this was to focus attention on the matter of theory choice. Whilst it is logically correct that a singular negative statement can falsify many positive statements, what is important is the status of the claim to falsification and the status of the theory that is to be falsified. As Popper himself admits the decision about whether a theory is falsified is a matter of intersubjective agreement – it is then the outcome of a social process. But so too is the original theory. Although single hypotheses or 'hunches' about data may be born of sudden and individual inspiration, fully formed theories rarely are. Popper's method may be adequate to the testing of specific hypotheses, or parts of theories, but only rarely in the history of science has a crucial experiment falsified a whole body of theory. It may, however, be important that this remains a possibility.

What perhaps lies at the heart of Popper's philosophy is a credo of self-criticism in science, that of the critical attitude. Whilst I will argue later a credo of rigorous methodological criticism is the key characteristic of science, it does not amount to a 'method', nor does it provide a clear science/non-science demarcation.

Nature and the social practice of science

The logical strategy of showing something to be wrong turns out to not be much more helpful to the accretion of reliable knowledge as the one of showing something to be right. Inductive and falsificationist strategies end up failing on similar grounds, that is they depend on evaluation of evidence from the world in the court of human consciousness. In other words the only means we have to assess whether something is right or wrong are our senses and previous standards of corroboration or falsification. The truth about the world will be the truth mediated through human consciousness and whilst this may indeed be the truth, we cannot know that it is. As the philosopher William James pointed out: ' ... theories are a man made language, a conceptual shorthand in which we write our reports of nature' (James 1949: 57). This does not necessarily mean that we can't know reality, just that we can't know that we know reality! Even when we think we have good grounds for saying that we know a particular thing, we can't be sure that what we know is all there is to know about that thing, or even that what we know is correct.

For Popper deductive logic in the form of the falsifiability of statements is the only bastion against the subjectivism of ideology, dogma and caprice in science. Yet scientists, even when using the methodological device of falsification, can nevertheless fall prey to subjectivity in their choice of theory or tests. Rarely do they simply accept or reject theories on the basis of what he calls 'crucial experiments' (Popper 1979: 14), but nor do they arbitrarily choose one theory over another. Discovery and justification so often intermesh in a complex structure of theory choice, probabilistic reasoning and subjective or serendipitous factors. In the remainder of this chapter I will take a brief look at some of these factors.

Theory choice

Observations do not occur innocent of some conceptual framework and in science that is usually one of theory and hypothesis. Observations, then, have a history, but so do theories. Popper's 'falibilism' allows that theories can arise from anywhere and perhaps everywhere, but in actuality this would be rare. Science does not proceed by testing theories in isolation of other theories and moreover the connections between theories, and between theories and earlier observations, both constrain and license the predictions of any given theory. A theory itself has properties other than its predictive content. William Newton-Smith (1981: 226–32) proposes eight characteristics of good theory:

Observational nesting: A new theory should explain observed phenomena as well as its predecessor. Increasing observational success is a primary indicator that we are moving nearer to the truth of the way the world is. Indeed it might be added here that a theory that can explain more should be preferred to one which explains the same range of phenomena.

Fertility: A theory should be capable of being developed further to explain a range of phenomena. In itself this is not enough of a characteristic. Newton-Smith notes that psychoanalysis was a fertile theory, but ultimately did not bear fruit.

Track record: The longer a theory has been around, the more important its track record becomes. What have been its observational successes? A theory with a good track record of success is to be preferred to one with a poor track record.

Inter-theory support: A theory which is compatible with other theories is to be preferred over one that is not. Even if two theories are each successful, but they are incompatible each with the other, then one or other must be incorrect as they stand. Newton-Smith cites the success but incompatibility of Quantum Mechanics and General Relativity as an example of this.

Smoothness: Most theories will explain only part of a range of phenomena it is wished to explain and to provide explanations for the remainder scientists often introduce auxiliary hypotheses. A counter-example will serve here. In this respect Marxism has failed, for in order to explain its predictive failures many more than one auxiliary hypothesis must be introduced.

Internal consistency: Are the various statements in the theory logically compatible with each other? Does it contain internal *non sequiturs*?

Compatibility with well grounded metaphysical beliefs: Scientific theories rest on a foundation of metaphysical beliefs about the world. A theory can in principle deny one or more of these to be true, but mostly such beliefs are not testable. Newton-Smith offers as an example the rejection of the proposal 'that something in the physical world happened because the time was ripe for it to happen' in favour of 'something happened in time to explain the event' (1981: 229)

Simplicity: There has been a historical preference for parsimony in theories, of ontological economy – the principle of Ockham's Razor (see Chapter 1). In other words the more a theory explains in the fewest terms the better it is. Thus two theories may explain a set of observations, but the simpler of the two is preferred provided it is consistent with other known facts. Nevertheless as Newton-Smith observes, simplicity expressed in this way is not always possible or desirable (1981: 231). Quantum Mechanics looks more complex than classical mechanics, but we have good reason to suppose the former to be a closer approximation to the truth and therefore to be preferred.

Others offer slightly different criteria of a good theory, but whichever one adopts the message is simple, that there are several 'tests' of a theory and the more of these a theory passes the more likely it is that it will commend itself to the scientist. Furthermore scientists are not just passive observers of nature and will do their utmost to empirically discriminate between theories through testing the consequences predicted by each theory. Only very rarely will two theories each pass a range of tests made by the scientist. Of course the scientist may end up picking the wrong theory, or both theories may be ultimately wrong (as was the case for wave and particle theories of light). Often though the scientist has only one theory to work with and when the test (often an experiment) result contradicts the theory the scientist will want to know why. A culprit is very often the 'initial conditions' that were assumed, or the instruments used in the test. Finally, though there is no sharp distinction between a theory and a hypothesis, a theory will usually consist of several hypotheses. Obviously if tests failed to confirm any of these then it is likely the theory would be abandoned, or extensively modified. Quite often only one hypothesis fails to agree with test results. It then seems reasonable to conclude that at least some of the theory is right and the search is on to find the bit of the theory that was wrong, or what might be error in other assumptions underlying the 'failed' test.

Inductive inference

Whilst inductive arguments are not syllogistically valid (the conclusion is not entailed in the premises as in a deductive argument), inductive inference seems to be substantively unavoidable. At an everyday level our survival must depend on inductive assumptions – as indeed Hume himself insisted (Hume [1739] 1911). It might well be the case that a child can play in a busy road without injury or death, but it would be a very irresponsible adult that lets it do so. A scientist whose theory predicts certain phenomena, which are subsequently found, is more likely to be right than wrong. That is not to say that the scientist has obtained *true* knowledge, but instead knowledge that is probably true. Alternatively we could say that whilst something is not proven, it is proven beyond reasonable doubt. The inductive reasoning is not 'cold', rather it is located within a framework of facts which are not offended by the findings. For example a concentration of cases of childhood leukaemia near a nuclear power station would *suggest* an association between location and the likelihood of developing leukaemia, given our existing knowledge of the effects of radiation. If on further investigation it was discovered that in all, or virtually all cases, a parent had carried out work on or near the reactor core, and that decontamination procedures were lax, it would be a reasonable *assumption* to associate these prior circumstances with the cases of leukaemia. There may of course be other explanations, but given the known facts this is the most likely. Although, strictly speaking, this is still inductive reasoning because it is still logically possible for there to be other explanations, it is intuitively very like a deductive inference (Couvalis 1997: 53). Such a procedure as this is known as inference to the best explanation.

Probability

The statement that theories are 'probably true' has not satisfied all philosophers of science by any means, but scientists (like bookmakers) would claim to be vindicated by predictive success. Moreover, as this century has progressed science has become more 'probabilistic' in its methods, mainly as a result of the realisation that the world itself is, at the quantum level, intrinsically unpredictable and indeed systems in the non-quantum world may also in principle be non-deterministic (Feynman 1965: 127–48). Thus the idea that science is about simple mechanical cause and effect relationships is simply a persistent myth. As long ago as the second decade of this century Bertrand Russell (cited in Miller 1995) was moved to remark that in advanced sciences such as gravitational astronomy the word 'cause' never occurs. Much of science is probabilistic. Two examples illustrate this.

Brownian motion describes the irregular movement of minute particles of matter when suspended in a liquid. Whilst the movement of any given particle cannot be known, when the liquid is heated the particles move faster, when it is cooled they move more slowly. Aggregate movement can be known and the movement of any given particle could be described probabilistically. The second example is that of turbulence in liquids, such as the water flow in a river. A characteristic of this is aptly illustrated by the game of Pooh Sticks. Pooh and Piglet each throw a stick into the river one side of a bridge and rush to the other side to see which will emerge first. Neither Pooh, Piglet or the watching scientist can determine which will emerge first. Turbulence, like Brownian motion, can be predicted but not determined.

Yet of course assuming the sticks are thrown into the river at the same time and assuming they are of equal weight and the same shape (the initial conditions), then there is a 50 per cent chance of either stick emerging first. The odds can be known. Even if the weight of the sticks differed, or one was thrown into the water earlier than the other, it would still be possible to mathematically calculate the changed probability of each stick arriving first. This is, in scientific terms, an easy problem to calculate, but for Pooh Sticks substitute ecological systems, complex chemical reactions, or the trajectory of a comet – the principle remains the same. Mathematical axioms can be used to calculate the probability of systems, or parts thereof, behaving in particular ways. Though mathematics in general, nor probability theory in particular, cannot themselves tell us much about the truth of the way the world is, they can at least help us to understand and accurately predict relationships between parts of the world. As our mathematical abilities have developed, so has our ability to more accurately predict. The development of Aristotelian logic, the development of the mathematical calculus and of the computer have all significantly aided the process of discovery and justification of findings. And of course the existence of the former two were essential to the possibility of the third as a scientific tool.

Mathematical modelling and simulations have become as important to the scientist as the laboratory experiment. The complexity of simulations, or the ability to deal with very large numbers, is the domain of the computer alone. Nature, it would seem, is too big and too complex to be known in its detail solely through human brain power.

Subjectivity and serendipity

The foregoing indicates that science and its method are much more complex than confirmationist or falsificationist accounts suggest. The HD model can be seen as an ideal type of reasoning, but perhaps more importantly the acceptance or rejection of a hypothesis must be seen in the context of the status of a whole web of theories and the nature of the connections between them. Moreover, findings are rarely 'true' or 'false', but usually assessed in terms of their probability, often within a hierarchy of knowledge, where the 'higher' one goes, the more 'certain' the knowledge is. Yet despite this complexity, particular researchers usually focus on just one problem at a time and they rarely have a knowledge of the hierarchy, or how their work affects its epistemological status (Sanitt 1996: 14). Particular standards are inherited, but the work of investigation is not determined beforehand. There will be many false trails, mistakes and reassessments of past work. This process of investigation itself combines several things: first it relies on a set of technical procedures, often particular to a discipline, or subdiscipline; second, it relies on the provisional belief that certain assumptions are true; and third, it relies on testing both of these through observation, experiment or deduction. The interface between all of these things is constantly in flux and whilst some things are held as constants, others change, though rarely does everything change at once in a discipline. In the history of astronomy and cosmology, for example, the development of optics made observations of distant bodies possible and the observation in turn allowed the development of theory such that we can trace an observational and theoretical history from Copernicus to Hawking. In the last few years alone the concept of 'Black Holes' in space has moved from the 'fringe' science that Isaac Asimov talked of only in 1987 (Asimov 1995), simply theoretical objects, to objects for which there is a growing body of empirical evidence. Black Holes were predicted as a logical consequence of Einstein's General Theory, were theorised by Karl Schwarzschild in 1916 (Gribben 1996: 62), but convincing evidence for their existence was not forthcoming until the advent of powerful radio telescopes, and particularly after the launch of the Hubble Space Telescope in 1990.

The sociologist of science Bruno Latour neatly illustrates the dynamic and indeed serendipitous nature of science in a series of 'flashbacks' directly and indirectly concerning DNA research (Latour 1987). In his first flashback molecular biologist John Whittaker is admiring a three-dimensional picture of the DNA double helix on his computer screen. Whittaker, Latour tells us, is uncertain whether his research programme will yield results, or whether his fellowship at the *Institut Pasteur* will be renewed, but what he can be certain of is 'the double helix shape of DNA and his Data General computer' (Latour 1987: 2). In further episodes Latour tells the story of the difficult development programme of the computer, the elaborate de-bugging necessary and how it was nearly never finished and marketed at all. The narrative of these two stories is punctuated by that of the discovery of the structure of DNA, in 1951, by Jim Watson and Francis Crick. The discovery of the structure of DNA (deoxyribonucleic acid), sometimes called the 'blueprint' of life, has made possible a vast amount of research since in genetics, pharmacology and oncology, and has made possible the 'Human Genome Project' (described in Chapter 6). In 1951 this discovery (like penicillin) was sought and indeed heralded to the point where there was a race between Watson and Crick and the (then much better known) American chemist Linus Pauling. Shortly before their 'breakthrough' Watson and Crick were presented with a paper showing that Pauling had discovered the structure, but appeared to have made a basic error in his chemistry. This is how Latour summarises Watson and Crick's dilemma:

To decide whether they are still in the game Watson and Crick have to evaluate simultaneously Linus Pauling's reputation, common chemistry, the tone of the paper, the level of Cal Tech's students [students who assisted Pauling]; they have to decide if a revolution is underway, in which case they have been beaten off, or if an enormous blunder has been committed, in which case they have to rush still faster because Pauling will not be long picking it up.

(Latour 1987: 6)

Watson, Crick and Pauling each depended on a vast body of 'firm' knowledge, indeed the mistake referred to Pauling's apparent failure to recognise the known part of hydrogen atoms in the structure. Thirty-four years later Whittaker was able to do his work only because he could build upon the even greater body of 'firm' knowledge bequeathed to him by Watson and Crick and DNA research since. In 1951 researchers had no computers (as we understand them), therefore the success of Whittaker's work depends not just on firm knowledge, but on technology and the techniques made possible because of it. Yet in each of the flashbacks we are struck by the serendipity of what happens, or even the luck. It could have been otherwise and frequently in science it is, yet most scientific literature, both specialist and popular, reports only the success of science. Experiments go wrong, theories are misconceived and errors of interpretation and calculation occur.

Latour's narrative is an attempt to present a picture of how science gets done, the nature of contingent connections, of serendipity, of rivalry and of competition. His story reads like soap opera, portraying science as a very human activity, which of course it is and indeed the intention of his work is to deny any useful distinction between science and, for example, politics (Chalmers 1990: 80). Whether or not this view is correct it remains that science getting done is messy with the methods and procedures hard to disentangle from the social relations of science. Whittaker's training would incline him to the formal reasoning of science, but also towards seeing the tools he uses (his computer for example) as a 'black box' and whilst he would have a firm understanding of the biology and chemistry of DNA he may be unfamiliar with more fundamental physical theories. These too would be black boxes. The competitive nature of science drives him towards wanting firm results as much for the sake of his salary and career as simply a thirst for knowledge. Though separated by decades Watson, Crick and Pauling could be similarly described, as could most scientists engaged in research.

Conclusion

At the beginning of this chapter I referred to scientific method as an ensemble of practices and knowledge. The question of this chapter has been what makes scientific method scientific? Popper's falsificationism illustrated the difficulty of pursuing a simple demarcation criterion between science and non-science. I have instead suggested that science is a heterogeneous system of methodological checks and balances involving testing, theory choice, and logical and mathematical reasoning. However, to this we must add the 'human' element of science. At a philosophical level what we 'know' of the world we know only through our knowledge as participating agents in the world. As Thomas Nagel observed, there is no 'view from nowhere' (Nagel 1986). At the level of scientific practice the activity is a social one and it would therefore be surprising if science did not take on at least some of the character of other social activities.

Scientific discovery, though usually directed toward more complex phenomena, nevertheless follows the same kinds of cognitive patterns as everyday discovery. Indeed as Jacob Bronowski (1960) noted much of what was once ground-breaking knowledge often becomes commonplace later. The discoveries of Galileo or Newton are now the basis of common sense knowledge. Yet what has been discovered is to a great extent cumulative and at least partially determines the discovery agenda of the future. The cumulative nature of knowledge and the refinement of the technical means to discovery are enough to account for the complexity and counter-intuitiveness of many of those discoveries Wolpert calls 'unnatural'. Any activity which has refined its practices and the means to its goals will be unnatural (to a greater or lesser degree) to the outsider. We can comprehend the outcomes of science, but not understand how scientists got there, just as we can comprehend great music without understanding the intricacies of its production.

Though science is in the business of discovery, this is shaped by and shapes theories. But theories come and go. Scientists insist at one point that X is right, but later that it isn't and Y is. For example at different times the scientific orthodoxy has supported both wave and particle theories of light, but nowadays neither are seen to be wholly true (Nagel 1979: 143–5). This surely must cause us to doubt all of their findings? There are three things to say here. First, a lot of science remains 'right' even after a very long time. Though many of the findings of Galileo or Copernicus are now part of the history of science, they are not wrong. In the few decades since the Watson and Crick discovery we have learnt considerably more about DNA, but their findings remain fundamentally correct. Even though it is commonplace to say Newtonian physics was superseded by Einsteinian physics, it remains the former is still 'right', but is limited in what it can explain. Since the advent of quantum physics the aforementioned theories of light have been 'incorporated' into a new theory, whereby light travels in discrete 'quanta', appearing as waves or particles depending on how it is measured.

Second, any old theory will not do. Scientists hold a concept of good theories and bad theories and as Newton-Smith shows, we can distinguish these on a number of criteria. A scientist's defence of 'getting it wrong' is that, as in everyday life, science learns by its mistakes and in doing so moves closer to the truth. Third, justification in science is complex. Theories do not exist in isolation but as part of what W.V. Quine called 'a web of belief' (Quine [1951] 1961). Though he was referring just to theories, we must also include accumulated techniques and standards of testing and inference.

Each of these components of 'good theory' or of justification through testing or inference is in itself neither a necessary or sufficient condition for scientific method. Yet the whole is greater than the sum of the parts, but not all of the parts need to be in place at the same time. Moreover at different times and in different circumstances particular aspects of method will be emphasised. This plurality in method is inevitable because scientists are part of that which they study. The final court of appeal is human consciousness, thus science in general and its method in particular are an attempt to render the workings of the natural world manifest to human consciousness. Yet it does not follow from this that method is subjective, or even arbitrary, but it is necessarily intersubjective. That is, within the scientific community certain procedures and certain knowledge will be taken to be scientific. What counts as method rests on the intersubjective *values* of the scientific community.

At this point controversy arises. Those whom we might loosely term 'realists' will claim that the methodological values of the scientific community arise out of the fact that science discovers objective facts about the world. That is, that the world exists independently of us and a successful method is marked by its ability to reveal the world to us; the 'realist' can be more specific here. She can cite particular values which are general to all science. The first is verisimilitude, or 'truth likeness'. Science aims for increasing our stock of truths about the world. Second, science is a fallible enterprise, that is, scientists can be wrong. Now this is not quite the same as Popperian falsification (though Popper would have claimed it should be), but simply a willingness to take seriously contrary evidence. The third value is that science is logical, being based upon sound reasoning. Although these may be consensual values held by the scientific community they do not simply derive from the social structure of science but instead from their efficacy as a means to explain reality.

Those who we might (again loosely) term social constructionists deny that science is an objective encounter with the world, as suggested by the 'realists'. The values of science do not arise out of any privileged access to nature, but are simply contingent social constructions. In this view science is just one story of many about the world and the privileged knowledge that scientists claim is just a manifestation of their ideological success in convincing us of this.

This controversy is important to social scientists, for if a version of social constructionism is right then any description of studies of the social world as 'scientific' would amount to no more than the claim that social science holds the same set of socially constructed values as natural science. In Chapter 4 I will return to this debate about the social character of science and in Chapter 6 the question of objectivity and social context, but in the next chapter I want to consider the case for the social sciences as 'scientific' in the narrower sense of whether or not its investigations can proceed in the same or similar ways to those of the physical world.

Suggested further reading

Gower, B. (1997) *Scientific Method: An Historical and Philosophical Introduction*, London: Routledge.

Newton-Smith, W. (1981) *The Rationality of Science*, London: Routledge & Kegan Paul.

Sanitt, N. (1996) *Science as a Questioning Process*, Bristol: Institute of Physics.

3 Social science as science

In the last two chapters I have described the historical and methodological context of science, concluding that whilst we must see it as historically contingent, it is nevertheless possible to discern cognitive and material progress. This progress, though not explicable through any universal methodological or logical criteria, may however be explained by the persistence of certain values over time. These in turn have led to (what we must assume is) the best iteration yet of scientific method. In this chapter I will argue that there is enough commonality between the methodological approach to studies of the physical world and the social world to qualify study of the latter as science. This qualification does, however, come warts and all and if social science is science then these objections apply to it equally. In the following chapter I discuss these generic objections, and in Chapter 5 I discuss an alternative approach to investigation that arises out of specific objections to science in social science.

I have divided this chapter into two sections: first, 'Conceptualising a Social *Science*' and second, 'Doing Social *Science*'. In the first I will set out some broad philosophical reasons for considering investigations of the social world as a subset of scientific investigations of the world in general and briefly reflect on an implication of a denial of this. In the second I will consider some key methodological similarities and differences between the social sciences and the natural sciences through some brief sketches of how social science is done.

Conceptualising a social *science*

Naturalism

The justification for adopting a position of a 'unity of method' rests on the philosophical principle of 'naturalism'. Naturalism is defined in a number of ways (Papineau 1993: 2–5; Kincaid 1996: 3–4; Gower 1997: 257–8), but in social science it is usually taken to mean that human beings belong to an objective natural order and that the social world is continuous with, or arises from, the physical world.

From this it is usually reasoned that we should explain the relation of humans to the world in terms of that order, therefore with appropriate adaptation, the methodological approach of natural science can be used to study the social world. Though of course as in the natural sciences, the phenomena themselves will lend difference to method, as is the case (for example) between astronomy and biology. Of course there may be reasons why natural science methods are not adequate to the task of studying the social world, in which case whilst science in social science is possible in principle, it is not so in practice (Kincaid 1996: 3). This, however, does not impair the philosophical argument, any more than an inability to study any part of the physical world disqualifies it as being itself natural.

Naturalism has historically taken a number of forms in social science, such as positivism and realism, and these epistemological positions are mirrored in the natural sciences. Though each takes different views on the properties of the world, how they are manifested or can be investigated, for the most part naturalism is usually taken to depend on an ontological principle of reduction. That is, whatever the fundamental basis of the universe is, all things are regarded as deriving from it. This often takes a physicalist form, claiming that the ultimate constituent of the universe is physical matter, say elementary particles, and all else exists by virtue of such fundamental arrangements (Papineau 1993: 7). This implies that biology is reducible to chemistry and chemistry to physics. Sociology would therefore be reducible to psychology and psychology to biology. By reducible it is meant that the antecedent or component characteristics of any phenomenon could, at least in principle, be followed back to earlier and lower states. This does not mean that the separate disciplines of science become redundant, simply that they study nature in its different manifestation. For the naturalist these manifestations of mind and matter are simply what philosophers sometimes call 'placeholders' for an all encompassing natural kind (Pettit 1993). Naturalism, as I argue later, does not imply determinism and is compatible with the view that aggregations can take on a character not apparent in their parts, that new characteristics can 'emerge' or arise *ex nihilo* from earlier ones.

Anti-naturalists rarely overtly claim that 'mind' and 'matter' are distinct entities, but rather that they are manifested as such. This was substantially the view of Wilhelm Windelband, an importance influence on early social science. In his view all science and knowledge refer to the same reality, but different disciplines have different concerns and approach reality accordingly. He divided disciplines into the 'nomothetic', the natural sciences, the aim of which is the identification of universal laws, and 'ideographic' disciplines such as history, which study the unique character of particular events (Hammersley 1989: 29). Even if there is no philosophical assertion of a divide between the world of 'mind' and that of 'matter' anti-naturalists maintain that in practice such a divide exists between the world of culture produced by autonomous, self-reflecting human agents and the world of nature. Thus the social world as manifested has a different ontological status. Physical and social (or mental) *properties* are not then of the same natural kind. The properties of the physical world, it is held, may be known objectively by human observers, but those of the social world must be studied subjectively through a strategy of interpretation.

The German philosopher Wilhelm Dilthey was an important early influence upon (what I have termed) anti-naturalism (Outhwaite 1975). Dilthey was not anti-scientific as such, but instead wished to set out a different road to objectivity and validity in (what he termed) the 'human sciences'. The human sciences, he held, should use the method of *verstehen* (understanding), whereas natural sciences should seek causal explanations. Social life, for Dilthey, was the outcome of minds and was composed of intersubjectively held, but changing meanings often passionately held. It was, therefore, a phenomenon not subject to causal explanation. Culture for Dilthey, and those who follow in this tradition, is the object of study for the social investigator, but it is also contingent. If cultures are contingent and rest upon intersubjectively held meaning, then the investigator too must be seen as part of such a milieu and is simply engaged in making one culture (or part thereof) intelligible to another. The best that social investigation can do is to create impressions, which despite the use of the word 'science' by Dilthey is actually closer to being an artistic not scientific enterprise. For example when I look at the Sisley print on my office wall I do not expect this to be an accurate detailed description, but rather Sisley's subjective impression of (in this case) the riverbank at Sainte Mamnès. I want to feel that the painting conveys something of the 'mood', or the 'feel' of the place, concepts hard to pin down into firm description. Indeed millions of people have looked at the painting, or its reproductions, and have gained an impression of the riverbank at Sainte Mamnès and there is no one 'right' or 'authoritative' view.

However, whether or not this view of what the social world is like and thus how we should come to know it, is right or wrong it does have important consequences. Kincaid (1996: 4–6) points out, for example, that it brings with it the acceptance that social science can neither explain nor predict the social world, that 'the best that social scientists can do is give us many different kinds of literary "thick" description of social reality' (Geertz 1994: 213–33). If this is so, according to Kincaid, social policy is groundless and 'government intervention in social and economic affairs would be inane. How could we evaluate educational programs, prison reform, economic policy and so on without having well-confirmed generalisations … [?]' (Kincaid 1996: 5–6).

Nevertheless it is claimed that anti-naturalism can give rise to a method of knowing the social world and I will consider this in Chapter 5, but now I will look at some general considerations of the process of discovery in the social world, contrasting it with that in the physical world.

Discovery in the social world

The first thing to say is that the 'social world' is a theoretical construction of the social scientist or philosopher. The constructs used to make the social world intelligible (such as forms of stratification, economic behaviour, etc.) are either alien concepts for those to which we apply them, or they are used in a different and simpler way. For example the common sense perception of class is quite different to that of the social scientist. In everyday life people are in what the phenomenologists call the *natural attitude* (Schutz [1932] 1967). That is they are unreflective participants and observers of the world.

Second, at a common sense level people do not sharply distinguish between the characteristics of the physical and social world, nor in how causal or purposive descriptions are ascribed. For example human beings commonly attribute purpose to nature and often anthropomorphise animal behaviour and elements of the natural world (Leakey and Lewin 1992: 307), ascribing human characteristics to forests, rocks, the wind etc. in many cultures. Conversely the dynamic and multi-faceted nature of personal identity is not usually captured in everyday characterisations. People are described as this kind of person, or that kind of person in much the same way as a car, a house or a dog is described. Perhaps these 'typifications', as Schutz (1967) describes them, are necessary to make intersubjective understanding possible?

Third, everyday language is causal language. That is to say, a response to a why question can be considered an explanation. Why were you late? Because I had to buy socks in Woolworths. Why didn't you eat your meat? Because I don't like liver. ... and so on. Reasons for action are treated in the same way (indeed reason and cause are often interchangeable in use) as physical causes. Whether or not the social scientist would wish to treat reasons as causes, in the natural attitude this does seem to be the case in everyday usage (Papineau 1978: chapter 4).

Finally what social scientists call the social world often has physical characteristics that are socially produced or interpreted (see for example Thrift 1996). In the natural attitude the social construction of a motor car or a pair of shoes is ignored in favour of their physical characteristics. Again that is not to say that fashion, for example, is not understood in the everyday attitude, but just that its sociological status is not apparent.

Social science can be seen both as 'common sense' and as 'unnatural' in the sense meant by Wolpert. The natural attitude towards the social world leads to everyday discovery in much the same way as the physical world and they are only really made separate as modes of discovery by the social scientist. Though the origins of social science are somewhat obscure (Heilbron 1995: 1–2) as with natural science, they almost certainly began with common sense curiosity about the world, but even though social science is newer than natural science and is arguably less sophisticated, its evolving methods and corpus of knowledge mean that many of its findings are counter-intuitive – 'unnatural' in Wolpert's sense. Indeed the whole point of social science is to produce explanations that transcend common sense knowledge, or at least to 'correct and improve upon notions used by actors themselves in interpreting their own actions and the actions of others' (Giddens 1993: 137–8).

It is not too surprising then that discovery of both physical and social aspects of the world should be similar in the natural attitude. In both cases discovery is socially mediated by psychological and social factors. This will shape (though as I argued in the last chapter not determine) what is to be discovered and how it is discovered. Accident, purpose and serendipity are present in all discovery. In both cases the 'unnatural nature' grew out of a natural attitude and remains mediated by psychological and social factors. Given this it is also not surprising that the early aim of social scientific knowledge was to produce truths about the social world with the same status as truths about the physical world, and that the motivations for investigations in each domain had many similarities. Indeed the interface of characteristics of the natural and social worlds and how these often conspired to produce ill health and poverty were a principal concern of early social policy (Mishra 1981: 11). Alan Murie (1983) emphasises, for example, the importance of public health concerns to early slum clearance. Knowledge of the effects of damp housing and poor ventilation on the human respiratory system arose from investigations in chemistry and biology, whereas knowledge of the social conditions of poor housing arose from studies such as those of Charles Booth in the East End of London and Seebohm Rowntree in York (Gauldie 1974). Although each approach had different disciplinary antecedents there was no explicit attempt to separate physical and social aspects of investigation, yet both kinds of investigation were problem-orientated. In both the natural and the social sciences discovery is motivated by a problem, which (again in both) might be inspired either by curiosity or a perceived social or political need. In this respect the sciences are similar and employ a problem-centred curiosity that is also found in everyday discovery.

Laws, causes and association

A psychological characteristic of humans and indeed most animals is a search for regularity. In everyday life this takes the form of habitual expectations, which have arisen from the awareness of past regularities in the world – the inductive principle. Whilst some (such as Popper) have sought to build a science which does not rely on induction, the existence and discovery of regularities are a major preoccupation of science. Regularities which are discovered to hold at all times and in all circumstances are laws of nature (see Chapter 2) and the aspiration of many supporters of naturalistic social science is to be able to identify their social equivalent (Hempel 1994).

Such a person was Karl Marx. Many of his concepts such as 'surplus value', the 'tendency of the rate of profit to decline' have the accents of nineteenth-century science writing and their articulation is the assertion of the existence of immutable laws in the social world, indeed a principal task in his later work was to identify the law of capital accumulation (Marx [1887] 1954: 574). There is no doubt that Marx thought he was producing science, though whether he meant quite the same thing by science as his contemporaries in physics or chemistry is doubtful (McLellan 1975: 58). However, we now know that Marx's 'law of capital accumulation' neither adequately explained nor predicted the future of capitalism. Profit has not declined, the first 'communist' revolution took place in a neo-peasant, not bourgeois society, and this revolution was, in its turn, overthrown by a capitalist one. Marx was not alone in proposing economic laws. Adam Smith, for example, proposed that an invisible hand was at work in so far as the individual pursuit of economic gain will result in beneficial outcomes for all (Smith [1776] 1970). Similarly, following Smith, David Ricardo declared that the principal problem of political economy was to determine the laws which regulated distribution between classes, proposing a causal link between profit, the needs of labourers and the rent yield of the land worked (Barber 1967: 79). The striking thing about these 'laws' and indeed virtually any we care to name in social science is that they are controversial. Whilst laws in the physical world get amended, superseded or very occasionally are shown to be false, the very existence of laws of the social world are disputed. This arises for two reasons. First, as in the case of Marx, the predictions they make are for the future, a future which for many Marxists remains just that. Second, in the case of Smith or Ricardo, they refer to phenomena which specified in particular historical or social contexts appear to obey the law, but in others do not. Smith's economic analysis, for example, though stressing the importance of a division of labour in the economy, was nevertheless based on a very simple economy, quite unlike those in more complex industrial societies. Similarly whilst Ricardo's analysis was sophisticated for its day it crucially depended upon an agricultural basis to political economy (Barber 1967: 81). To be a follower of Smith or Ricardo nowadays is to adhere to their 'laws' only in the most general way. Unlike laws in natural science specific effects cannot be deduced. Does this mean there can be no social laws of the kind favoured by Marx, Smith or Ricardo, or is it that social science is not yet sufficiently developed to produce laws?

For some the ability to explain the phenomena relevant to its domain in terms of laws is the hallmark of science. Carl Hempel, for example, attached particular importance to laws because only in them can we 'ground' causal explanations. An event, or set of events can only be said to have caused an effect if there are general laws connecting the former with the latter, so that if we are given a description of the antecedent events, we can deduce the effect with the help of the laws (Hempel 1965: 299–301).

In this view there would need to be social laws if there are any events in the social world that we could say are 'caused'.

This condition does not bode well for social science and indeed many have claimed that social laws are impossible for several reasons, all of which turn upon the contingent nature of the social world (Searle 1984; Fay 1996: 157–9). Humans have free will and there is nothing which determines that the social world must exist in particular way. The creations of the social world, even those with a physical manifestation such as money for example, can hold different meanings at various times and places. Moreover, there is no universal regularity in the social world, across time or place, or necessary connections with the physical world that would allow logical connectives between social laws (if they existed) and physical ones.

It is said, however, that these objections either draw the definition of a law too tightly (Kincaid 1996: 59–62), or they assume a deterministic version of causality. The two are related.

Laws in the physical world are rarely universal in scope, they have different statuses and they can be locally 'broken'. Laws can refer to a correlation of facts about the world, for example Boyle's law of the relationship between the pressure and volume of gases, or they might refer to sequential events in, for example, Galileo's laws of free fall and the parabolic trajectory of projectiles (Losee 1980: 117). That they can be 'broken' is illustrated by the second law of thermodynamics, which says that though entropy will increase in the universe, yet locally we can create, or nature creates, anti-entropic systems (even though there must be an eventual 'pay back').

On this basis a defence of social laws could be readily made. First, laws could relate to particular historical or cultural manifestations of the social world and this would not preclude a search for higher more general laws that would unify a group of more 'local' ones, as is the case in the physicists' search for a Grand Unified Theory (Horgan 1996: 60–92), uniting relativity and quantum theory. This in turn would allow at least rather general logical connectives with physical laws to be made, in for example economic laws which relate finite resources to economic behaviour. Second, social 'laws' are likely to be probabilistic. That is it may be possible to specify laws of aggregate behaviour, but impossible to specify laws of individual action. Lastly, laws may be locally 'broken', but that may not invalidate the law in the long term.

Whilst I am persuaded that these propositions are reasonable I would not want to defend them to the death, because I do not think that 'laws' are a necessary requirement for science. To begin with, as I noted in Chapter 2, there is no clear distinction between a 'theory' and a 'law'; both are generalisations, and both are capable of being partially (or completely) falsified. What counts is the firmness of evidence for the theory, or law. Laws are just those generalisations for which there are compelling reasons to think hold under specified circumstances. Generalisations are, however, a necessary requirement and the goal of making these as 'general' and firm as possible is one which natural and social scientists can each sign up to. A defence of generalisation (as opposed to laws) in the social world is much easier, especially if we can dispense with deterministic versions of causality.

The two principal philosophical versions of causality can be, roughly speaking, subsumed under the headings of 'natural necessity', or 'association' (Hospers 1973: chapter 5; Hage and Foley-Meeker 1988). In both cases a cause manifests itself when one event is preceded by another in time and the first event is seen to bring about the second. A 'natural necessity' version of causality holds, accidental association aside, that the second event had to be brought about, it could be no other way, that it was *determined* by nature. The Laplacian view of nature, discussed in Chapter 1, is underwritten by this principle. In contrast causality as association is a more sceptical view. This version, in a sense not 'causality' at all, originated with David Hume. His view, a bedrock of empiricism, was that there is no evidence in the observed association of two events that the first must bring about the second (Hume [1739] 1972: 148–9). For Hume it is all in the mind, a psychological expectation arising from our experience of similar associations in the past. Whilst Hume's version of causality is rarely upheld today in its original form, the idea of association – often statistical association – is the nearest most science gets to 'causality'. As I noted in Chapter 2, Russell claimed that an advanced scientific understanding of the world could dispense with causality. Certainly causality, in its natural necessity form, is more trouble than it is worth. There are two main problems. First, the necessity of identifying how X brings about Y requires us to posit a mechanism. For example the cause of a bridge collapsing might be poor maintenance, which led to the failure to identify sheared bolts, which in turn were the result of poor quality steel etc. Eventually we would follow this chain back to quantum description, itself a probabilistic one based on indeterminacy (Feynman 1965: 127–48). Second, it is difficult to identify all of the conditions that are necessary for a bridge to collapse and all of those which are sufficient. Some poorly maintained bridges don't collapse, some with sheared bolts don't and sometimes poor quality steel does not mean bolts will shear. Whilst it is possible to have a pretty good idea of the conditions under which bolts shear, bridges collapse etc., it is impossible to show how this was determined, for it could have been otherwise. Causality, or its denial, is very much bound up with mathematical complexity, or 'chaos', and I want to say much more about this in Chapter 7, but for the moment suffice to say that the search for 'certainty' in science (Casti 1991) is actually a search for damned near certainty! It might be the case that the world is ultimately 'determined' and some philosophers still argue this (see Honderich 1979), but most of the time scientists are just very probably right!

There is an exception to this, that is where a cause and effect can be locally deduced. By 'locally' I mean within a system, which could be bigger than a solar system, or just could be to do with bridges collapsing. A simple example suffices. The collapse of a bridge which was the result of the shearing of (say) 20 per cent of bolts securing it at one end cannot be seen to be determined. In another case there could have been a 20 per cent shearing of bolts and the bridge would have stayed up. If, however, all the bolts at one end were sheared then the bridge had to collapse because nothing was holding it up. This event was locally determined. This form of necessity is not quite the same thing, but is instead logical necessity, i.e. if bridges collapse when nothing holds them up, bridge X must collapse if there is nothing to hold it up.

Generalisation in the social world is then the same kind of enterprise as that in the physical world. I mean that at both the common sense level, where we do not really distinguish between the two when generalising from our discoveries, and I mean it at the scientific level where both the natural and social scientist generalise on the basis of an acceptable strength of association between variables. Of course in both cases logical necessity or local determinism is possible, though in the social sciences this is less common. Where they differ is the extent to which generalisations can apply. A physicist can sometimes make (literally) universal generalisations, which are known as 'laws', whereas a social scientist may not be able to generalise much beyond a specific community. At the beginning of the chapter I touched upon a philosophical justification for the rejection of naturalism, that the social world is contingent upon individuals who are free to interpret and construct the world in a number of ways. This argument is not the same as the one which holds that the social world is more complex than the physical world and for this reason alone generalisation will always be limited. The complexity is, however, said to arise from the contingency of culture but can be considered separately.

I do not want to dispute that the social world is complex and with reservations, which I will spell out in Chapter 5, I am prepared to admit that this complexity does arise from individual subjectivity and cultural heterogeneity, and further that the social world is more complex than the physical one. However, I believe that the manifestation of that complexity in the relationship of variables to each other is not in principle different and the strategies for measurement just the same. Although possibly the antecedent states of physical and social settings may be different they can both exhibit varying degrees of indeterminacy. The natural scientist, by virtue of experimental method, is able to control and manipulate a discrete set of variables. But not all measurement in natural science is conducted within the confines of the laboratory, much (as in the social world) is measurement within systems which are 'open' to one extent or another. This is the case, for example, in much of the biological sciences, meteorology, astronomy and oceanography. An open system is one within which we cannot know the possible effects of unseen variables either in producing observed effects, or in bringing about unpredictable change over time. Indeed even within the laboratory, in relatively 'closed' systems indeterminacy can be present, in the case of Brownian motion (discussed in Chapter 2) for instance. For the social scientist the indeterminacy is very much greater for she must always work within open systems, and even when laboratory experiments are possible (rare in social science as opposed to psychology), the 'social' variables being manipulated may be produced or changed by psychological or biological variables unidentified and not subject to manipulation.

The test of a law is that it leads to successful predictions. If predictions failed, then, as in the case of Marx or Smith, the law will be called into question. Laws require successful predictions, but successful predictions do not require laws. In open systems statistical prediction is possible and of course if Hume was right then there is reason to suppose that all patterns of events are ultimately statistical. The following from Alvin Sapperstein (1995) provides a nice example of indeterminism and the possibility of prediction in a hypothetical social setting. Suppose a circular table is set for dinner with four plates set around the circumference of the table and midway between each plate there is a wine glass. The first person to sit down is in the position of being able to choose whether she will use the glass to the left, or to the right. If she chooses the right then so must her fellow diners. Meanwhile other diners are milling around waiting to be seated at other similarly laid tables. Some will prefer a left handed wine glass, others a right, yet others will be indifferent, but the first person to choose on each table will determine the side each of the others on her table will take their wine. In this way those with a left preference, those with a right preference and those with no preference become distributed through the room. Now further suppose on some arbitrary whim it is decided to serve left-handed diners from one pot of food and right-handed from another. The 'left hand' pot contains contaminated food and those diners suffer food poisoning. Even if we had known left- and right-handed preference we could not have predicted deterministically which diners would be poisoned. A deterministic causal explanation would be inadequate because on following the causal chain back we would reach a point where outcomes depended wholly on a chance set of circumstances.

A criticism of Sapperstein's scenario is that it is too simplistic and it is likely that there would be a number of other intervening variables. This can be readily conceded, but in this case and in more realistic open systems indeterminacy is not necessarily a barrier to generalisation. Specifically we can know enough about a system to allow us to produce explanations of why something happened and to be able to predict, within certain parameters, future events. But let me stay with the Sapperstein example for the moment to show how prediction in open systems is possible.

The stages of the scenario from diners waiting to be seated to the subsequent food poisoning could be represented as A B C D E, where E is those persons suffering from food poisoning. Something like a Markov chain exists here whereby the state of a future system is effected only by its immediate past. So E is produced by D, but not directly by C. We cannot therefore determine the state E from any point other than D. However, what we can do is probabilistically predict E from A if we know two things: the total number of diners and the total number of portions of poisoned food. If there are 20 portions and 100 diners then the odds of any given person being in E are 1:5. This of course assumes that all those given poisoned food will eat it and subsequently suffer the effects. This is a very simple example and generalisation possibilities would be limited or vague, but I think it nevertheless neatly illustrates both social indeterminacy and how this is so much like indeterminacy in physical systems such as weather, water turbulence or biological systems (see Ruelle 1991).

In the natural sciences laws exist where there are well-established regularities. However, whilst the former may or may not be possible in the social world, generalisations are. The limits of generalisation in the social world are greater than the physical world, but both the physical and social world and systems within them are measurable at least probabilistically suggesting that the social world, like the physical world, is ordered – at least at a macroscopic level. Evidence for the ordered nature of the social world lies in our ability to measure and successfully predict future states. In the remainder of this chapter I will look at some of the ways in which this is done in empirical social science.

Doing social *science*

How do social scientists investigate the social world and how might it differ from that undertaken by their colleagues in the natural sciences? Much of the natural scientist's explanatory schema is located within a framework of laws, which themselves are governed by higher laws. The natural scientist's findings should not offend those laws and if they do the findings are in error, or the laws must be amended. The social scientist's explanatory schema is very much less rigid. The latter's investigations, like those of the natural scientist, will be underwritten by theory. However, unlike the natural sciences the findings could confirm or refute a part or all of a particular theory with few or no consequences for other theories.

Theories

The nearest social scientists get to a corpus of law is to operate within the context of Grand Theory (see Skinner 1985). Indeed at certain times in the history of social science particular grand theories have dominated, or at least hugely influenced, empirical work. One can cite Parsonian functionalism in the United States in the 1950s, and Marxism in Europe in the 1960s and 1970s (Swingewood 1991), but for much of the time, what Ken Menzies (1982: 1–8) describes as 'theoreticians' theory' (as opposed to research theory) does not inform empirical work. The strength of the links between Grand Theory and empirical social science do, however, depend upon the discipline. In sociology the links are rather weak and indeed this weakness led Robert Merton (1968) to suggest the need for 'theories of the middle range' to bridge the local hypotheses of empirical research with the Grand Theories of (say) Functionalism. Even in economics, often regarded as the most 'scientific' of the social sciences, rival ideologies have competed to establish economic laws (Schumpeter 1965).

Grand Theory, in social science, has a number of emphases and has followed diverse philosophical paths, particularly in this century (May 1996: chapter 2), but one matter that is at the centre of most theories is the question of action and structure. Classical theory such as that of Durkheim ([1896] 1952, [1912] 1961) holds that social structures exist autonomously of particular individuals and that such structures will have a great deal of influence upon (or even determine) the character and action of individuals. Conversely the social theory of Weber (1949, [1904] 1958) claims that individuals create the social world through their own meaningful action arising in individual interpretations of the world. In recent years there has been a concerted effort to resolve the action–structure problem with theorists such as Giddens (1984), Bourdieu (1977) and Habermas (1984, 1987) each having produced a theory which emphasises how social structure is reproduced, but changed by individuals. This debate and indeed how it can inform empirical social science is very important, but cannot be the focus of our attention here. It is mentioned because most theoretical positions informing research will, at least implicitly, be informed by a view of action or structure (Giddens 1984: 327–34). If one subscribes to Rational Action Theory, for example, then the assumption is that social structure simply exists as an outcome of the rational behaviour of individuals (see Elster 1986). The unit of analysis will be the individual and although this does not mean that research cannot be conducted on collectives, the focus will be how individual rationality is deployed and what are its outcomes for the collective. If, however, the theoretical underpinning of a research question was that of functionalism, the aim would be to explain a social institution or practice in terms of its consequences for the social system, or part of the social system (Foster 1974).

The theoretical basis will have consequences for the hypotheses produced and very likely the methods deployed. For example if one maintains that social structure is the unintended consequence of individual agents acting in their own perceived best interests then research will focus on individual reasoning and goals (Little 1991: 41). Conversely if it is held that the social character of individuals is a function of a given culture then research will focus on evidence for this in individual practices and attitudes.

Action and structure are not the only dichotomies that will drive theories. Emphases on conflict, or consensus, on language or material existence, on constructionism or on realism will shape not just the interpretation of findings, but the research question in the first place. Does this mean that social science is hopelessly compromised by theoretical in-fighting? The answer, I think, is a qualified 'no'. It is qualified in so much that sectarianism is not absent from social science, but such theoretical disagreements do not diminish the empirical adequacy of its constituent disciplines for two reasons:

First, within the disciplines a great deal of research is not about theory testing as such. Now by this I do not want to imply that it is 'empiricist', or anti-theoretical, just that theories are either not spelt out into conjectural statements, or the theoretical background is much looser. In quantitative research (the approach most usually associated with naturalism in social science) this takes two main forms. The first is of large scale data gathering, often through 'omnibus' surveys or censuses. In Britain there are a number of such large scale surveys, such as the General Household Survey, the Labour Force Survey, the Family Expenditure Survey, etc. The 'theory' here is often not specified and takes the form of a number of topics to be investigated which are arrived at in a relatively consensual way. The Census, in England and Wales, is a good example of this. After each Census a consultation period seeks to establish the topics that should be added, or subtracted in the following Census. In practice this consultation, though theoretically open to all, is usually amongst professional social scientists or policy-makers. The decision, for example, to exclude questions on whether a household had access to cooking facilities (1981), or include one on central heating (1991) indicates changing views on the importance of these topics (Dale and Marsh 1993: 7). Though the ensuing data sets are themselves 'atheoretical', they can become the raw material for secondary analysis which is itself theory driven (Dale *et al.* 1988: 28–9).

The second type of research is exemplified by large scale 'one off' surveys which are often topical. One example of this was the National Survey of Sexual Attitudes and Lifestyles, conducted in Britain in the early 1990s. In the book reporting on the findings of the study, the section entitled 'Theoretical Framework' occupies less than two pages (Wellings *et al.* 1994: 7–8) and consists of a brief discussion of the history of beliefs about sexual behaviour. No specific theories are tested, but instead the study explores a wide range of sexual practices and beliefs about sex – for example the final chapter is concerned with 'risk reduction strategies', mainly those associated with AIDS risk. In one sense the study is actually very 'theoretical', or even 'ideological', yet its findings could provide usable data for a wide range of particular theoretical positions on social structure.

Whilst these kinds of study are very large scale, it is also the case that because the theoretical framework of social science is looser than natural science, then even small scale studies will provide data that will have utility beyond the theoretical perspective that underlies them.

Second, as Merton recognised, not that much social research is influenced by Grand Theory. The dichotomous positions of action and structure, for instance, will influence research but usually this is not through any specific theoretical position such as 'functionalism' etc. More often than not debate will be around a substantive question in 'middle range' theory (though presumably to Merton's disappointment this will often have only a tangential relationship to Grand Theory; see Maynard 1998: 134–7 for a discussion of this). Current research in population geography, on urban to rural migration, illustrates this.

Classical migration theory was based upon the idea that migrants were rational economic agents who held perfect knowledge of the economic system (Jackson, 1986: 14). This model was quite sophisticated and employed a number of variables, and for many years enjoyed some success, at least whilst most migration was rural to urban. In the 1960s, however, it was noticed, mainly from a secondary analysis of census data, in Europe and the United States, that the direction of migration changed. This kind of urban–rural migration has been termed 'counter-urbanisation' (Berry 1976: 17). The problems for counter-urbanisation have been both definitional and empirical. Definitional in that it is difficult to pinpoint exactly what is meant by 'urban' or 'rural' and empirical in that the focus of research has been both at a macro level (what are the aggregate characteristics of movers?) and at a micro level (what motivates movers?) Nevertheless research progress has been made and a great deal of consensus exists. First, it is clear that there has been some form of large scale population 'deconcentration' (whatever the definitional difficulties), that motivation for moving is not always economic (and may be more to do with lifestyle) and that agents do not enjoy perfect economic knowledge. Indeed quite often urban to rural migrants come to occupy weaker economic positions than prior to moving (Williams and Champion 1998).

Counter-urbanisation refutes an important premise of classical (Grand) theory – that is, migrants are always rational, knowledgeable economic agents – though it is not intended as a test of such theory and any consequence of this kind is unintended. Indeed it is firmly middle range theory, in that whilst specific theories are advanced to explain observations and these inform subsequent research, connections with Grand Theory are tangential. Counter-urbanisation theory proposes generalisations within limited circumstances. Logically these are the same as laws, or Grand Theory, in so far as they take the form of $P{\rightarrow}Q$, that is, if circumstances P hold, Q will follow. However, unlike laws and Grand Theory both P and Q are less tightly specified. Indeed a key argument in counter-urbanisation (Cloke 1985) has been that urban–rural migration is very heterogeneous.

Now that is not the same as saying that we can't know the circumstances under which people move, but rather their characteristics are too diverse to more tightly specify the theory. What can be said is that (a) under a number of specifications of 'urban' or 'rural' the decades since the 1960s have been marked by an increase of urban–rural moves; (b) that motivations for these moves are not always economic and are often multiple and complex; (c) that motivations for moving may change over time. On the face of it then counter-urbanisation seems to be better at telling us the limits of what we don't know. But this is so often the way it goes in the social sciences. Firm results can be obtained on aggregate data, in this case that such a phenomenon as urban–rural movement took place, but on further investigation motivations for moving are so varied as to apparently defy a classification, that would allow an elegant specification of counter-urbanisation. Either we cannot move from the level of description to any kind of explanation, or the explanation is so wide as to be trivial.

As I noted above, the complexity of the social world seems to render it explicable only probabilistically. The apparent indeterminacy almost certainly arises at least partially as a result of free will, but even if this is the case then the outcome is no different. Aggregates can be shown to exist, but deterministic causal patterns leading to the aggregates cannot. In the second case what do we mean by aggregates here? At what level must we throw in the towel and say that we cannot specify the precise circumstances under which X will happen? The social scientist, like her counterpart in the natural sciences, is seeking explanations that will incorporate as many circumstances as possible. If we can move from the broadest level of aggregate description of a population, to describing a subset of that population and how the former and the latter are related, we have at least achieved some degree of explanation. For example if we could show that those at, or nearing retirement age, or those with property assets, are more likely to make urban–rural moves for reasons of lifestyle, whilst younger working people move for employment or career-related reasons, then we have made at least some progress toward an explanation of counter-urbanisation. Researchers can make progress towards explanations that can incorporate more and more circumstances, though at the end of all of this the explanations will be probabilistic, because the individual actions that lead to the aggregate outcomes arise partially out of free will and partially out of other complex antecedents, themselves indeterminate.

In natural science experiments particular variables can be held constant (temperature, pressure etc.) in order to measure the effect of one specific variable. Although occasionally it is possible to do this in the social world it is unusual, partly because we cannot control all of the variables and partly because we often do not know what all of them might be. Sometimes survey researchers will conduct 'quasi experiments'. This strategy features some of the characteristics of classical experiments, but there is less control over variables and subjects are not randomly assigned

(Pettigrew 1996: 52–7). One simple, but commonly used strategy, is one where two groups of respondents will be surveyed at time *T1*. At *T1* the variables to be measured are the same in each group, but by *T2* one of the groups will have undergone some change, which can be measured and compared to the group which has not experienced change in the relevant areas (Williams and May 1996: 144–7). Of course, as I have noted, not all natural science relies on experimental method, the variables that constitute the analyses exist in open systems, they can be measured, but they cannot be isolated from other intervening variables. This is the regime under which the social scientist must also mostly operate and it is to the procedures within this regime I want to now turn.

Measurement and explanation

Variables are those characteristics and attributes in the world that can be identified and measured. Variables vary, that is they will have more than one value or category within them (the opposite of a variable is a constant). Our theories identify what shall be variables and constants and whether we treat them as one or the other. Variables could be age, sex, ethic group, social class, type of housing tenure, attitudes, opinions, beliefs, intentions or experience. Unlike the natural sciences, the social sciences measure a mixture of ontological categories. The categories of the social world can relate to physical characteristics (e.g. sex), social or individual interpretations of those characteristics (e.g. again sex, ethnic group), or purely subjective or intersubjective mental or social properties. In the natural sciences because all ontological kinds are (supposed) to be physical properties only one level of social construction can occur, that is of the observer (in this case the scientist). In the social world there are two levels of social construction available. First, that of how 'people' socially construct the physical (or social) world and second, how the social scientist then categorises those constructions. Ethnicity is a good example of this. The UK Census recognises 35 ethnic groups, but for most purposes these are condensed to 10 categories and in certain analyses (Small Area Statistics) only five categories are used (Dale and Marsh 1993: 34). This categorisation consists of: White, Black, Indian/Pakistani/Bangladeshi, Chinese and Other.

So what is being measured here? The derivation of ethnicity is very complex and is a mixture of physical categories, social description and subjective decision. The categories used by the Census, or social scientists generally, could probably never be the subject of mutual agreement amongst those it is wished to describe. Second, sometimes physical characteristics are used to count as ethnicity (e.g. 'white', 'black') and other times a mixture of cultural and physical characteristics are used (e.g. 'Chinese'). In the larger Census classification there is a political/cultural distinction between Indian, Pakistani and Bangladeshi and in the 35 category classification the 'white' group is further broken down. Whichever definition of the variable 'ethnicity' is used it will be a construct of the social scientist and when analysed with another variable will differ accordingly. The conclusion must therefore be that the results of such a bivariate analysis will also be a social construction. Well, yes and no.

This is a question of operationalisation and a matter for both natural and social scientists. The former can choose to measure temperature in centigrade, Fahrenheit or Kelvin. Certain scientists (such as those doing work in superconductivity) often use the Kelvin scale where zero Kelvin is equivalent to − 273.1° centigrade. The freezing point of water is 273° Kelvin and boiling point is 373°. Immediately it can be seen that the Kelvin measurement is of limited use in everyday life, but valuable to scientists because it expresses the range of temperatures (not usually encountered in everyday life) without using a minus sign. Different operationalisations will provide different answers, but we do have the potential to measure differently. For example if we produce a contingency table with five category ethnicity variable and type of housing tenure we will see that 'white' people are more likely to be owner occupiers and Indian/Pakistani/Bangladeshi people very much less, but if we use the ten category variable we will see that Indians are much more likely to be owner occupiers than Bangladeshis (Dale *et al.* 1996: 28). More sophisticated analyses, perhaps in one city, will show that such differences are much more complex than this even within any given ethnic group (Vertovek 1994).

The social scientist also gets excited by differences of a few percentage points between categories in a variable. For example in the 1991 Census, in England and Wales, 72 per cent of White people and 53 per cent of Afro-Caribbeans lived in owner-occupation. In housing terms this 19 percentage point difference is large enough to be of concern, suggesting that the latter group will suffer disadvantage in housing chances. Thus any given 'white' person has about a 7:10 chance of living in owner occupation whereas an Afro-Caribbean has slightly better than a 1:2 chance. But these odds of course assume that all other things are held as constants, but it is easy to see that an unemployed 'white' teenager living in an inner city is likely to have different odds to (say) the comedian Lenny Henry! Nevertheless a fairly simple analysis of ethnicity and tenure is useful as much that it then provides us with a hypothesis that Afro-Caribbeans are *more likely* to experience poorer housing chances than 'whites'.

How might we test this? Here the social scientist becomes rather sophisticated. First of all, she could produce a number of bi-variate contingency tables where a third variable is 'controlled' for, testing (say) for differences in location or socio-economic status on the likelihood of each ethnic group living in owner-occupation. We might find that location makes little difference to the distribution, whereas class or socio-economic status does. But how do we find out which of these variables is the most important 'predictor' of living in owner occupation? Multivariate analysis is where several variables are examined at the same time. This might be through any one of a number of techniques: simple regression, log linear analysis, stepwise regression, logistic regression etc. (Tacq 1997). In the latter, for example, we could measure the comparative 'odds' of an Afro-Caribbean, a person in Social Class IV, or someone unemployed living in owner occupation. We could repeat this holding constant ethnic group and so on. But of course living in owner occupation may not be a good measure of good housing chances. We might therefore wish to look at whether the property is owned outright, where it is situated, or its condition.

Whilst then it is true that the results of a bi-variate analysis (or for that matter multivariate analyses) are a social construction of the social scientist they do seem to describe the world, though maybe not in sharp focus and they can lead to further analyses where the focus can be made sharper. Yet in most analyses there will come the point where events appear to become contingent and arise from individual action or circumstances (Giddens 1984: 333). Mr A is Afro-Caribbean and became an owner-occupier because his local council offered a particularly generous discount scheme to its tenants to enable them to buy. Ms B is in the same ethnic group, is offered the same deal, but chooses not to take it up because she has been saving for a holiday. If we were asked to say beforehand which of Mr A or Ms B would buy their flat, we could not say. Afterwards we could ask each (along with others given the same opportunity) the reasons for buying or not. This would increase our predictive power in future situations. Thus given enough information about antecedent characteristics of people like Mr A or Ms B we could perhaps give a probability estimate, but that is all. Individuals rarely act randomly or arbitrarily, they will give reasons for their actions and sometimes those reasons can be categorised. But for many social scientists this is not enough. Scriven (1964: 171) has likened the problem to the natural scientist being unable to predict the fall of a particular leaf from a tree. Such an ability, he notes, is not seen as important for the scientist, but as Lee McIntyre notes (1994: 134), 'The unfortunate situation for social science, however, is that we *have* been concerned to know how a particular leaf fall from a particular tree.' Is it at this point where social science must abandon 'science' for 'folk psychology' (Rosenberg 1988: 23–7)?

Interpretation

One of the strengths of 'macro-level' explanations is that a chain of reasoning can be uncovered as to why the relationships are what they are. The scientist (natural or social) can tell us how variables are constructed and what the margin of error in any purported relationship might be. The reasoning is transparent. However, at the micro level in social science ethnographic methods are deployed which depend on the social scientist attempting to 'understand' why an agent did X or believes Y, or why a group behaves as it does. Now whilst the survey researcher will 'socially construct' a variable, how it is done can be shown. Conversely the process of 'understanding' is more complex and less transparent.

The strategy of understanding, *verstehen*, is often effective and I would maintain indispensable, but is it 'scientific' in the broadest sense? The argument for the efficacy of this approach is that humans have the ability to understand, or at least attempt to understand their own actions through introspection and therefore are able to interpret the motives of the conduct of others in terms of their professed or ascribed intentions (Gerth and Mills [1948] 1991: 57). Of course we cannot know another mind as we know our own, but in everyday life we are rather good at interpreting the actions or the utterances of others and acting upon them – at least within our own cultural milieu. Social life works because of a well developed 'folk psychology'. Understanding and interpretation of the actions and utterances of others as a research strategy, is then utilising the successful strategy of folk psychology to produce explanations of the social world.

As I have suggested earlier, many of those who practise interpretivist methods (these include participant observation, 'depth' interviewing, focus groups) are either not concerned by the science debate or would avow that they are not doing science at all. Leaving that debate aside for the moment I want to briefly explore the methodological dilemma of interpretivism from the point of view of science. The dilemma is that whatever some enthusiasts say about survey research as being the only means to test conjectures about the social world (Marsh 1982: 6–7), as a researcher I cannot conceive of a social science without interpretive methods. Such methods are indispensable, particularly when one wishes to research, for example, 'closed' organisations or sensitive issues. Nigel Fielding's study of the British 'National Front' (an extreme right wing political party), or Simon Holdaway's study of the police, whilst serving as a police officer, would have been impossible if they could not have used participant observation to gather data (Fielding 1981; Holdaway 1982). Similarly issues such as intimate emotions in personal relationships (Dunscombe and Marsden 1996), deviancy (Hobbs 1988) or sensitive health issues, such as AIDS (Bowser and Seiber 1993). Yet can interpretive methods be scientific?

For 'anti-naturalists' who deny that generalisation is possible, or even desirable (Guba and Lincoln 1982; Denzin 1983), understanding is considered sufficient in itself and there is no need to produce explanations or predictions. The naturalist using interpretive methods, conversely, will wish to generalise, she will require explanations which lead to predictions. Interpretivism, whether intended or not, produces *moderatum* generalisations, as does the deployment of folk psychological methods in everyday life, indeed as I have noted the pattern of discovery in everyday life is a precursor of scientific discovery. The process in which science became 'unnatural' was long and complex and there is no sharp divide between everyday and scientific discovery. *Moderatum* generalisations arise from everyday discovery, so it seems plausible that everyday generalisations in the social world have the same kind of relationship to social science as their equivalent ones in the physical world have to natural science. They are pre-scientific, which means they are potentially *scientific* (Williams 1998: 19–21).

A *moderatum* generalisation is simply a generalisation about key intersubjectively understood features in the social landscape of a particular culture. For example, Holdaway can describe the workings of a particular police force in Britain and it would be reasonable to expect that much of what he describes would be found in other British police forces, and some of that described in police forces outside of Britain. Now for most purposes such generalisation is enough, but if we were policy-makers and wished to utilise his findings to change policy we might want to test some of these generalisations by operationalising them into variables that could be tested through (say) survey research. We would then turn *moderatum* generalisations into statistical ones. Let me reiterate. Methodologically this may not always be desirable and sometimes ethically questionable, but from a scientific viewpoint interpretive methods are pre-scientific, yet they can provide testable hypotheses and therefore are an indispensable strategy of social *science*. Indeed to embrace interpretivism does not imply anti-naturalism, a theme I will return to in Chapter 5.

Conclusion

In this chapter I have sketched out the key features of naturalism, the underlying philosophical justification for a 'scientific' approach to social science. I have suggested that although the social world has a number of complex and unique features, it both intermeshes with the physical world and is continuous with it. Indeed it seems that explanation and prediction are just as possible in the social as the physical world, if we accept that the social world is probabilistic. Conversely deterministic causal explanations do not seem to be possible in the social world, but of course this seems also to be the case in the study of much of the physical world. Although the latter comports itself in more regular and stable patterns, allowing us to identify 'laws' and 'local' causal determinism, the study of the social world scientifically is just as possible as the study of any other complex system in nature. The social world, like many physical systems, displays statistical regularity and is clearly predictable.

But of course this is only half of social 'science'. The other half seeks to understand and interpret the world, because the 'scientific' strategies of survey method, or even experiment, cannot get at the underlying reasons for action. Or, methodologically, only covert methods could be used to find out about a particular aspect of the social world. Here I have suggested that such methods are indispensable and at least pre-scientific – that is they can generate testable hypotheses. As I write these words I realise that many will be unhappy with the apparent conclusion that the only role for interpretivism is somehow that of the labourer who prepares the ground for the altogether more serious enterprise of survey research. This is not my intention and it is a matter I will return to in Chapter 5. However, I must first turn my attention to two angry crowds gathering at the gates. The first is denouncing science as a project *per se* and the second is denouncing the idea of social science as science.

Suggested further reading

Bryman, A. (1988) *Quantity and Quality in Social Research*, London: Routledge.

Fay, B. (1996) *Contemporary Philosophy of Social Science*, Oxford: Blackwell.

Kincaid, H. (1996) *Philosophical Foundations of the Social Sciences: Analyzing Controversies in Social Research*, Cambridge: Cambridge University Press.

Williams, M. and May, T. (1996) *Introduction to Philosophy of Social Research*, London: UCL Press.

4   Against science

It is possible to be against science in many ways. In this chapter I will present a view of science that is 'against' in the same way as it is possible to be against fox hunting or smoking. There is however another view, or more properly views, which regard science as a contingent social construction, no more privileged in its accounts of the world than (say) astrology or voodoo. In Bruno Latour's words they aim 'to abolish the distinction between science and fiction' (Latour 1988: 166). I will argue that the first of these, (what I will call) the *rejectionist* view of science, is naïve and incoherent and the second view of science (what I will call *social constructionist*) is (mostly) in error. Nevertheless both positions do raise important issues around the question of the social and ethical basis of science, matters I will return to in Chapter 6. Though many of the arguments 'against' and 'for' science are specifically aimed at the natural sciences they mostly would be equally applicable to the social sciences. However, some are specifically critical of the idea of social science as science and I will consider these particular criticisms in the next chapter.

The 'science' debate has produced an enormous literature and at the end of this chapter I make a few suggestions for further reading. The three 'views' I present are therefore not intended as a comprehensive account of the debate, but rather as exemplars – which of course others may have chosen differently.

Rejectionism

The position I characterise as 'rejectionism' comes in many shades. It can take a humanist academic form where literature and art are taken as culturally superior to science. It can take the form of the 'technophobia' of those who see science and technology as dehumanising, environmentally destructive, or both (Alvares 1988). Finally there are those who see science as simply a form of ideology or cultural hegemony (Roszak [1968] 1995). These positions shade both into each other and into social constructionism or revisionism. Usually they are polemical and rarely they are offered as a more considered position. An example of the latter might be Brian

Appleyard's (1992) *Understanding the Present* – though in this case there are hints of 'revisionism' towards an alternative view of science. However, rejectionism mostly exhibits a naïveté that is characterised by a blindness to the *de facto* nature of science and technology in our lives and a mistaken view of what science is.

Outright opposition to science has a long history, its beginnings coinciding with the first perceived widespread effects of science through industrialisation, in the late eighteenth century. Raymond Tallis (1995) locates the origins of this opposition in what he terms 'romanticism'. The poet William Blake, for example, spoke of art as the tree of life and science as the tree of death. The objections of the Romantics arose both from the perceived effects of technological progress in 'dark satanic mills' and, according to Tallis, in a misunderstanding of Newtonianism as deterministic, a mistaken view put about (as I noted in Chapter 1) by Laplace and Voltaire and in Britain especially by Alexander Pope. For those that exchanged the pastoral ' … for the cacophonic roar of the machine were rewarded with appalling working and living conditions, uncertain employment, poverty, ill health, execrable surroundings and early death' (Tallis 1995: 14).

Since the Industrial Revolution art and literature have become associated with the pure and natural, science with the synthetic and cruel. Science, it was said, had diminished emotional, aesthetic, ethical, sensory, imaginative and intentional qualities, those things that were seen as most constitutive of what it is to be human (Tarnas 1991: 326).

For many who opposed science in the nineteenth century the barbarity of the 'terror' that followed the French Revolution was testimony to its evil potential when applied to human affairs. At the height of the killing between 1792–4, as well as establishing the foundations of scientific research and education, the regime sought to utilise scientific expertise by appointing the most famous scientists of the day to key posts: Carnot in charge of the war effort, and Lavoisier in charge of national accounting (Hobsbawm 1977: 337). Even its method of killing – the guillotine – was considered the most scientifically advanced and therefore the most humane. The terror prefigured worse to come, not only through the development of more efficient means of killing on the battlefield but in the utilisation and invocation of science for the purposes of massive social engineering. Forced collectivisation and the five year plans of the early Soviet Union killed or incarcerated millions in the name of 'scientific socialism', and whilst the Nazi regime was 'anti-scientific' in many ways, it nevertheless reached new levels of technological efficiency in its extermination camps (Visvanathan 1988: 269–70).

My own generation, born in the West since Hiroshima and Nagasaki, has had a complex and sometimes contradictory relationship with science. From when we were born and throughout our lives, we have been dependent on technology for shelter, food and health, yet opposition to science has perhaps never been more widespread than amongst those born after the Second World War. This opposition has been described by Theodore Roszak ([1968] 1995) as 'counter-culture', a widespread rejection of the technocratic society by youth. This work was first published in a period which saw the student rising in France and the opposition to the Vietnam War. The imagery of that opposition was bells, poetry, hallucinogenic drugs and peace, thus whilst it was in many ways an opposition of youth, it was also an opposition of 'progressive' anti-science against 'reactionary' science. Anti-science became associated with the left and indeed was given intellectual weight by the writings of Hannah Arendt (1958) and Herbert Marcuse (1964). On the other hand science was associated with the bomb, with the execution of faceless political power at a distance and never more so than in the United States of the 1960s. The then US President, Lyndon Johnson, took his place in history as the man who was responsible for the use of the greatest tonnage of explosives ever in wartime, the awareness and opposition to this typified by the popular slogan 'Hey, hey, LBJ/ How many kids did you burn today?' (Inglis 1992: 240). At the same time as ever more efficient means of killing were deployed in Vietnam there was a growing awareness, on the anti-scientific left, that the 'technocratic society' was no longer environ-mentally sustainable. The defence of ever greater consumer consumption in the name of progress was made by the technocratic right long after it became indefensible. These things contributed to a widespread (as Gerald Holton puts it) 'delegitimation of science' (Holton 1993). Since 1968 what might be termed the 'new left', the wide and shifting alliance of socialists, Trotskyists, green and anti-nuclear activists, left-libertarians and anar-chists, has been dominated by anti-science views. To express an alternative is so often to align oneself with the forces of reaction, of conservatism, fascism or Stalinism.

This view reached political and intellectual respectability in the address of the former dissident, playwright and later President of the Czech Republic, Vaclev Havel, to the World Economic Forum in Davos, in 1992 (Holton 1993: 175–7). In Havel, it might be said, Roszak's counter-culture came of age. Havel's address eloquently traced the history of scientific evil, its cult of depersonalised objectivity, from the Renaissance to the Soviet Union. His rejection was not simply that of the technological and political evils made possible by science, but of scientific thought and scientific culture in total. His sentiments were little different to those of Blake:

> Modern rationalism and modern science, through the work of man that, as all human works, developed within our natural world, now systematically leave it behind, deny it, degrade and defame it – and, of course, at the same time colonize it.
>
> (Havel quoted in Holton 1993: 177)

Havel's rejectionism was perhaps intended as an epitaph for modernity, but if taken seriously would constitute an end to rationality, seen by him (and others) as a quintessentially scientific phenomenon. Of course if the rejection of science implies a rejection of its underlying rationality then it is not surprising that the rejection of science is often incoherent or illogical. Nevertheless it is worth trying to dissect what exactly is being rejected in science, though such a dissection must inevitably be conducted using the reasoning rejected by the rejectionists!

What is rejected in science can be placed under three headings: its material products (usually in the form of technology), its knowledge products, or its values.

Material products

The complaint is often that science and technology have created the materials of our moral and actual destruction (see for example McKibben 1990). For our very survival it is said we should at least partially withdraw material products. However, there is a difficulty here in *which* products we should withdraw. Which products of science and technology do we reject and which do we keep? To reject them all would be a return to the Neolithic, but the rejectionist is presumably not suggesting this. Perhaps instead we should opt for a low-grade technology, or technology with a human face? Tallis points to the contradiction inherent in this position too:

> ... at the very least, [it] would rule out the production, quality control and distribution of safe and reliable self-propelled vehicles, effective antibiotics, radios upon which it was possible to make out Bach from static, and much else besides. It would not just be a matter of doing without Arcade games. Only a little bit of the technology we currently take for granted has to be withdrawn to remove most of the comfort we also take for granted. Technology is so interdependent – mass production, quality control and distribution are all very hi-tech matters, even if the commodity in question is fairly low-tech – that a modest retrenchment will have major effects, especially on the under privileged (who, in a low-tech world, will be the majority).
>
> (Tallis 1995: 45)

Maybe we should reject the products of military technology, or those which are environmentally damaging? In this I, presumably along with many scientists, would heartily agree, but far from a rejection of science this implies a need for more (perhaps different and better) science. Whilst the decision to deploy and use military technology is often made by politicians for a range of reasons, at least some wars, in Africa in particular, have been about competition for scarce resources, resources which through the deployment of technology can often be increased or their effectiveness maximised. Environmental pollution will obviously decrease through the use of fewer pollutants, but in order to use fewer pollutants less 'dirty' manufacturing and processing techniques must be developed. To put the matter starkly, once the damaging effects of CFCs were known and agreed there were two choices, to withdraw completely all aerosol-based products and to stop manufacturing refrigerators, or to develop an alternative.

Knowledge

Perhaps instead the argument can be directed against scientific knowledge? In recent years the postmodernists have been foremost in the criticism of the legitimacy of scientific knowledge. For the postmodernists science is a 'metanarrative', indeed its culture might be said to be *the* metanarrative of the past two hundred years. Metanarratives assume the validity of their own truth claims. In other words the rationality that underlies science must be taken as an unchallengeable given for science to make any sense. But according to the postmodernists the metanarrative of science has broken down, science has become delegitimised and exposed as an ideological project rather than a path to true knowledge of the world (Lyotard 1984). Again with this kind of denunciation it is hard to know whether all scientific knowledge is to be rejected, or just particular scientific knowledge? If it is to be rejected because it is no longer legitimate, then is there a knowledge that bears a greater legitimacy? Postmodernists would, of course, reply that it is not 'legitimacy' that is being claimed, simply that local narratives, rooted in specific times and places paint a more meaningful picture of the world to those who live in such times and places. To attempt to generalise knowledge from one time or place to another would be to create a metanarrative.

Two kinds of knowledge upon which science depends might be rejected. That is knowledge of how to do things – technological knowledge – or new knowledge through discovery. To reject the first brings us back to rejecting further material development. However, the possibility of remaining as we are is not viable, because the materials used in present technology are finite and new technologies and therefore new knowledge are inevitably required just to 'stay put'. To reject the second is to reject the possibility of knowing anything new about the world – an absurd proposition. Curiosity, and therefore discovery, is necessary to everyday survival.

Perhaps then it is the form of knowledge accretion that science takes, as 'positivist, empiricist, rational-logical' (Rosenau 1992: 9)? Well of course not that many scientists would today sign up to empiricism, or positivism, but to reject these hardly requires a rejection of the metanarrative of science. So is it the logical-rational? Maybe – but if it is then presumably science should be illogical and irrational, though would this still be science?

The rejection of knowledge often takes the form of 'alternative', or 'para' science, but here the rejection is even more confused. The whole point of (say) 'ufology', or para-psychology is to be taken seriously as a science. Whilst alternative science rejects mainstream scientific knowledge as narrow and unimaginative, it seeks legitimacy in a deployment of the vocabulary and method of science (see for example Blake 1979).

Moral values

This view implies both an 'end of innocence' and a belief that the 'morality' of science can be replaced with a different nobler morality. The 'moral' critics rightly point out, as Carl Sagan notes, that

> Scientists have on occasion given aid and comfort to a variety of noxious doctrines (including the supposed 'superiority' of one ethnic group or gender over another from measurement of brain size or skull bumps or IQ tests). Scientists are often reluctant to offend the rich and the powerful ... many worked without a trace of moral regret for the Nazis.
>
> (Sagan 1996: 242)

To that, of course, could be added the evil of the atomic bomb and the irresponsibility of global pollution. Indeed, it is hard to deny the weight of evidence of the manipulation of science by what Roszak called 'technocracy'. It is indubitably correct that many of the products of science are evil and that scientists themselves have often been morally irresponsible, or even 'evil' in the service of the technocracy, or earlier technocratic-political regimes. What is incorrect is that all of that which science produces is evil. Science, or its derivative technology gave us chemical and biological weapons, but it also gave us anaesthetics and the means to eradicate smallpox.

What about the scientists themselves? Is it really held that Josef Mengele, Edward Teller, Marie Curie, Albert Einstein and Niels Bohr are equal in the attribution of evil intent or moral fecklessness? Teller and Bohr, for example, were both leading physicists in the period spanning the Second World War. The former incessantly lobbied Roosevelt to build the hydrogen bomb (and indeed was an early advocate of the 'Star Wars' project), whilst the latter refused to allow his work to be used for war purposes and worked towards using the internationalism of science to reduce the hostility between the USA and the USSR (Inglis 1992: 43–4). Other scientists, such as Hans Beth or Freeman Dyson (Visvanathan 1988: 124–5; Inglis 1992: 171–9), were extraordinarily complex in their moral views, variously working on weapons programmes and opposing them at different stages of their careers. I do not want to suggest that science, or scientists, are innocent, simply that science should not be seen as morally homogeneous in intention or deed.

A second kind of moral criticism is that science is unnatural, artificial and in being so separates us from 'nature'. But the nature from which we are said to be separated is portrayed as innocent, gentle, non-threatening and pastoral. It can be glimpsed from the pastel colours and sweet smells of the Body Shop and partially achieved through consumption of organic food and the avoidance of 'artificial' additives. But of course other things are just as natural. As Tallis observes ' ... nothing could be more natural than a 90 per cent infant mortality rate, that pus pouring from one's leg is as natural as song pouring from a bird's throat, and starvation is as natural as satiety' (Tallis 1995: 53–4).

Rejectionism is naïve and incoherent. It is naïve because in its denunciation of science it assumes the option of a return to a pre-scientific age as not just desirable, but also possible. Of course such a return would require the abandonment of the very means of communication (the PC, modern printing and all forms of electronic communication) that makes the dissemination of such a message possible. It is incoherent because apart from a generalised complaint about the effects of science, for example in 'dehumanising us' (Appleyard 1992: Chapter 8), or in its potential for environmental destruction (McKibben 1990), we are not told what it is in science that is being objected to. Or if it is, it is stated in vague or incoherent terms. An example of this comes from Vandana Shiva (1988). In a paper concerned to show the evils of what she terms 'reductionist science', she cites evidence from Thomas Kuhn and Paul Feyerabend to argue (a) that there is no such thing as a scientific method and (b) that the belief that such a method is attainable has resulted in a 'reductionist ecology' geared to industrial agricultural production and a 'scientific' management of the ecosystem. Much (though not all) of this argument is plausible, but is then completely undermined when Shiva complains that the Indian forestry establishment had rejected 'all recognized and established scientific information' (Shiva 1988: 245) and had continued with its environmentally destructive policy of eucalyptus planting!

On closer examination there might actually be a lot of common ground in the objections to environmental destruction or the military uses of technology, between scientists and their critics. But of course, as Tallis points out, the role of the scientist as critic is so often unrecognised outside of science.

Social constructionism

Whilst the foregoing are straightforwardly 'against science', many of those holding to variants of social constructionism intend to be reformers and do not explicitly admit to being anti-science, yet it is the case that many social constructionist prescriptions would, if upheld, have the unintended consequence of making science impossible or unbelievable.

Social constructionism embraces a wide range of positions including postmodern and post-structural critiques of science that go beyond simple rejection. However, in this section I want to concentrate on just two manifestations: that within the sociology of science and that within feminism. Even within these areas there are a number of divisions and nuances, but my aim here is to show that whilst the criticisms of science advanced by social constructionists are often well made, what they claim does, or should, follow from these is mistaken.

Sociology of science

Social constructionists in the sociology of science take seriously particular aspects of the claims of Thomas Kuhn (1970). His *Structure of Scientific Revolutions*, first published in 1962, became something of a revolutionary icon itself. Kuhn was a philosopher of science, turned historian, who supported his radical claim with illustrations from the history of science. Broadly, this was that scientific knowledge was not based on a process of gradual accretion through the scientists' encounters with the natural world, but was instead shaped by historical form, by what he termed 'revolutions'. Every so often in science a discovery, or series of discoveries served to undermine the fundamental beliefs of the scientific community. Eventually these beliefs would be overthrown by a scientific revolution and a new 'paradigm' would be established. Within this all science took place. It contained not just established scientific principles and laws, but also the way of doing science and the metaphysical basis upon which its methodological and justificatory procedures rested. What is important for Kuhn is that the paradigm itself shapes what the scientist looks for. Whilst it is true that data are often open to interpretation by more than one theory, it is equally true that the theory one adopts will shape what it is one discovers. The theories that are permitted are those permitted within the paradigm, as are the assessments of those theories. With a change of paradigm will come not just new theories, but also a different evaluation of what counts as a good theory. Theories themselves are psychological and social constructions which arise from the way we perceive and understand the world.

However Kuhn's claim was not that scientists are irrational, indeed new theories replace old ones on the entirely rational grounds that the newer theories solve more problems than the old ones (Kuhn 1977: 321–3). In that sense there is progress in science; how else could we explain the historical 'progress' from Galileo's simple experiments to the launch of a space probe? Sociologists of science have, however, been particularly interested in developing the social constructionist claims in Kuhn's work. The position of the social constructionist sociologists of science (represented, for example, by Latour and Woolgar [1979] 1986; Barnes and Bloor 1982; Collins 1981; Latour 1987; and Woolgar 1988) is summed up by Harry Collins in his conclusion that 'the natural world has a small or non-existent role in the construction of scientific knowledge' (Collins 1981: 3). How is this position arrived at?

Sociologists of science have often likened themselves to anthropologists in the laboratory. Studies such as those of Harry Collins (1975) or Bruno Latour and Steve Woolgar ([1979] 1986) have concentrated on what it is that scientists do in relation to what they say they do. Collins (1975), for example, concentrates on the principle of replication, that the procedures used to produce data should be replicable. He claims, however, that replication confers no advantage upon a scientist, that if an experiment can be replicated then the work of the original scientist is given greater credibility and the scientist carrying out the replication gains little. On the other hand if no replication was possible then there would be nothing to show for the work.

Others, such as Latour (1987), as we saw in Chapter 2, point to the role of serendipity in discovery. James Watson's discovery of the double helix, for example, rested partially on a misunderstanding of the underlying chemistry. Other social factors such as peer review or citation act as justificatory strategies in science, whilst Barry Barnes and David Bloor (1982) claim the importance of the class interests of scientists as a shaping factor. Put perhaps crudely the citation of a Penrose or a Hawking in support of one's view is as valuable, or more so, than empirical data.

These things could have perhaps been denied or explained away as aberrations if it were not that in the history of science today's truth is so often yesterday's heresy and tomorrow's error. A sociological account of how scientific theories become adopted, are legitimised and discarded lends support to Kuhn's paradigmatic view of the history of science. It has the ability not just to explain how the 'social factors' I spoke of in Chapter 1 have crucially shaped various moments in its history, but also it can explain the adoption of alternative world views in other contemporary (or historical) cultures. In other words if the social studies of science are seen as anthropological then they are comparative in terms of the rationality of the views held by their practitioners.

This cross-cultural evaluation of 'scientific' belief is at the basis of what Barnes and Bloor (1982) have called the 'strong programme'. The 'strong programme' is openly relativistic. Now as Barnes and Bloor point out (1982: 22) relativism comes in many forms, but presents problems for those who claim a truth equivalent for all beliefs – that is all knowledge claims are equally true, or equally false. This presents a paradox for if A is the belief that X is true and B is the belief that X is false, then both are equally true or false. The consequence being that there can be no mechanism to choose between A or B (the mechanism itself would fall foul of the same problem). Instead Barnes and Bloor propose that if they are right then what counts as scientific knowledge at any one time will be determined by social influences, specifically interests, that are not connected with the empirical data. This is not to say that any given theory is true or false empirically, whether rationally or irrationally held. They propose then an equivalence postulate which holds that:

> ... all beliefs are on a par with one another with respect to the causes of their credibility. It is not that all beliefs are equally true or equally false, but that regardless of truth or falsity the fact of their credibility is seen to be equally problematic. ... the incidence of all beliefs without exception calls for empirical investigation and must be accounted for by finding the specific, local causes of this credibility.
>
> (Barnes and Bloor 1982: 23)

Barnes and Bloor, like most of the other 'social constructionist' sociologists, are well aware of the relativistic implications of social constructionism, i.e. a full blown epistemological relativism would end up asserting that the knowledge claims of voodoo and biology are equivalent. Their view is that we can be catholic on whether one or the other is right empirically, but both sets of beliefs have social antecedents. Moreover, they recommend that the 'strong programme' itself should be likewise evaluated.

The 'strong programme' is sophisticated and as George Couvalis (1997) has pointed out is both consistent and productive, but is it right?

Couvalis cites several objections to the 'strong programme' (Couvalis 1997: 145–51). Two in particular are telling:

First, it is paradoxical. Its strength is that it relies on a number of detailed and rigorous studies to demonstrate the social causes of the scientific beliefs. These are the empirical evidence of the strong programme, but of course if the Kuhnian view that theories are undetermined by the data is right, these data alone would not be reason enough for opponents of the 'strong programme' to change their minds. If the strong programmers are right then we should be as sceptical about their claims as we are about those of the scientific community.

Second, whilst it is possible that any number of theories could be compatible with the data, it doesn't follow that more than one existing theory is thus. As Couvalis notes, 'Scientists often find it very hard to produce even one relatively simple explanation of the data in an area' (Couvalis 1997: 147; see also Chalmers 1990: 85). Larry Laudan has made a similar point:

> ... the rules and evidence of biology, although they do not establish the unique correctness of evolutionary theory, do exclude numerous creationist hypotheses – for example, the claim that the earth is between 10,000 and 20,000 years old – from the permissible realm and thus provide a warrant for a rational preference for evolutionary over creationist biology.
>
> (Laudan 1984: 30)

Thus the 'strong programmer' in particular and the social construction-ist sociologist in general slide from what is true, that theories are underde-termined, to one that is untrue, that theories are *always* underdetermined. Nevertheless the value of the 'strong programme' is that it can show in detail how social factors shape science, but in accepting this as valuable we do not have to agree that science is wholly socially determined.

Feminism

Feminist perspectives on science arise out of a concern that science and technology have been important instruments 'in the continuing subordina-tion of women and in the degradation of the environment' (Fox Keller and Longino 1996: 1). But the thinking about science goes deeper in feminism and there is a philosophical reconstruction of the epistemological justification for science. Thus feminists see science as a direct manifesta-tion of patriarchy in its actions, its social composition and even its language (Fox Keller 1985: 139–50), but also that the epistemological justification of science in objectivity is patriarchal and in turn perpetuates patriarchy. I will concentrate on the latter epistemological critique here because in its implications it transcends feminism and raises more general questions of objectivity in science (to which I will return in Chapter 6). However, even with 'feminist epistemology' there are a variety of positions (see for example essays in Lennon and Whitford 1994; Fox Keller and Longino 1996). Here I will consider that of the 'standpoint epistemologies' associated with (for example) Sandra Harding (1986, 1996), Hilary Rose (1983), and Donna Haraway (1989).

'Standpoint' epistemology has two principal components: that science is a gendered activity and that women (or variously feminists) have the potential for a more objective knowledge of the world as a result of their subordinate position. Though advocates of 'standpoint' epistemologies make different emphases, there are some common assumptions:

- That the social practices of society are patriarchal
- That all knowledge, including scientific knowledge, is a social product
- That it follows from this that science is patriarchal.

According to Hilary Rose (1983: 88) a feminist epistemology cannot begin from a consideration of women in the laboratory, for in this role they are forced into being 'men', but at the same time excluded from the production of scientific knowledge. Instead it is proposed that the position of women *vis-à-vis* science and their potential for a more objective scientific knowledge, begins from a consideration of women's experience. Women's experience has been in caring and child-rearing roles, but also of subjugation by men, legitimated by a biological determinism which sees the social role of women as a product of their genes (Rose 1983: 83).

Knowledge for women is quite a different thing to that of men and arises out of such experience. As Nancy Hartsock puts it producing a human being is quite a different matter to producing a chair (Hartsock 1983: 293). It is said that whilst men, through their socialisation, come to see themselves as isolated from nature, women – especially through child-bearing – are united with nature. The scientific distinction between the subject as knower and the object as known is, for women, not meaningful.

The assertion that knowledge is a social product is closely bound to this differential experience of women and men. The subject–object distinction in male socialisation is the basis of an objective, value-free science. Lorraine Code holds that:

> For positivist-empiricists, knowers are detached and neutral specta-tors, and objects of knowledge are separate from them, inert items in knowledge gathering processes, yielding knowledge best verified by appealing to observational data ... it is from this positivist legacy that the fact/value distinction that regulates inquiry also derives.
>
> (Code 1995: 17)

It is asserted that the working class, gays, blacks etc. are regarded by holders of this value free perspective as 'special interest groups', whose perspectives are value laden and not objective. For standpoint feminists, what Code calls 'positivist-empiricists', knowledge is actually seen as a distortion, a knowledge that is deeply bound to the values of white, middle class, heterosexual men. This is seen as the inevitable result of the kind of society we live in. A key claim of standpoint feminism is, in Sandra Harding's words:

> that in societies stratified by race, ethnicity, class, gender, sexuality or some other such politics shaping the very structure of a society, the *activities* of those at the top both organize and set limits on what persons who perform such activities can understand about themselves and the world around them.
>
> (Harding 1996: 240; original emphasis)

Thus, as in Marx, the ideas of the ruling class are the ruling ideas. It follows because the ruling ideas are those of patriarchy they will be the ruling ideas of science. This viewpoint, it is claimed, distorts the practice and results of science and standpoint feminists call instead for a successor science that can better reflect the experiences of the oppressed groups.

There is one further assertion: that the feminist standpoint offers the potential for a liberating, less distorted knowledge than that of oppressive patriarchy. The result is rather confusingly both a denial of the existence of any universal questions free of historical values and interests (Harding 1996: 242) and a claim for a 'rigorous logic of discovery intended to maximise the objectivity of the results of research and thereby to produce knowledge that can be *for* marginalized people' (Harding 1996: 242, original emphasis).

What Harding has come to describe as 'strong objectivity' (*ibid.*) can perhaps be seen as an attempted answer to the problems of either essentialism or relativism implicit in the 'standpoint' position (Halberg 1989). The question of what the standpoint consists of is a vexed one. If it is held that all women either hold, or have the potential for a less distorted knowledge, then what is it about all women that confers this ability upon them? Conversely what is it about men that prevents them from attaining such a standpoint? In such an assertion is the implication of an 'essential' woman, or 'man', presumably defined through either biological character-istics or some kind of universal psychology? Such an essentialism is deeply pessimistic and potentially harmful to feminism in that it leaves men incapable of transcending patriarchy and both women and men as determined in their roles, a position not so very different to certain forms of sociobiology (see Chapter 7). If on the other hand, as is usually held, there are many standpoints and that men are capable of transcending patriarchy (Harding 1996: 242), then this suggests a fractured, relativised knowledge that potentially divides women into many (possibly antagonis-tic) standpoints – 'black women', 'disabled women', 'black disabled women', etc. Unless the claim to the privileged knowledge of a standpoint can be grounded in an experience unified enough to give a common knowledge upon which to build science, then there is an epistemological equivalence between the knowledge of every woman.

'Strong objectivity' is a call for 'strong reflexivity' (Harding 1996: 244). She maintains that whilst the most critical (and therefore best) research comes from those whose lives have been marginalised, they too must be aware that at every stage of scientific enquiry beliefs will function as evidence. The 'subject' of knowledge, that is the bearers of the beliefs, must therefore also be the object of knowledge.

The objectivity that reflexivity is said to provide arises because the research is conducted from the standpoint of marginalisation. But does this resolve the essentialism–relativism problem? Harding doesn't claim that it does, but nevertheless the claim of strong objectivity is a recasting of the feminist standpoint so it seems reasonable to judge the ensemble of ideas in the reiterated form. By shifting the focus of the object of enquiry to what was originally the subject does address an important cause for concern in science, namely the apparent gendering of knowledge. Evidence for this comes mainly in the scientific metaphor, the descriptions of the world scientists use. Evelyn Fox Keller points to a number of examples: 'hard' and 'soft' sciences (i.e. the masculinity of physics as opposed to the femininity of more subjective branches of knowledge) and the deeply embedded representations of science as 'male' in our culture (Fox Keller 1985: 77). Masculine linguistic representations in science no doubt arise from the male dominance of the culture of science, which in turn arises, as the standpoint feminists argue, from a patriarchal society.

This raises fundamental questions for science: just how much do issues such as class and gender, etc. shape questions or results? The answer is probably quite a lot and this is a matter I will return to in Chapter 6. Nevertheless, here, the resolution of the essentialism–relativism problem is not convincing. First, it does not distinguish between gendered and non-gendered concepts. Some concepts such as metaphors, or divisions of labour, are gendered, but is mathematical expression gendered? Harding's response to this is to cite evidence from Pierre Duhem, N.R. Campbell and Mary Hesse to the effect that science needs metaphor to make itself understood (Harding 1986: 232–6). This doesn't really answer the objection, but merely skirts around it. Perhaps in the attempt to rid science of metaphors and replace them with abstract symbols is evidence for the androcentric value of objectivity? It may well be, but of course to strip science of mathematical language would not only render it descriptively weakened, but would also rid it of machine readable codes that make computer software run.

Second, is it actually the case that a successor science shaped on standpoint principles would discover different things about the world to an androcentric one? It may seem fatuous to ask, but none of the standpoint feminists really addresses this: would a non-androcentric science have discovered the same gravitational laws, for example, or would gravity not be an important topic for science? Here one reads the arguments for a feminist standpoint, or standpoints, but rarely do Harding, Code, Rose or Haraway etc. actually get down to saying how the science itself would be different. Harding is aware of these contradictions and others and her plea is that the epistemology of the standpoint(s) is transitional. Therefore trying to imagine a feminist science in a contemporary society is rather like asking a medieval peasant to imagine a theory of genetics (Harding 1986: 139). This seems a reasonable point, but of course if we cannot know what a feminist science would look like, then we also cannot know beforehand if it would better describe the world than androcentric science.

But what is the point of science? Who does it serve? The usual answer from science is that science is about objective enquiry, it does not serve anyone, but simply helps us to explain the world. This answer is not good enough. The twentieth century is replete with examples of discovery motivated by military or economic ambition – science has and does serve interests. Indeed, we would want it to serve interests, much of the social sciences consist of identifying social ills in order that these can be addressed (Williams and May 1996: 114–15). Feminism itself is, at root, a political project and to use knowledge to further that project is an alternative moral agenda to the development of nuclear weapons. It simply serves a different constituency. Presumably a successor science based on a feminist agenda would have no use for weaponry or many other outcomes of androcentric science and technology, but does this mean a successor science would also have no interest in the development of medicines, or environmentally sustainable forms of production? In other words if we accept the correct premise that science is interest-based does that lead us to the conclusion that there can be no agendas in common across interests? I do not think it does. Harding could respond to this by saying yes, but that is the point of 'strong objectivity' to overcome these interests. This opens a wider issue about what is (or should be) meant by objectivity, a matter I will take up in Chapter 6.

Conclusion

Anti-science has intended and unintended consequences. The intended consequences are often not to be 'anti' at all, but to make clear the intellectual basis of science and to make it relevant to wider or different constituencies. Despite the relativism so often evident in social construc-tionism, few claim to be 'anti-science'. Indeed Bruno Latour has gone on record to protest that he is actually 'pro-science' (Latour 1998). Relativism is, however, an addictive powerful brew and once a small amount is imbibed larger draughts must follow.

The 'strong programme' presents convincing evidence of the importance of social determinants in science, but the insistence that social antecedents can account solely for science does indeed end up abolishing the distinction between science and fiction, whatever the intention. In judging accounts of what the world is like (social or physical) we must be in a position to weigh evidence, to be able to say that whilst accounts *A* and *B* possibly do not tell the whole truth of the matter, one is to be preferred over the other, or if neither is to be preferred *why* they are equal. The abolition of this possibility alone would render science impossible, or irrelevant.

In 'standpoint feminism' the intention appears to be that one account should be preferred over another, but here it is the proposed 'court of appeal' that ends up as problematic. Assuming that it is wished to avoid a standpoint that is biologically (or psychologically) reductionist then which standpoint will provide the best experience to make scientific decisions? Marginalisation is not itself sufficient as a standpoint because marginalisa-tion takes many and often contradictory forms. If all standpoints provide knowledge that must be judged as equivalent once again the court of appeal is abolished.

I have taken Harding's 'strong objectivity' as an attempt to address this problem, but reflexivity (though a valuable strategy) in making subjects the objects of enquiry doesn't touch questions about the adequacy of data. The social antecedents of Professor X's and Professor Y's findings might be quite different, but if their findings turned out to show the same results how could we account for this?

The further problem for social constructionism is that it is social constructionist! That is, ultimately findings are to be seen as social constructions – not some, but all findings. Is this right? My own view is that whilst quite a lot of the world is socially constructed many things within it exist independently of how we perceive, or construct them. An important task of science and one in which it is (I think) partially successful is to distinguish between the 'real' and what is socially constructed as real. A caveat to this is that a meta-problem of what counts as 'real' also exists. Social constructionism dodges the question altogether and substitutes subjective and intersubjective constructions of the world for any independently existing reality. Apart from being counter-intuitive – gravity for example does not differentially affect cultures in time or space – it fails to explain the huge predictive success and consistency of explanations. That is, whilst counter-examples of theories being overthrown or superseded can be found, many core theories of science have remarkably long lives and moreover (as in the well known case of Einstein's theories superseding Newton's) older theories very often become core components of newer theories.

The unintended consequences of social constructionism are anti-scientific. The intended consequences of rejectionism are anti-scientific, but what the rejectionists are anti is either unclear or incoherent. However, the basis of much of the rejectionist complaint seems to be with the ideological, cultural and ecological aspects of science. Havel (rightly) expresses the frustrations and anger of generations who have seen their freedom and creativity crushed by regimes legitimating their ideological posture in science. The '68 generation Roszak describes, though children of the affluent West, could see suffering and injustice around them. The suffering and injustice were made technologically possible by scientific knowledge.

Yet rejectionism throws out the baby with the bath water. Whether or not the pastoral yearnings of William Blake were ever realisable after the Pandora's box of science was opened cannot be known, but in the last years of the twentieth century the lid doesn't even fit any more. Pre-scientific ways of thinking would be unrecognisable to us. What we would now call irrationality is not intellectually viable, once discourse becomes rational. An attempt to persuade us to return to pre-scientific forms of thinking by giving good reasons is to employ rational discourse and is paradoxical (for an example of such an attempt see Alvares 1988). Harding quite rightly says that it would be absurd to expect a medieval peasant to imagine a theory of genetics, but equally it is absurd to expect someone who can understand a theory of genetics to forget her genetics and take on the world view and cognitive abilities of a medieval peasant.

Suggested further reading

Appleyard, B. (1992) *Understanding the Present: Science and the Soul of Modern Man*, London: Pan.

Couvalis, G. (1997) *The Philosophy of Science: Science and Objectivity*, London: Sage.

Holton, G. (1993) *Science and Anti-Science*, Cambridge, MA: Harvard University Press.

Lennon, K. and Whitford, M. (1994) *Knowing the Difference: Feminist Perspectives in Epistemology*, London: Routledge.

Tallis, R. (1995) *Newton's Sleep: Two Cultures and Two Kingdoms*, London: Macmillan.

5 Against science in social science

Anti-science in social science sometimes takes the more generalised rejectionist or social constructionist forms described in the previous chapter. That is, rejectionist motivations for being against science apply equally to social science with the most usual articulation to be found in postmodernist writings (see, for example, Rosenau 1992; Sarup 1993 for a discussion of this). Similarly 'standpoint theorists' or 'strong programmers' usually apply their prescriptions to both the natural and social sciences. Indeed the methodological justification for the latter lies in it being subject to the same form of analysis (see for example McCarl Neilsen 1990) as it applies to the natural sciences. However, on the whole the problems I raise for these positions would apply equally when they are held in the social sciences so I will not discuss them further here.

There are, however, 'anti-science in social science positions' which exist independently of the above, apply only to social science and are rejectionist specifically of social science as science, positions I described in Chapter 3 as 'anti-naturalist'. A consequence of this rejection is a non-scientific methodology for the social sciences, that of interpretivism. Though I use the term 'interpretivism' here this position is variously described as 'hermeneutics', 'ethnography', 'field research' or 'qualitative methods'. No one term entirely describes what is a huge range of theoretical views and technical procedures within this broad methodological approach. Therefore in using the term 'interpretivism' I mean all of those approaches to research that prioritise the interpretation of the actions and meanings of agents, over measurement, explanation and prediction. Interpretivism is mostly, though not entirely confined to sociology and anthropology and forms the basis of symbolic interactionism, ethnomethodology and some forms of critical theory (Hobbs and May 1993).

There is often a coincidence of methodological view between those who hold the positions I described in the previous chapter and the anti-naturalists I describe below. For example most (though not all) standpoint feminists advocate the use of interpretivist methods in investigating the social world even though their epistemological critique does not usually distinguish between 'knowledge production' in the natural or social sciences. Interpretivism, though a methodological consequence of anti-naturalism, does not itself imply anti-naturalism. Indeed one of the founders of interpretivism, Max Weber, believed that what he was doing was contributing to the *science* of sociology in that an understanding of meaning can form the basis of causal explanation (Weber 1978b: 15). For the sake of simplicity, in much of this chapter, I shall use the term 'interpretivism' to imply an anti-naturalist methodology. However in the conclusion I shall take a position similar to that of Weber, namely that interpretation is a necessary strategy to know the social world and that it can (and must) lead to explanations that are meaningful. It can neverthe-less answer 'why' questions about the social world. I will further argue that whilst the strategy of interpretivism is an essential methodological tool in social science, it cannot be the only tool available.

First, however, I will briefly set out the ontological position of interpre-tivism and second, the methodological position which arises from this. I will then argue that anti-naturalist interpretivists (hereafter for the sake of simplicity I will call 'interpretivists') are forced by their ontological stance into making methodological injunctions which they themselves must break.

The ontological basis of interpretivism

Interpretivism has taken the role of the opposition in social science. To borrow a Marxist term, the ruling ideology of social science up until the 1960s was, as I discussed in Chapter 1, that of naturalism, often in the guise of the continental positivism of Durkheim, or influenced by the logical positivism of the Vienna Circle. Nevertheless throughout this period and indeed since the time of Vico there existed an alternative view of how we can know the social world. Indeed, as I suggested in Chapter 1, the pedigree of this view predates the 'scientific revolution'.

Philosophically and even emotionally this alternative approach was influenced by the rejectionist views of Romanticism during the nineteenth century. Indeed the divide between science and the Romantic opposition was essentially philosophical (Tarnas 1991: 366–75) with the former adopting a position of materialist reduction (see Chapter 3) and the latter philosophical idealism. The divide is not quite as tidy as this, mainly because idealism takes many different forms (Rescher 1993), but for the purpose of clarifying the interpretivist position it is helpful.

Idealism, though taking different forms, has a central tenet that 'reality' as we know it reflects the workings of the mind (Rescher 1993: 187). It does not deny the existence of an independent reality, but the effect is to reduce the concept of reality to that which can be grasped by mind. Though this view underlies social constructionism and rejectionism in science generally, most interpretivists have been content to allow that even if descriptions and explanations of the physical world are mind dependent they are nevertheless reliable and universal. This, interpretivists maintain, is not the case in the social world. Indeed some philosophers, notably Rom Harré (Harré and Secord 1972; Harré 1986, 1998), are 'realists' about the physical world, but 'anti-realists' about the social world. In other words they hold that the physical world has a real existence beyond that which we perceive of it (and potentially knowable), but contrawise the social world is the intersubjective construction of its participants and is not 'knowable' in the same sense. Whilst there might be disagreement about the ontological characteristics of the physical world, there is agreement amongst interpretivists about some key ontological characteristics of the social world. What we call the 'social world' is an intersubjective creation. It is created and perhaps more importantly recreated continuously, by its participants as a result of their subjective understanding of it. This view allocates a special role to human consciousness; as Charles Taylor puts it, humans are 'self-interpreting animals' and necessarily so, 'for there is no such thing as the structure of meanings for him independently of his interpretation of them; one is woven into the other' (Taylor 1994: 189).

What we call 'social reality' is the outcome of those interpretations. Ontologically 'marriage', 'parenting', 'crime' and 'work' are of different categories to chemical compounds, or physical structures, for they are free to vary in their characteristics as a result of how they are interpreted and then recreated by their participants. It follows from this that individuals can attribute different meanings to the same action or circumstances and conversely different actions can arise out of similarly expressed meanings (Williams 1998). There is then, in Norman Denzin's words, 'an inherent indeterminateness in the lifeworld' (Denzin 1983: 133). The ontological character of the social world places limits on what we can know of it.

Specifically such a character denies the possibility of a causal explanation, either in a Humean sense whereby causes are seen as observable constant conjunctions between events, or in the form of 'natural necessity', whereby there is an underlying mechanism which will explain why two events are conjoined (Williams and May 1996: 53). Whilst on the face of it people will commonly talk as if their behaviour was 'caused', the causes are underdetermined. Ten different people performing the same action could give ten different reasons (or causes) for their doing it. And of course ten different actions could be motivated by the same reason (or cause). The long held scientific principle of 'same cause–same effect' does not hold in the social world. Therefore an individual giving an explanation of her actions would be giving an explanation adequate to her, but this would not necessarily explain that same action in others. There is, then, too much 'variability' between actions and meaning in the social world to allow causal explanation.

This situation has major implications for method; principally it is alleged that the strategy of explanation used in the natural sciences must be replaced by one of interpretive understanding.

Interpretive method

Interpretivism has its philosophical roots in idealism and its methodological roots in hermeneutics. The method of hermeneutics was originally used by biblical scholars in the Middle Ages and involved a search for and interpretation of meaning in scriptures. The translation of biblical texts was made complex by the tendency for them to have been already translated several times before. The hermeneuticist, in order to discover their original meaning, had then to attempt to understand the wider social context within which they were produced (see Bauman 1978; Hughes 1990). An extension of this method to an understanding of history, though advocated by Vico in the seventeenth century, was first adopted by Frederich Schleiermacher in the nineteenth century, but its use as a strategy in contemporary social investigation was not widely applied until well into the twentieth century. Rather ironically an important advocate of interpretivism in social science was Weber, who in his injunction that any explanation must be adequate at the level of cause and meaning advocated a methodological pluralism (Weber [1922] 1947). I will return to Weber in due course.

The central methodological principle of interpretivism is that individual actions, utterances and beliefs can only by understood through an act of interpretation, through which the investigator attempts to discover their meaning for the agent. As Daniel Little describes it:

> The goal of interpretation is to make sense of an action or practice –
> to discern the meaning of the practice in the context of a system of
> meaningful cultural symbols and representations.
>
> (Little 1991: 70)

As an investigative method interpretation is quite unlike scientific method (or methods). In the latter whilst there is disagreement about what should count as scientific method, there is no shortage of candidates. In interpretivism things are much vaguer (Little 1991: 72), with the coherence of the account provided by the investigator regarded as the principal criterion of validation. In other words the investigator, like her counterpart in biblical studies, is constrained to make interpretations of interpretations within the context of what is known of the particular culture. The less prescriptive approach shows in the methods of data collection used. Apart from the analysis of pre-given texts (books, film, archive material etc.) interpretivists use two principal methods (Hobbs and May 1993; Bryman 1988: chapter 3) of Participant Observation and Unstructured Interviewing. Often these are combined.

The technique of participant observation requires the investigator to partially, or wholly immerse herself in the culture of those she investigates. This might be within an 'alien' culture, such as that investigated by the anthropologist Clifford Geertz (1979) in Bali, or more 'familiar' cultures such as the inner city (see for example Hobbs 1988; Robins and Cohen 1978; Whyte 1943). The participant comes to understand (it is claimed) the culture from the point of view of an agent within that culture. There are no firm prescriptions for the collection of data, or what kind of data are collected. The investigator uses whatever is best or possible (notebook, tape recorder or just memory) and records those things that help to build a coherent picture of the culture that faithfully captures the meanings of its participants. Likewise the unstructured interview (confusingly sometimes called the focused interview), though possibly guided initially by some questions from the interviewer, is intended to allow those investigated to develop their perspective (Bryman 1988: 47). No hypothesis is being tested, standardisation of the interview (questions, format etc.) is unnecessary, the aim simply being 'to make sense of an object of study' (Taylor 1994: 181). This can perhaps be likened to a stranger who turns up to a tennis game. What is going on, in terms of the rules or the point of the game, is made intelligible to her by someone who already understands the game. In this way interpretivism is rather like everyday life in that we make adequate sense of events, sufficient to be able to recapitulate them, or act upon them.

Geertz's study of Balinese cockfighting (Geertz 1979) is a well known example of participant observation. Though unlike some interventions of this kind Geertz's role would have been apparent to the Balinese, often in such studies the observations are covert (see Fielding 1981 for example). At the time of Geertz's investigation, 1958, young Balinese males spent a great deal of their time at illegal cockfights. Superficially this appeared simply to be just a popular sport in Bali, but Geertz's observation is an attempt to go beyond the scenario as it appears. First, Geertz sets out to describe the surface appearance of the phenomenon of the cockfight as well as the context of Balinese society at that time. He provides some contextual detail of his arrival, with his wife, in a Balinese village, the indifference of the villagers towards them, the attitude of the government towards cockfighting, that the police officers were Javanese and not Balinese, and so on (Geertz 1979: 180–6).

The rules of the cockfight are described as are the specific relationships of aspects of the contest to Balinese life, for example 'If an outside cock is fighting any cock from your village, you will tend to support the local one', or 'Cocks which come from any distance are almost always favourites, for the theory is that the man would not have dared bring it if it were not a good cock' (Geertz 1979: 207). He then seeks to uncover the symbolic meaning of the ritual for Balinese men by selecting particular features and interpreting what they might symbolise. Gradually Geertz's account moves from the general and descriptive to interpretations of what was going on. The following gives some sense of the inferences Geertz draws:

Every people, the proverb has it, loves its own form of violence. The cockfight is the Balinese reflection on theirs: on its look, its uses, its force, its fascination. Drawing on almost every level of Balinese experience, it brings together themes – animal savagery, male narcissism, opponent gambling, status rivalry, mass excitement, blood sacrifice – whose main connection is their involvement with rage and the fear of rage, and, binding them into a set of rules which at once contains them and allows them play, builds a symbolic structure in which, over and over again, the reality of their inner affiliation can be felt.

(Geertz 1979: 219)

Geertz describes this strategy as 'thick description' (Geertz 1994: 213–31). Such studies are conducted at a micro level, they require dense, detailed and contextualised description from which, again in his words, it is possible 'to say something of something' (Geertz 1979: 218). The micro level detail of a small part of a society is used to paint a picture of that wider society. The reader of the 'Balinese Cockfight' comes away feeling that she has learned something, not just of a particular ritual in Balinese life, but something of Balinese culture in general. When reading the work of Geertz, or William Foote Whyte's classic study of an American Italian community in the 1940s (Whyte 1943), or even more recently Dick Hobbs' work on underworld culture (Hobbs 1988, 1995), one is drawn into the detail reminiscent of a rich travelogue, or descriptive novel. Rather like the tennis game analogy I used above one comes away with a feeling that something has now been made intelligible. Of course such intelligibility is not simply the outcome of interpretive investigation, but is available to the reader of a work of fiction, or in the appreciation of art. What does it mean then for an interpretivist to 'say something of something'? For Geertz it is to strain to read the 'texts' of a particular society over the shoulders of those to whom they properly belong (Geertz 1979: 222). In using the term 'text' Geertz was prefiguring the postmodern use of this word to denote something to be read and interpreted as a literary form (Rosenau 1992: 25). Geertz's 'thick description' has a similarity with the painstaking efforts of biblical scholars, to uncover layers of meaning within their context. His work and others in this tradition are, then, much closer to the understanding of art than the explanation of science. Metaphorically it is the difference between a Sisley painting and a surveyor's photograph.

To continue that metaphor the claim of interpretivism is that in the social world only the Sisley can represent social life. The fuzzy edges and the subjective interpretation of impressionism is a better metaphor for the complex creativity of the social world than the sharp edged unambiguous snapshot in time. Thus the 'anti-science' of interpretivism comes not in the assertion that such methods can produce *a* faithful representation, but in the claim that this is the *only* valid representation.

Can interpretivists know the social world?

This begs the question of what we can mean by knowing the social world, which in turn poses questions of what it is we can, or should know and questions of how we might know these things. These are perhaps the fundamental philosophical questions of social science (May and Williams 1998: Introduction) and not something that can anywhere near be resolved here. I think, however, that if this is posed as a pragmatic methodological question then a few things become clear, though this does not entirely avoid philosophical questions.

One of the difficulties, it will be recalled, of defining science and its method is that historically science has been a dynamic interplay between social, cognitive and material factors. Science arose out of common sense, though as Wolpert claims it became 'unnatural' later. Nevertheless because science is a human enterprise even at its most complex it retains the hallmark of human cognition. We pose questions to which we hope to find answers. Either at a practical or abstract level science is about problem-solving. However different the social world might be ontologically from the physical world (though as I noted in Chapter 3, in everyday life we do not seem to always notice such distinctions) problem-solving has equally been the hallmark of social science. In social science, as in natural science, to say we know something of X is a knowledge claim that arose from an earlier question about X, or about Y – the knowledge of X being accidentally obtained. We may, of course, be wrong and may have to revise our views, but again (put rather crudely) whether we are seen as right or wrong about X will depend on how well the knowledge claim holds up over time. Whatever the philosophical objections to modes of 'knowing' in the social world our investigations have yielded at least some empirical success in contributing to knowledge that can resolve social ills. Only the most sceptical would say otherwise.

However, the anti-naturalist claim does turn on an ontological differ-ence which leads, at least implicitly, to a difference in what we can mean by the verb 'to know' when applied to the social, as opposed to the physical world (Harré 1998: 37). When, for example, a biologist says she knows what somatotrophin is, she is claiming that she is aware that it is a growth hormone secreted by mammals and we would also assume that her statement implies that she knows why this happens and what the outcomes arise from it happening or not. If, on the other hand, I say to someone who has just undergone an emotional trauma 'I know how you feel', I am saying that I have imagined myself into your position and I think I can understand how you feel. I am claiming an empathic understanding. Unless I am very arrogant I am not saying that the way I feel is the only way to feel, or that it captures the totality of how you feel, but that I have *some* understanding of how you feel. For interpretivists knowledge of the social world is more like the second than the first. Whilst there is an algorithm that will allow us to express knowledge of somatotrophin and one that is potentially available to everyone, knowledge of how someone feels (and how this might lead to subsequent actions or utterances) is subjective. There is no algorithm and moreover the interpretation that arises from that understanding could be different if achieved by another person.

Now let us suppose this view is right. The implication is that to 'know' the social world in the second sense above, we must 'feel' our way into it, a process for which there can be no algorithm. Empathy can perhaps only be learnt through experience, maybe not direct experience, but at least enough to know what something is like. One does not have to be a survivor of Auschwitz to empathise with its victims, but that empathy cannot be learnt as we can learn the periodic table of elements. To base one's interpretations upon such understanding is a subjective exercise, it is about feeling, and others could feel differently. There is no algorithm of method, or of outcome. If this is right then a methodological contradiction arises. There cannot be a method of empathic understanding, yet in order to provide knowledge (in the second sense) of the wider social world, as opposed to the individual, anti-naturalists need a method. The paradox leads to a number of specific problems.

Method

Interpretivism needs a method that is more than the injunction to interpret and above I have touched on some examples of how interpretivists go about their investigations. Geertz's account of the Balinese cockfight is, perhaps rightfully, cited as a fine example of interpretive 'thick description', but what makes it better than say that of an untrained observer (say a UN worker) who happened to be in Bali at the same time? If it is the case that the strategy of 'thick description' has advantages over other methods of data collection then it should follow that Geertz's account is better than that of the untrained observer. If on the other hand interpretivists remain true to a principle of epistemological equivalence in interpretation then what purpose does the strategy of 'thick description' (or any other for that matter) serve?

Plausibility

If epistemological equivalence in the matter of interpretations holds, then why should we believe interpretivist accounts? Perhaps we shouldn't, but then if none are 'true' then what separates interpretation from fiction? It is claimed that all interpretations are subjective accounts with epistemological equivalence, but is it also claimed that interpretation is better than fiction? If it is then there must be a criterion of what an interpretation is, as opposed to any old story. If no claim of privilege of interpretation over fiction is being made, then why bother with the interpretation at all?

Notwithstanding the problem of whether we should believe interpretivist accounts at all, there is the problem of whether we should believe particular accounts. This is a point made by Todd Jones (Jones 1998) specifically in relation to Geertz's work:

> Geertz looks for deeper meaning by selecting central features of the cockfight and speculating about what they symbolize. The method for this is somewhat crude. One item is considered a candidate for being a symbol of something else if it is associated with by convention, resemblance, or spacio-temporal contiguity. Cocks, for example, are read to be phallic symbols because of their vague resemblance to penises, their tendencies to be held by men between their thighs and stroked, their tendencies to be cared for and fussed over exclusively by men, and so on.
>
> (Jones 1998: 43)

Jones concludes that this interpretation is entirely arbitrary, that is the characteristics of what Geertz describes are equally consistent with alternative interpretations. In this, as in other instances of interpretation, there seems to be nothing separating the account from fiction.

The impossibility of generalisation?

Even if we ignore the above difficulties there remains the problem of generalisation. Interpretivists such as Norman Denzin (1983: 133), Taylor (1994: 208–9) and Guba and Lincoln (1982) have explicitly denied the possibility of generalisation and indeed if they are right about the variability of accounts that will arise from subjective interpretations (that is variability in the actions of the observed and in the accounts of the observer) then generalisation is impossible. Yet to 'say something of something' implies at least a *moderatum* generalisation (Williams 1998: 9), that is where aspects of any given situation (the outcomes of interpretation) must be seen to be instances of a broader recognisable set of features. For example on the basis of his 'thick description' of the Balinese cockfight, Geertz feels able to make a number of claims about wider Balinese society.

If interpretivists follow their own injunctions that arise from their ontological claims about the social world then their knowledge of the social world cannot be in any sense privileged. Yet if there is to be any point to interpretivism then it must claim to produce results that are better knowledge of the world than that available to the lay person. But to do this it must abandon anti-naturalism.

Towards a naturalist interpretivism

In this final section of the chapter I want to first consider what I believe to be some methodological confusions in interpretivism. I also want to defend interpretivism as a method, but as part of a methodologically pluralist social science. Thus in the remainder of this chapter I will distinguish between anti-naturalist (AN) interpretivism and naturalist (N) interpretivism.

Anti-naturalism and the method of (AN) interpretivism arising from it are based on a number of confusions. Here I will briefly examine four of those I consider to be the most important (for a fuller discussion see Kincaid 1996: chapter 6).

Variability

Anti-naturalists claim an ontological distinction between the physical and social world. That is, the social world is the outcome of the actions of 'self-interpreting animals'. Our knowledge of the social world as agents in it is subjective as are our actions or utterances that arise from that knowledge. It follows from this, it is said by anti-naturalists, that there is an action–meaning variability in the social world that prevents us from saying that an explanation of *A*'s actions will hold for others, or for other times. *A* could have acted differently to the way she did and *B* ... *Z* would each act differently. There is, then, no one to one relationship between any given meaning and any given action.

Denzin and others holding this view are right to say that this *could* be the case, but in assuming that this *will* be the case they are wrong. Specifically they are right to say a deterministic causal account, on the principle same cause–same effect, is not possible, but wrong to say that human beings will always act or think differently to each other. Of course in any given circumstance we cannot be sure that one person is thinking the same thoughts, but we can know that people will often act in the same way as a result of the same stimuli. For example in the 1997 British General Election the Labour Party secured a landslide victory. It is just possible that every Labour voter had a slightly different suite of reasons for voting Labour, or least weighted them differently, but what is important is that a considerable number acted in the same way. Moreover, this outcome was predictable and it was possible to broadly predict the socio-economic and geographical distribution of voters for each party. The claim of action–meaning variability confuses the impossibility of knowing, deterministically, aggregate outcomes from single cases, with the possibility of making statistical predictions about aggregates. As I noted in Chapter 3 this is often a limitation in complex systems within the physical world also.

As well as action–meaning variability there is also the matter of the variability of interpretations on the part of the investigator. As we have seen (AN) interpretivists are modest in this regard and do not make claims to any privileged interpretation. All that is held is the hermeneutic principle that we can only understand a specific meaning in relation to (say) a whole world view or discourse within which it is embedded. The problem here, as we have seen, is if one does not make the claim that one's interpretation is the best available then all interpretations become equally believable or unbelievable. Knowing the context itself within which the interpretation is made is simply anchoring the interpretation within other interpretations. There is only what Taylor and others have termed the 'hermeneutic circle' (Taylor 1994: 206–7; Blaikie 1993: 29). This seems to me to be too pessimistic by far. Translated into the language of the natural sciences we could say that researchers will hold different theories to explain the phenomena and hold different background assumptions (Kincaid 1996: 206). Where the difficulty lies is not in having different interpretations, but in not showing how we can adjudicate between them. Why is it not possible to devise 'fair tests' between interpretations as would be the case in the natural sciences (Kincaid 1996: 206)? Suppose there was a rival and contradictory interpretation of the Balinese cockfight to that offered by Geertz, then the proposer of each interpretation should be able to make clear the underlying premises of each interpretation, which should be then operationalisable into tests. If this is not the case then they must remain untested conjectures and cannot amount to a knowledge claim. If, as is so often the case, there is only one interpretation made of specific data, the reasons for making this interpretation should be clear if it is not to be regarded as simply arbitrary (Jones 1998: 45).

The existence of variability, either as that between action and meaning, or arising from investigators' interpretations, does not seem to be sufficient reason to abandon naturalism. However, if the resolution of the action–meaning problem lies in restricting social science to description and prediction of aggregate phenomena then this surely makes for a very 'thin' social science. Anti-naturalists are right to claim that actions are meaningful and any successful investigative strategy must surely tell us something about those meanings. Naturalist social science cannot ignore meaning and I will try to show how a naturalist methodology can incorporate meaning into investigation, but first I would like to say something about explanation and understanding.

Explanation – understanding and meaning

The rejection of explanation is likewise on the grounds of variability, that an explanation makes intelligible a mechanism underlying a phenomenon and no such mechanisms exist in the social world. For example the presence of non-ferrous metals in rocks is *explained* by metamorphosis, itself the result of the nearby intrusion of hot igneous rocks, but no mechanism can be posited to explain why people laugh (other than physiological description). People may laugh at the same things and this might be predictable, but there is no encompassing explanation for laughter. Against this it is said that it would be quite possible to come to understand why a particular individual will laugh at something. The route to getting at meanings is to understand. The assumption is, then, that understanding and explanation are not the same thing. But is this the case? Moreover do we have to posit a mechanism to be in possession of an explanation?

In everyday English speech the concepts of explanation and under-standing are run together. We even talk of 'understanding an explanation'. In most cases the one word could fairly readily be substituted for the other. To say one understands how to programme a video, is to be in possession of an explanation of how to programme a video. If Denzil explains the reasons for leaving his partner to Jan, then Jan can under-stand why Denzil left. Indeed as is the case with causes and reasons (see Chapter 3) in everyday speech, explanation and understanding are used interchangeably. Weber makes things clearer by distinguishing between descriptive understanding (*aktuelles verstehen*) where one understands what is happening (for example someone is digging with a shovel) and explanatory understanding (*erklärendes verstehen*) where one comes to know why (to plant potatoes). Though Weber's distinction has been criticised, most famously by Schutz ([1932] 1967), it is at least a starting point. Weber also alludes to the concept of empathy (Weber 1949: 74), though whether (or under what circumstances) he was advocating empathic understanding is likewise controversial. Empathic understanding is, of course, when we 'put ourselves in someone else's shoes' in order to understand their actions, feelings etc. Clearly not only must one be clear about what kind of understanding is being talked about, but also it is the case that by no means all understandings of social life are empathic. They do not require a deep understanding of particular individual reasons, but simply (in the case of explanatory understanding) an identification with a known cultural norm. Thus if I observe someone digging and ask them to tell me why and they respond 'to plant potatoes' I have an explanation of their actions consistent with what I know about what one needs to do to plant potatoes and that this is a common occurrence in my society. This seems little different to the kind of question we might ask in respect of the physical world.

There is then no sharp division between an explanation and an under-standing, though we might want to treat empathic understanding as a special case. To achieve explanatory understanding is to have answered a 'why' question by reference to the norms obtaining in any given society. Therefore we do not need a 'mechanism', indeed (as Harold Kincaid points out, 1996: 55) an explanation might simply be to show how diverse phenomena fit into a common pattern.

Whilst it is true that the actions (or utterances) for which we seek an 'explanation' or 'understanding' are meaningful to their authors, what we mean by 'meaning' can itself differ considerably and is rarely defined or specified. This point is noted by Kincaid and in his efforts to specify a possible 'science of interpretivism' he lists six different uses of the term by those who claim human behaviour is meaningful.

Perceptual meaning	how a subject perceives the world, including the actions of others and him- or herself.
Doxastic meaning	what a subject believes.
Intentional meaning	what a subject intends, desires etc., to bring it about.
Linguistic meaning	how the verbal behaviour of the subject is to be translated.
Symbolic meaning	what the behaviour of the subject – verbal or non-verbal – symbolizes.
Normative meaning	what norms the behaviour of the individual reflects or embodies.

(Kincaid 1996: 192)

It seems unnecessary to elaborate upon these in order to make the point that when an investigator claims to understand agents' meanings, a number of things (possibly contradictory) could be involved, furthermore in different contexts one meaning might be more readily understood than another. The kind of meaning sought or found will often be linked to the kind of understanding required or achieved. Whilst it is quite reasonable to claim that human action is meaningful, this is far too vague. Moreover, once it is more tightly specified, then the meaning of agents can constitute hypotheses. Indeed it would seem that this is exactly what Weber intended when he advocated the method of *verstehen*. For Weber, in the social sciences, grasping the complex meaning of an action comes to constitute an explanation (Weber 1978b: 8–16). We can add to that that the nature of the meaning grasped (perceptual, symbolic, or normative, for example) will determine the extent or power of the explanation.

The possibility of generalisation?

To be in possession of an explanation allows at least some kind of inference between (say) a present and future action in an individual, or from one to another individual or over time. In other words explanations are linked to generalisations. Now, as I noted above, (AN) interpretivists tend to either ignore or explicitly deny generalisation can arise from interpretation, but much turns on what one means by generalisation. We can identify three kinds of generalisation:

1   Total generalisations, where situation *S1* is identical to *S* in every detail. Thus *S1* is not a copy of *S* but an instance of a general deterministic law that governs *S* also.

2   Statistical generalisations, where the probability of situation *S* occurring more widely can be estimated from instances of *S*.

3   *Moderatum* generalisations, where aspects of *S* can be seen to be instances of a broader recognisable set of features.

The first of these are almost certainly impossible in the social sciences and in the natural sciences mostly restricted to a few fundamental laws of nature. The second, as I have indicated, form the basis of aggregate description in the social sciences. Both, I would agree, are neither possible or desirable outcomes of interpretive data, but, as I suggested above, the third seems to be an attainable goal.

An explanation of how diverse phenomena fit into common patterns is made possible by the existence of cultural consistency (the hermeneutic context in which interpretations are made). This is perhaps best illustrated through example.

In the late 1980s the British Economic and Social Research Council (ESRC) commissioned longitudinal research on the practices and attitudes of a sample of 16–19 year olds through their transition to adulthood. The 16–19 Initiative, as it is known, was conducted in Swindon, Liverpool, Sheffield and Kirkcaldy. Though most of this study was quantitative, a sub-sample of young people were selected for interview. This section of the study was conducted by Pat Ainley (Ainley 1991) and concentrated on the views of young people about leaving home. In Ainley's part of the study there was some standardisation of questions, but nevertheless it aimed to answer questions about practices and attitudes unanswered in the main quantitative study. For example, why was there such a difference between the locations in the number of young people leaving home to live with other relatives (Ainley 1991: 15)? The search then is to answer 'why' questions about difference, but in order to do this the assumption must be of at least some cultural consistency between the locations. For example all of the young people (with the possible exception of Kirkcaldy) would have emerged from any education system that is organised in approximately the same way and shares certain values. Most of the youngsters would be English speaking and be the product of similar familial norms. Most would have been exposed to similar media images and all grew up exposed to the ruling political ideology of the period – Thatcherism. One could go on to talk about the built environment, kinship cultures and so on. Difference attributable to cultural *in*consistency would be the exception, rather than the rule.

It seems quite reasonable then to make *moderatum* generalisations from the instances where cultural consistency between locations was found and reasonable to assume that findings which held in Swindon and Sheffield would hold in Peterborough and Penzance. Moreover, in reading Ainley's findings, one is left with the impression that many of the youth experiences (of for example retaining links with home) would enjoy a very much wider cultural consistency than just that of Britain. *Moderatum* generalisations are not just possible, they seem unavoidable. Moreover in many cases they are capable of formation into specific testable hypotheses, thus fulfilling Weber's dictum that an explanation must be adequate at the level of cause and meaning. I have, it will be recalled, shown caution about the use of causal language and I will consider this again in Chapter 7, but nevertheless research such as Ainley's is capable of generating further hypotheses testable within and beyond the specific culture.

The limits of interpretivism

There are two main limits to even a recast (N) interpretivism. The first concerns the limits to understanding, the second concerns the limits to generalisation.

1. *Understanding.* If, as I suggest, the claims of interpretation should be subject to testing then this will inevitably set limits on what can be claimed as understood. A long-standing critique from within anti-naturalism places the limits of understanding with language.

In the foregoing I have said little about language because I do not believe the debate about language in social life is central to the question of whether the subjectivity of human consciousness rules out scientific methods in social science. Social scientists place different emphases on the importance of language, though few would maintain that it is unimportant. An influential view originated with Peter Winch ([1958] 1990) which maintained that the task of social investigation is to elaborate the 'forms of life' of a particular society (Winch 1990: 42). The forms of life are embodied in rules which are expressed and known through language. To understand a form of life one must understand the language. An even more radical version of this thesis is known as the Sapir–Whorf hypothesis (Whorf 1956; see also Mennell 1974 for a discussion of this) which holds that language does not simply reproduce ideas, but actually shapes the ideas themselves. Thus Newtonian space and time are not intuitions, but instead are the product of linguistically produced culture (Whorf 1956: 153). Language then allows us a richer experience of reality. For example (reputedly) the Eskimos have over 100 words for snow, allowing a much finer differentiation of a concept we see in a unitary way. The consequence of this is that certain aspects of cultures may never be understandable to outsiders.

Of course, as Steven Lukes has pointed out, in order to begin to understand a society through its language, we must have some starting point, some referential categories upon which we can agree (Lukes 1994: 293).

The views of Winch, or Sapir and Whorf, are much too pessimistic. This said, where cultural consistency does not obtain, then interpretations require at least some cultural translation on the part of the researcher, or at least to her audience. This must have its limits and whether or not the Sapir–Whorf hypothesis about cultural relativity holds, knowing a language seems to be a prerequisite for interpretation and the extent to which one knows that language may limit what can be known (Jones 1998: 55). It may also mean that Kincaid's plea for 'fair tests' may not be workable unless there is a fair amount of cultural consistency to allow such intersubjective testing.

2.   *Generalisation.* The limit to *moderatum* generalisations is that they can probably only ever amount to provisional hypotheses, because the nature of their further testing means they cannot be too specific. However, in my view, this is not an impossible problem provided it is accepted that there are generalising limits to interpretations. To use an analogy, one would not expect an artist's brush to be much use for painting a building. A rigorous and informative social science needs the accounts of meaningful action available from interpretive methods, but it also needs quantitative methods in order to move beyond *moderatum* generalisations.

Conclusion

There will be many anti-naturalists who will not be convinced by my plea for a naturalistic interpretivism. They will complain that I have missed the point that interpretivism belongs to the humanities, that it is not anti-scientific because it has no more to do with science than does Impressionist painting. In one sense they may be right. I would certainly agree, for example, that multiple interpretations in the humanities are enriching and if an investigation of the social world was part of the humanities then I would have to concede that they are right that this is how we should treat the social world.

But from the point of view of giving us workable knowledge (that can be employed in policy-making etc.) then I must agree with Raymond Tallis when he describes art as 'useless' (Tallis 1991: part II). Though I concede that the social world may be of a different 'kind' to the physical world I do not believe that this inhibits a scientific investigation of it. Actually, (as I touched on in Chapter 3 and will say more about in Chapter 7), I do not believe that the ontological disjuncture between the physical and social worlds is a disjuncture, but that phenomena of different ontological kinds can be emergent from each other.

Interpretivists, including those I have categorised as anti-naturalist interpretivists, claim for their method, at least implicitly, as much as a naturalist would claim. Unfortunately their anti-naturalism leads to confusions over understanding, explanation, meaning and generalisation and their methodological claims rest on shaky philosophical foundations. When these confusions are cleared up (a task I have tackled only in a fairly perfunctory way here) nothing of the richness of interpretivist method is lost and indeed in a pluralistic social science can only enhance other methods. Fortunately the argument for pluralism is one that largely won, at least amongst empirical researchers. Multi-method research is both commonplace and well defended for the practical benefits it brings to social investigation (see for example Brewer and Hunter 1989).

Suggested further reading

Collin, F. (1997) *Social Reality*, London: Routledge.

Elster, J. (1989) *Nuts and Bolts for the Social Sciences*, Cambridge: Cambridge University Press.

Kincaid, H. (1996) *Philosophical Foundations of the Social Sciences: Analyzing Controversies in Social Research*, Cambridge: Cambridge University Press.

Phillips, D. (1987) *Philosophy, Science and Social Inquiry: Contemporary Methodological Controversies in Social Science and Related Applied Fields of Research*, Oxford: Pergamon.

6   Science, objectivity and ethics

Objectivity and ethics are often considered as two separate issues in science, but the position I will set out in this chapter assigns them both to the status of normative values. This is a position that the social constructionists I spoke of, in Chapter 5, would have no difficulty in supporting. Indeed I concluded in that chapter that both social constructionists and rejectionists raised important issues about the social nature of science and the outcomes of scientific practice for the wider society. However I argued that the rejectionist view was incoherent because it ignored the interpenetration of science and technology into wider society and that furthermore the relativism of social constructionism would make science impossible or unrecognisable.

The opposite of relativism is objectivism, and it is the certainty of the existence of an objective reality, about which scientists can be objective, that has characterised most of science since the time of Newton. However, in the philosophy of science (a discipline not always treated with reverence by practising scientists!) a wider range of views has been canvassed (see for example Laudan 1977; Newton-Smith 1981; Howson and Urbach 1989; Chalmers 1990; Trigg 1993), but most are characterised by a belief that some criterion of objectivity must be retained in order that science can describe and explain the world – and indeed, so that we can explain how it is we can come to have a knowledge of the world sufficient to build atom bombs, undertake genetic engineering or produce medicines that work, or in the social sciences to accurately predict voting patterns or market preferences.

Because science has been successful at doing these things its knowledge has been at the service of those who wish to use or control this knowledge. Not all of the clients or sponsors of science are 'bad', but a problem for science is how can we decide which are bad or good, or more generally what is the 'right' thing to do? Scientists once believed it was enough just to be objective, but if objectivity is a value itself how can it stand apart from other normative values? Is objectivity itself an *ethical* value, or is it a value of a different kind?

Reality and objectivity

For a natural scientist to believe that what she did was not an objective encounter with reality would represent a loss of faith. Objectivity and reality might be seen as the epistemological and ontological cornerstones of science and are rarely held to question by scientists themselves – though of course the lack of questioning does not necessarily indicate philosophical introspection in arriving at such views.

Scientific realism (there are many varieties of realism, see Harré 1986) holds that over time science produces ever more accurate theories to bring us closer to what is the reality and moreover that science is the most effective instrument with which to discover reality (Laudan 1997: 139). What is interesting is that what counts as 'reality' has changed as a result of scientific discoveries and is not just something out there to be discovered, but is redefined as a result of scientific endeavour. In Chapter 1 I showed how this was the case in the shift from a Newtonian to an Einsteinian world view in physics. This is not the same as saying we socially construct reality, simply that what we understand by it is subject to revision.

Postmodernists are fond of using the term 'multiple realities' (see Rosenau 1992: 109–12) to capture the different experiences that people have, but also to suggest that there is no privileged account of reality. The term is unfortunate for if reality is to retain its meaning, then as a concept it must encompass all experiences of it. Nevertheless the notion of reality as experienced is important, because the only evidence we have of a reality is through our experiences, through logical relations between those things we can experience, or through the accounts of others of these things. The problem is an old one in philosophy and was recognised by Immanuel Kant when he distinguished between phenomena, those things we experience, and noumena, those things which are the source of experience, but cannot themselves be experienced (see Körner 1955: 91–6). For example the reality of water is in the everyday sense a colourless, odourless liquid, but to the chemist it is atoms of two gases joined together in a particular way to produce a molecular structure possessing its own chemical properties. Both accounts are equally 'real', but reality is differentially experienced and will depend on past knowledge and upon what we are looking for. There is no one experience we can point to and say that is what water *really* is. Social reality is even more problematic, because whilst intersubjective agreement about the commonplace (or molecular) properties of water is readily achieved, the 'reality' of disability will be subject to social definition which may change between time and place. Disability, though experienced as a reality and possessing properties not subject to individual definition, nevertheless is a social construction. As I noted in the last chapter it is this characteristic that leads some philosophers, such as Rom Harré, to be realists about the physical world, but not the social world.

Notwithstanding the particular ontological problem of social 'reality', that reality is differentially experienced means there is the wider problem of knowing which accounts should be privileged, even within science. Scientific realism holds that a growth of knowledge about the world requires the scientist, through her theories, to produce better accounts of it. The scientist will claim that she is able to do this by being objective about her investigations. A scientist, if pressed on the matter, would probably say that to be objective about enquiry is to rely on non-arbitrary and non-subjective criteria for the development, acceptance or rejection of theories and hypotheses (Longino 1990: 62). Is the scientist therefore claiming that to do science is to engage in a process that is free from the caprice, emotion, convenience or aesthetic preferences that guide our everyday judgements? For example, if I say a wine is too 'acid' I am expressing a statement of opinion as fact. Others may express contrary opinions, but the chemist, by measuring the pH of the wine, would be able to say it was more, or less acid than another wine. But is it always this simple?

Measurement and the adoption of particular forms of measurement (like objectivity itself) have social antecedents. Either as the result of habit, or through the conscious adoption of particular measures, measurements started with people. They are then values that arose socially. So what makes these values (measurement, or other methodological procedures) different to values such as 'loud', 'tasty' or 'astringent', or even moral values such as 'good', 'kind' or 'honest'? The scientist may say that the former are objective and the latter subjective, but the difficulty is that they are not sharply divided (Putnam 1997).

For example to adopt a set of measurement values might be to unwittingly adopt particular moral, or political values, or even not be aware that underlying values are anything other than scientific ones. Steven Shapin (1979) provides a nice example in the 'science' of phrenology. Phrenology, in the nineteenth century, used measured characteristics of cranial topography to infer that head and/or brain size was an indication of its power or functioning. The measurement techniques applied were detailed and accurate for their day and provided useful descriptive knowledge of a cerebral and neuro-anatomy that is of scientific value today (Shapin 1979: 147), but of course phrenology is now an object of ridicule and as Shapin clearly shows its motivations were social and political. Other measurement values used in science have less obvious social antecedents. In physics and cosmology, for example, the decision to adopt the Kelvin measurement for extreme ranges of temperatures resolved the difficulty of expressing such extremes within the narrow range afforded by existing measurements (see Chapter 3). But of course the scale itself was 'invented' by William Thomson (Lord Kelvin) in 1848.

Science has long tried to hold on to a distinction between facts and values, whereby (to use Hume's distinction) facts correspond to 'is' statements and values to 'ought' statements (see Williams and May 1996:

chapter 5, for a discussion of this). The former are statements about the way the world is and the latter statements about opinion. But this distinction breaks down when values such as measurement, which are used to establish facts, are seen to have subjective antecedents. Science turns out to be an ensemble of values and though I do not suggest that these are all derived as a result of caprice or aesthetic preference, it remains that the value base of science emerged socially.

The sociology of science is rich with examples to illustrate how social values enter, or become scientific ones (see for example studies reported in Barnes and Edge 1982, or Mulkay 1991). The matter could rest there with victory for social constructionism if it were not for two inconvenient matters. First without the value of objectivity, that is without some criteria of selection that allows the scientist to privilege one theory, or one explanation (etc.) over another, science is just as believable as any other story about 'reality'. Second, though scientific values have social antecedents their adoption does lead science to produce testable conclusions about both the physical and the social world. The adoption of particular measurement scales may be a social convention, but when applied do seem to help us distinguish aspects of reality. For example though the Kelvin scale is a social construct, 2.7 Kelvin *is* the temperature of cosmic background radiation and a cosmologist or an astronomer would claim that this is a description of an actual characteristic of nature (that it is not 2.6 or 2.8) and would be so regardless of our ability to measure it, or the type of measurement employed.

Redefining objectivity

Most natural scientists, I would conjecture, would not see the need to redefine objectivity, though the matter of objectivity has been a concern in social science for much of this century. Positivism held that the scientist, whether natural or social, conducted 'value free' science, that scientists were (or should be) neutral in terms of moral or political values. But of course the social world consists, to a great extent, of values that are moral or political and this is the subject matter of social science. This was recognised by Max Weber who regarded values as a defining characteristic of human beings. However, he also recognised (Albrow 1990: 243) that if we accept that all values are subjective or historically contingent, then relativism would ensue. Weber instead believed that only by embracing values wholeheartedly can a scientist achieve value freedom. Furthermore, he too recognised that science itself is founded on values such as truth, rigour and clarity. Weber's position rests on the acceptance that in science in general and specifically sociology, there will be a debate about 'ends', about what policy should achieve and therefore what research should be done (Weber 1974: 75). However, it does not follow from this that the investigation itself need be biased by those values. For example through *verstehen* we can come to know the meaning of social practices for the agents involved, but it does not mean we have to take sides on these values. One does not have to be a Fascist to understand Mussolini and why he took Italy into the Second World War; one does not have to be deviant to understand deviance. In sociology Weber's objectivity is to make the subjective values of those investigated the subject matter of the discipline, to show how their values guided their actions. Objectivity does not imply neutrality, as the positivists believed. Alfred Tauber (1997: 30) cites Robert Proctor's distinction between the two. Neutrality implies that science does not take a stand, whereas objectivity is about whether science is *reliable*. Particular sciences may be completely objective, but may serve economic or political interests. Geologists, for example, know more about oil bearing rocks (because of the demand for oil) than any other sort, but their knowledge is no less reliable for that.

Weber's position would, I think, be a resolution of the objectivity problem if it were possible to say that methodological values were objective and separable from external values about ends. The ends of science will often make a difference to the science itself. This is a point central to Helen Longino's argument about science and objectivity. Longino, like the Standpoint Feminists, is concerned to show why science is androcentric and how it might be otherwise. Her project is, however, broader and she wishes to show *how* science is value laden. As Couvalis (1997: 152) points out her position initially looks similar to that of the Strong Programmers (see Chapter 4). Both parties agree to the underdetermination thesis with the Strong Programmers emphasising the role of interests in determining standards and evidence in science, whilst Longino emphasises underlying values in science.

For Longino there is no sharp divide between social values and methodological values. She uses the terms *constitutive* values to describe the internal values of science, such as accuracy, explanation etc., and *contextual* values which approximate to the social or subjective values I describe above. Two conclusions arise from this. First, that science must adopt constitutive values though these may be disputed in (say) the debate between induction and falsification (see Chapter 2). Second, and unlike the 'Strong Programmers', Longino accepts that contextual values will not always influence underlying assumptions about the science itself. There then comes a further twist however, that she thinks that contextual values can legitimately influence constitutive ones, but despite this science can still be objective. How can this be?

First she sets out a number of criteria that would produce a critical science based upon intersubjectively agreed standards – what she terms the 'transformative interrogation by the scientific community' (Longino 1990: 216). Somewhat akin to Harding she calls for scientists to be aware, and make other scientists aware, of the background assumptions held, though this amounts to a communal reflexivity rather than one simply on the part of the single investigator. Thus

> Values are not incompatible with objectivity, but objectivity is ana-lyzed as a function of community practices rather than an attitude of individual researchers toward their material ...
>
> (Longino 1990: 216)

Like Popper before her, she points out that observation is an interactive, not passive process and will be directed by a theory. Therefore 'What is observational and what is theoretical changes depending on what can be contested or what can be taken for granted' (Longino 1990: 220). Science is essentially social knowledge and she criticises the tendency in Anglo-American philosophy of science to reduce knowledge of a particular thing to individual knowledge. How we know something and how we validate that knowledge should, according to Longino, therefore take place in the social domain. Unlike Weber, Longino is less concerned with how the individual comes to see her value orientation, but how those values can be examined communally. One could suppose that Weberian 'value freedom' within science would sanction the use of particular methods as 'neutral'. For instance, a scientist could use (in Longino's example) induction, which would apply as a general principle whatever the 'ends' of science are. But as Longino reminds us these kinds of general principles have been called into question by Popper, Kuhn and others (Longino 1990: 32–4). Longino's scientist, unlike Weber's, cannot (metaphorically speaking) shut herself in her laboratory and believe she left her values outside.

A number of writers since Kuhn, and specifically here, Longino, have provided accounts of how values outside of science shape those inside science, suggesting a deficiency in a Weberian view that the act of investigation itself can be value neutral. A constitutive value (to use Longino's term), that might appear to be a neutral instrument of investigation, or regulatory principle in science, turns out to have been shaped by non-scientific values. However, as Longino recognises even though constitutive values may be underwritten by contextual ones, this is unavoidable and necessary. If it were not science would be an impossible project. Scientists, then, embrace a set of values in order to do science. Once we have accepted this to be the case, then the question is which values should scientists adopt?

The principal value that Longino wants to adopt is that of objectivity (though she redefines it). The problem she faces, as does anyone who takes the view that the epistemology and methodology of science are social, is what will serve as a guarantee of that objectivity (one could substitute 'truth' for objectivity here)? More traditional views of science, maintaining the fact–value distinction, could anchor objectivity or truth in a corre-spondence with the 'facts' (Nagel 1979: 485–90), specifically in the case of empiricist observation statements. Once, however, one accepts that observation statements are guided by theoretical or cognitive preconceptions, which in turn might even have a basis in normative values, then an alternative social 'guarantee' must be substituted. As we have seen Longino uses the device of transformative interrogation by the scientific community. Objectivity becomes redefined as intersubjective agreement. What is objective becomes the consensus of that community. There are, I believe, four problems with this.

First, the effect of Longino's social epistemology is (laudably) to widen the ownership of knowledge. The transformative interrogation would then not be limited to the present mechanisms of peer review of work, replication etc. (Cole 1992: chapter 6), but would expose the scientist and her theories, methods and regulatory principles to wider social scrutiny. Whilst one can see how this would produce an interrogation, how the transformation that Longino wants would occur, is less clear and such a process seems no more protected from the hijacking by powerful interests than the present regime. Couvalis, for example, maintains that she fails to show how such an ideal community could come to agree on the choice of one theory over another (Couvalis 1997: 161). The consensus of such a community could just as easily be based upon caprice, or particular social interests, as a desire to get at the truth. Once truth becomes a function of social agreement as a goal, then it becomes the social agreement of a particular community and it follows that any alternative account would be epistemologically deviant to that community.

Second, although Longino's 'contextual empiricism', as she names it, maintains a distinction between the observational–experimental dimension of science and the theoretical one (Longino 1990: 219), this does not seem strong enough, particularly in respect of the history of science. The importation of interests or contexts into science can have a disastrous effect on its methodology or regulatory principles. We can cite here, for example, Lysenkian genetics in the Soviet Union (Medvedev 1969), or of course the aforementioned phrenology. When this happens it can take science a long while to discredit such importations, but in the long run this will usually happen because the predicted results will usually fail to materialise. Lysenko predicted that his approach to genetics would have a beneficial effect on crop yields (which is partly why it was so attractive to Stalin), but of course it didn't. Whilst a 'transformative interrogation' by the scientific community may well reveal contextual values underlying constitutive ones, in the long run the powerful court of empirical adequacy will rule.

Third, whilst we can agree with Longino that criteria of objectivity are intersubjective, there has to be something external to the community to be objective about. For instance whilst there would be intersubjective agreement that t = 4.66, p<0.01, the reference category is a state of the world that is that state and no other one.

Lastly there is an elision of ethical values and epistemological–methodological values. Once it is accepted that science is built on social values there is the danger that one can slide from what is true, that normative values will often underlie scientific ones, to what is untrue, that all normative values have equal status, or effect. Scientists bring a range of 'normative' values to their work. These may be an epistemological world view, or particular techniques acquired from a mentor and they may be political, moral or more general metaphysical world views acquired from outside of science. Compare, for example, the motivating moral and political values in phrenology with the pragmatic methodological values underlying the 'invention' of the Kelvin scale. The 'right thing to do' in terms of how to do science should not be conflated with the 'right thing to do' in terms of ethics. I will discuss these separately. First, ethics.

Ethics and science

Ethical judgements are normative ones, they are socially derived, but for much of human history there has been an attempt to derive ethical principles that can be universal, that is applicable in all times and places. The growth of science, but in particular the attendant culture of rationality, gave impetus to the search for ethical principles. The growth of scientific rationality is culturally specific to the West and like the science it has facilitated has had a long period of gestation. Put like this it would seem that 'science' and its accompanying 'rationality' are two separate things, but the ability to reason (the hallmark of scientific rationality) is as much part of science as experimental method. As I indicated in Chapter 1 the cultural success of science was attributable to its empirical and technological achievements. Consequently scientific rationality became the gold standard and as Weber ([1925] 1978a) and more recently Habermas ([1968] 1989) have argued, that rationality has become increasingly institutionalised. In particular scientific rationality successfully challenged mystic beliefs and in a secular (or virtually) secular society reason becomes the hallmark of normal social conduct. The persecution of 'witches' and heretics by the Inquisition, in the late Middle Ages, could be justified as being sanctioned by 'God's will'. But in the twentieth century, in the West at least, it is no longer socially acceptable to attribute the reasoning for one's actions to the will of God, particularly if this involves mass slaughter.

Scientific rationality is a secular form of rationality in so far as actions are justified in relation to human standards. This, however, requires a different approach to justification in the social world; it requires an ethics. Attempts to produce an ethical principle as a foundation to society have been various (Glover 1990; Smart and Williams 1973), but most importantly have included the 'rights' based ethics of Kant (Körner 1955: chapter 6) and more recently John Rawls (1971) or Robert Nozick (1974), which holds a respect for the individual person as a guiding principle. Utilitarian ethics (associated with Jeremy Bentham, John Stuart Mill and G.E. Moore) conversely holds either, in its consequentialist form, that the rightness of any action must judged by its consequences and the greater the good the better the action, or, in its 'hedonistic' form, that the only thing that is good is happiness and an absence of pain. The emphasis in utilitarian ethics, then, is on maximising the sum of goods in society.

It is not my intention to discuss these particular ethics, instead I mention them in order to demonstrate how, with the removal of god as an ethical guarantor, there is a need to rationally justify action with reference to a different principle, that of what it is reasonable to do. Ethical reasoning and scientific reasoning become rather similar. For example a scientist who chose one particular theory over another on the grounds that it was proposed by her best friend would be seen to have offended scientific rationality. Similarly if a judge recommended a 'not guilty' verdict because the defendant was a member of the same secret society as the judge, he would have been considered to have acted against ethical principles. The reasons for condemning the scientist, or the judge, could be reasoned from universal principles applying in the domains of science and law respectively.

Rights and utilitarian ethics are examples of specific ethics, ways in which it is said we should live. However, beyond particular ethics science gave rise to the search for meta-ethical principles, which would begin from a clarification of what can be meant by 'duty', 'rights' or 'virtue' (Smart 1984: 2). The impetus to do this was the ability of science to describe and explain the world. If, as Laplace believed, science could come to know the position, velocity and mass of every particle in the universe, present, past and into the future, then it must follow from this that human lives are also determined by those same (to be discovered) laws.

Unsurprisingly, the search for a 'naturalistic' meta-ethic had its opponents, such as G.E. Moore who maintained words such as 'kind', 'good', 'pleased', etc. can only be known intuitively and cannot be defined ([1903] 1959: 12), though of course this does beg the question of where intuition came from in the first place. Whether or not the search for a naturalistic meta-ethic can be regarded as successful, it must be seen as an attempt to replace the 'ought' of human subjective behaviour with the 'is' of science. Perhaps more importantly the debate about whether or not this is possible has been conducted through a form of analytic discourse that is manifestly scientific in form (see for example Hospers 1973: chapter 9).

The problem with using science as a source of ethics, or the language of science to derive ethical principles, is that it is tautological with regard to the way science and scientists should behave. Thus if it is held that scientific practice must be ethical and the source of that ethic lies in it either being scientifically established as natural, or scientifically reasoned as deriving in some other way, then the ethic itself can only be validated by the science that is supposed to be ethical! Ethical decisions are about how humans should treat each other, they are then recipes about how social life should be. Questions of ethics arose only with social life and it would seem therefore they can only be derived from social life. Science too is a social practice and like other social practices changes over time. Social life and science change, so it would seem to follow that an ethic of science would change too.

Scientific knowledge and ethics

Epistemological (and methodological) standards in science may have social antecedents and these may be subject to change, but what is also important is that they have consequences that transcend any contemporary ethical standards. Put simply, today's scientific knowledge may lie at the root of tomorrow's ethical problem.

One of the greatest ethical dilemmas facing scientists is that connected with what has become known as the Human Genome Project. The 'project' is actually a number of interrelated and co-ordinated projects, the aim of which is a complete map of the entire human genetic code (Davis 1990: 3). A genome is defined as all the genetic information of a particular species, and variations in this create the variety in a species. They also account for genetic 'defects' that lead to inherited conditions such as cystic fibrosis and Huntington's Disease (see Harper and Morris 1991). Indeed knowledge of any given human being's individual genetic composition allows probabilistic prediction of a range of diseases, including cancer. The potential of the research to medical science is enormous, because once such information is known corrective measures may possibly be undertaken. But of course this kind of information has potentially harming effects for individuals. An individual known to have a high likelihood of developing a fatal disease early in life may have difficulty in obtaining insurance, or indeed insurance companies may insist (when this becomes practicable) that proposers undertake a mapping of their genomes. Associated projects in animal genetics have led to some success in 'cloning', suggesting that the science required to successfully clone humans is possible.

In genetic research the science has 'run ahead' of the ethics, but the science itself has a long pedigree (one could say going back to Darwin!), directly traceable to the work of Gregor Mendel in the nineteenth century. He was able to produce the first evidence of heredity, the transmission of the characteristics of organisms from one generation to the next, but the key milestone along the road to the 'genome' project was the discovery of the structure of DNA by Watson and Crick. Mendel showed that heredity existed and Watson and Crick were able to show what was the key to understanding it. Since Watson and Crick (what is called) the New Genetics allows the manipulation or re-arrangement of genetic material to alter hereditary traits (Roberts 1991), a move from passive explanation to active control.

It seems very unlikely that Mendel, a Franciscan monk, could have imagined the consequence of his work and although Watson and Crick may have anticipated some outcomes, the idea of genetic mapping, or 'gene splicing', may well have sounded like science fiction to them in 1953. The problem for science is that ethical dilemmas are quite often unintended consequences, but a further problem arises as to when should a scientist say no to following a particular research programme, lest it lead to such dilemmas? At what point, if at all, should molecular biologists draw a line under their research programmes?

This is perhaps an impossible question to answer, for quite apart from the scientist not always knowing what consequences will ensue, even if she does how does she make an ethical decision? The dilemma for molecular biologists is summed up by Joel Davis: 'The human genome is *our* genome – mine, and yours. It belongs to no one. And to everyone. It is a creation of 4.5 billion years of evolution' (Davis 1990: vi, original emphasis).

The genome itself is ethically neutral, as are most of the data of science. It is what humans do with those data that may offend one or other ethical code. The scientist, then, cannot look to her data for guidance, but must look outside of science. But when she looks she will see that ethical principles have a normative character. How does she distinguish the 'goods' implied by one ethical principle over another? Here the scientist is as ill- or as well-equipped as any citizen.

The scientist in the social world

The ethical questions raised by the Human Genome Project are not just narrowly ethical in the sense of what is a particular scientist to do (though this is important), but have wider social implications and antecedents. In the case of the Human Genome Project, factors such as the character it should take, who funds it, what it is intended for etc., are decisions made in a wider social context than the laboratory. Science, though a social product, itself produces knowledge that has social consequences, and moreover science itself (as I suggested in Chapter 1) changes as the result of a number of factors, but importantly as the result of a symbiotic relationship between it and society. The ethical decisions of science are not just the ethical decisions of scientists as individuals, or even as a group, but arise as an outcome of a wider social process. These decisions will shape (though not wholly determine) the nature of scientific knowledge and the effects may well transcend science and the groups making the decisions about it. Social constructionists and particularly sociologists of science such as Woolgar, Barnes, Bloor and Latour maintain that such interests determine entirely the character of science. I think this is too strong, for the reasons I set out in Chapter 4, but nevertheless there is a case to answer in respect of the scientist's role.

For much of this century the symbiosis between science and society has been one dominated by particular social interests – those of the military and industry. Major funders of the Human Genome Research include the US Department of Defense as well as multinational companies. One must presume that not all of the funding is motivated by a search for knowledge for its own sake, or even for the medical advances that it might bring. Since Second World War defence interests have provided a major source of funds for science. The period known as the 'Cold War', from 1945 to 1989, saw the greatest military expansion, in terms of hardware and killing capability, that the world has ever known. Unsurprisingly it was also a period of an exponential growth in scientific knowledge. A question that historians of science will no doubt ask is to what extent would this growth have occurred in the absence of such military expansion? In 1986, in the final years of the Cold War, 69 per cent of the US government research and development budget was allocated to military research (in the UK it was 49 per cent) (ACOST 1989: 14). Indeed there has been widespread concern at the possible impact on science and technology in the post-Cold War world (Coopey *et al.* 1993). Donald MacKenzie and Graham Spinardi (1993) present a number of case studies demonstrating the impacts that a defence research establishment has on more general developments in science and technology. The examples include infrared sensing, silicon integrated circuits, parallel computing and liquid crystal displays. Each of these have been important tools in further military and non-military research and each resulted from the application of 'pure' scientific findings. The science–military–industrial link is implicitly present through much of the natural sciences inevitably changing and shaping their character.

The social sciences too have been implicated, often too in the area of defence. Allan Kimmel describes a number of studies conducted by the US military (Kimmel 1996: 121–2), where the reaction of recruits to simulated emergencies (for example radiation release, or the belief that the soldiers were under artillery fire) was measured. One of these studies involved an innovative use of the social survey. Attitudinal questionnaires were distributed to recruits on an aircraft which they were duped into believing was about to crash! Other research has been less obviously ethically controversial. For example in the UK and US, during the Cold War, a number of academic 'think tanks' were established. Although presented as neutral and objective centres of learning in the field of International Relations, they often embraced a core ideology deriving from particular political and defence interests (Higgott and Stone 1994). The Hoover Institution, an important US 'think tank', though located at Stanford University, was founded on the principle that 'it would demonstrate the evils of the doctrines of Karl Marx' (Higgott and Stone 1994: 20). What is complex, however, is that the output from the think tanks, or in some cases more directly from social research funded by the military, has a knowledge value that transcends its original ideological basis. For example work by Lyn Bryant *et al.* (1995) on the integration of women on British naval ships has implications for an understanding of the role and position of women in male dominated occupations more generally.

Science is, as I have argued, a social product and we must understand it historically. Steve Fuller (1988; 1997) maintains that science takes on a distinct social character at particular times. The military–industrial character of science in the second half of the twentieth century reflects in so many ways the character of Western society generally, or at least it reflects and promotes many of the social values held. Though feminists would want to date the androcentric tendencies of science to an earlier date; they argue that science now is an embodiment of male (often aggressively militaristic) values (Rose 1983). In this view science can be seen as just one part of a patriarchal hegemony, but one which has the ability to shape and reinforce that hegemony through its activities. The argument is then made by Harding and Longino (though in different ways) that science should serve a different constituency and in doing so it would become more objective. Between different writers the emphasis changes, but the ethic to replace is an androcentric, militaristic one which favours those groups in society with wealth and power. The ethic to put in its place is feminist, pacifist, 'green', democratic and empowering. At the risk of oversimplification the claim can be summarised as the replacement of one normative ethic with another which has the potential to change, for the better, the transcendental outcomes of science.

If science and scientific knowledge are a reflection or embodiment of the society in which it resides then this strategy, if executed, would change the transcendental nature of science, because different programmes of research would be promoted. What is not clear is how and how much it would change it. Would we, for example, have the technology of infrared sensing, silicon integrated circuits, parallel computing and liquid crystal displays (all results of military promoted research), or would we have different technologies? Would social scientists be interested in reaction to fear, or how male-centred 'total institutions' such as warships (if there were any) function?

As a citizen I think that a more democratic, pluralist science is a legitimate aim to pursue, but I have to accept that other citizens would disagree with me. That there are differences in the vision of science held by Fuller, Longino or Harding is testimony to at least some ideological difference amongst an oppositional view. Moreover, the people who are the powerful and shape science from within or outside have a vested interest in not changing things. But also it is more complex than that, because science is not monolithic and scientists are citizens who pursue their own ethical agendas. The story of the physicist Robert Oppenheimer illustrates this. Oppenheimer was a principal scientist in the development of the atomic bomb in 1945, but went on to campaign against nuclear weapons, apparently telling President Truman that 'scientists had known sin' (Maddox 1972: 10). Within a few years his politics led to him being brought before the House Un-American Activities Committee, subsequently losing his security clearance and thus, in effect, his career, for his views (Inglis 1992: 119).

But his conversion from being 'pro-' to 'anti-' bomb was no Paulian conversion. In the 1940s Oppenheimer reluctantly worked on the atomic bomb project, because as a Jew he feared fascism and as a scientist he had good reason to believe the Germans had the science capable of building an atomic weapon (Rouzé 1965). The object of his fears disappeared with the defeat of the Axis powers in 1945, and he believed that further atomic weapon development was unnecessary and their projected use morally wrong. Edward Teller, who worked with Oppenheimer at Los Alamos, continued to enthusiastically advocate the development of such weapons and played a central role in the development of the hydrogen bomb. Teller was a Hungarian who had been driven out of Germany by the Nazis, but also hated communism and feared the Russians. The Soviet Union, the object of his fears, was not defeated and went on to build its own hydrogen bomb in 1949 (the kind of moral choices faced by scientists at this time are captured well in C.P. Snow's 1959 novel *The New Men*).

Likewise research programmes have very mixed potential for 'good' or 'harm' (however one defines that), and the Human Genome Project is an example of this. Other 'big science' requires huge budgets, for example particle accelerators. Often these projects and their huge budgets are defended on pure knowledge grounds, that they bring us that bit closer to knowing reality (Sagan 1996: 300–17), but of course an alternative argument could be advanced, that the investment put in other areas of science would have different (and better) knowledge, or humanitarian pay-offs. As Fuller notes, 'big science' research is increasingly the aspiration of all countries (Fuller 1997: 141). Each view can be defended on alternative grounds of what is the right thing to do, or what kind of knowledge counts as a public 'good'? For those able to influence the direction, or the existence of research programmes, as for scientists in respect of particular decisions, the answer is subjectively or intersubjectively derived. Changing the social relations within science and between science and society will change science. On contemporary ethical grounds this can perhaps be justified, but equally we have to accept that the views about what science should be and should do will change historically. This said, is there anything about science that could be consensually agreed should transcend all normative conceptions of it?

Objectivity as a scientific 'good'

Like that of Longino, my candidate for this role is objectivity, though the version of objectivity I want to defend is not the same as Longino's and is of the more 'traditional' kind she rejects. Longino's conception of objectivity is inadequate because it renders what is 'objective' as subject to (normative) ethical decisions. Proctor, it will be recalled, construed objectivity as 'reliability' and it is this quality that would be necessary for science in any society, whatever its ethical orientation. In order to illustrate this it is helpful to consider an example where science is 'unreliable' and therefore, in the traditional sense, not objective.

The Bell Curve

The Bell Curve is a study published by Richard Herrnstein and Charles Murray in 1994 (the full title was *The Bell Curve: Intelligence and Class Structure in American Life*) and claimed to present evidence that 'low intelligence is largely a matter of genetic inheritance and underlies the majority of America's pressing social and economic problems (including poverty, educational failure, unemployment, illegitimacy, chronic welfare dependency and crime)' (Drew *et al.* 1995: 2).

Not surprisingly right wing politicians, fundamentalist Christians and creationists saw these findings as scientific support for their views, although the science itself has been subject to detailed criticism. David Drew, Bekia Fossam and David Gilborn have criticised *The Bell Curve* in respect of its underlying assumptions and its statistical sleights of hand, and these assumptions will now be examined.

Herrnstein and Murray, though acknowledging the debate about intelligence and IQ testing (what is it such tests measure and how can they be constructed), simply substitute the word 'cognitive ability' as a 'generic synonym for intelligence test score' (Herrnstein and Murray 1994: 22). They assert:

> ... high intelligence has earmarks that correspond to a first approximation to the commonly understood meaning of being *smart* ...
>
> (Herrnstein and Murray 1994: 21, original emphasis)

The basis of Herrnstein and Murray's claim is biological, yet a key variable, that of intelligence, turns out to be what Americans (one could add WASP Americans) see as being 'smart', a cultural construction if ever there was one.

However, they do itemise six conclusions about the testing of cognitive ability that they claim are now beyond technical dispute. These conclusions, as Drew *et al.* (1995: 4–5) note, are far from beyond technical dispute and are simply crude assertions about the notion of intelligence as being: a real thing inside us equated with the common sense use of the word; capable of being measured by IQ tests; capable of being measured regardless of class or ethnicity; stable; fixed; and genetically inherited.

Herrnstein and Murray's work is a secondary analysis of a longitudinal study of young people aged 14 to 22 at the study's inception in 1979 and it contains two main strands.

The first strand is 'to establish that intelligence, as measured by IQ test, is the primary determinant of success in occupational attainment, parenting, citizenship and so on ... ' and second 'to establish the relationship between race and intelligence' (Drew *et al.*: 1995: 8).

The analyses are mainly logistic regression models of dependent variables such as: being under the official poverty line; parents being divorced; being in a correctional facility; etc. The independent (or predictor) variables were IQ scores, socio-economic status and age. That the above relationships were shown to hold depends on how well the models 'fit'. A 'perfect' model would be a 100 per cent fit between the dependent and independent variables with all the variability explained. Though a perfect fit would not be expected, in this case in 18 of the 60 models presented a maximum of only 10 per cent of the variability in any one model is explained. This means, of course, that 90 per cent, or more, of the variability remains unexplained. Drew *et al.* (1995) conclude that the outcome of these models does not support Herrnstein and Murray's assertions and if presented at all should have carried a warning of their inadequacy.

Herrnstein and Murray failed to be objective (their work lacked 'reliability') on two counts. First they ignored counter evidence about their initial assumptions regarding the definition and measurement of intelligence and second, they formed unwarranted conclusions (supporting their hypotheses) from the data. The question of measuring intelligence is far from settled (see Kamin 1981 and Eysenck 1981 for quite different views on this) and many would say that the project was flawed to begin with. However, lack of a widespread acceptance of a theory does not necessarily disqualify its use. An equivalent in the natural sciences would be that of 'superstring theory' (see Kaku 1994: chapter 7), which is far from being universally accepted by physicists and cosmologists. It is then legitimate for scientists to say 'let S be correct then X would follow'. This is what John Horgan (1996) has called 'ironic science'. In this case the difference is that Herrnstein and Murray are maintaining that their preferred view on intelligence and testing is 'squarely in the middle of the scientific road' (Herrnstein and Murray 1994: 23), a claim not usually made by practitioners of 'ironic' science. For Herrnstein and Murray S is an established fact. The statistical 'sleight of hand' that Drew *et al.* complain of arises from the use of an established method of analysis, the results of which, if honestly interpreted, would have yielded conclusions less favourable to the hypotheses.

The assessment of Herrnstein and Murray's work rests on questions of truth. The former claim they are presenting evidence that is *truth* and their critics are saying that this is *untruth*. Who is right? On the question of 'intelligence' Drew *et al.* are right to say Herrnstein and Murray's claims of consensus are *untrue*, but whether biologically based theories of intelligence are *true* or *untrue* has not been established. On the other hand logistic regression analyses are independent of any particular contexts and variability explained, or unexplained, is a function of the terms in the model. In this then Herrnstein and Murray's claims can be considered *untrue*.

This assessment of the rival truth claims rests on a criterion of truth that postulates the existence of a reality that is beyond how either party wishes the world to be. It is based on what is called a correspondence theory of truth, that is what is regarded as true corresponds with reality (Williams and May 1996: 37). In this case the reality that is contested is, first, the social reality of whether scientists agree, or disagree, on matters of intelligence, and second, the interpretation of the mathematical reality of the logistic regression results. As a foundation of objectivity, it seems to me, such a definition of truth is unavoidable. Of course it has its philosophical weaknesses and what comes to count as truth may be the result of delusion, error or malpractice. Indeed a common criticism is that because any number of theories may support particular observations, that correspondence with reality becomes itself a social norm. For this and the other reasons I suggested, reality is a slippery concept, but actually much of science is not about direct, or even indirect observation, but about relationships between terms. What is true or untrue is quite clearly a function of those relations. Drew *et al.*'s critique of *The Bell Curve* rested on analytic relationships; in the first case between the concept 'intelligence' and the concept of 'scientific agreement' and in the second case between mathematical and rhetorical conclusions.

Conclusion

In this chapter I have argued that the cornerstone of science, objectivity, is a social value, but is a value necessary to science. This is a view widely supported, but in quite different ways. Weber believed that the scientist could embrace values, but act objectively in her scientific work. Longino conversely believes that if social values underlie all of science then the constitutive values necessary to pursue objective science will be founded on socially derived conceptual ones. I agreed that in this she is right, but that the values influencing science are not all the same. Instead I proposed that they can be approximately divided into ethical (including political and moral values) and epistemological–methodological. With George Couvalis I believe that Longino elides these two kinds of values.

The interface of ethics and science presents scientists with particular difficulties because scientific knowledge, though it will have ethical impacts, does not in itself have its own ethical character. In other words scientific knowledge can transcend particular concepts of good or right. This problem is made more complex because of the specific science–society relationships that reflect or embody the character of the wider society. Scientists and citizens (and scientists as citizens) will hold a range of complex ethical positions, they will differ within and between societies and these positions will impact on the character of science. If, then, science is to have any existence other than an epiphenomenon of particular societies, it must have at least one enduring character. This I suggested is objectivity, but objectivity rendered as intersubjective agreement is inadequate because it is then hostage to a particular ethic in a time and place. My conclusion, then, amounts to support for a variant of Weberian objectivity, with the caveat that the constitutive values upon which it depends will have a contextual basis in society and this is unavoidable. Contexts, however, do not necessarily have ethical implications (in for example measurement values) and even if they did their ability to transcend any particular ethical context is itself a test of their reliability.

Suggested further reading

Chalmers, A. (1990) *Science and its Fabrication*, Buckingham: Open University Press.

Morley, D. (ed.) (1978) *The Sensitive Scientist*, London: SCM.

Tauber, A. (ed.) (1997) *Science and the Quest for Reality*, London: Macmillan.

Trigg, R. (1993) *Rationality and Science: Can Science Explain Everything?*, Oxford: Blackwell.

7 New science and new social science

Science might be visualised as hierarchical knowledge of diverse aspects of the world. It could perhaps be represented as an inverted triangle. Near the (upturned) base, at the top, would be sciences such as zoology or botany, which in turn rest on principles of biology closer to the apex, lower still comes chemistry, finally physics at the apex. Much of physics depends on a few relatively simple classical laws, such as those touched on in Chapters 1 and 2. However, this is not the very tip of the triangle. There lie particle physics and relativity, each describing and at least partially explaining the very small and very large scale structure of the universe respectively. Up until this century the tip of the triangle would have been the laws of classical physics. It is possible that in the next century the tip will be even sharper, ending (possibly) with something called 'superstrings', a new theory that may yet provide the 'fundamental' laws of the universe (Kaku 1994). Not all of the relationships are hierarchical, some like those between zoology and botany, or biology and geology, take the form of complex networks of theories. A (usually) implicit task of science is an explication not just of theoretical relationships within sciences, but also between phenomena known under the rubric of one science and phenomena known under the rubric of another. Indeed the overwhelming tendency in Western science is towards explaining the more complex in terms of the less complex.

It is one thing to claim, as I have done, that the social sciences are just as much sciences as the natural ones, but where do the social sciences fit in the triangle? Superficially one could say that social behaviour rests upon a biological basis, but what is the nature of the relationship between the social and biological realm? The relationship must pass through the individual in some way, but how much of individual behaviour is due to heredity and how much is due to environment? Notwithstanding this, the social world has characteristics which seem to require a different kind of explanation to those within other sciences. This explanation is that social life is constructed (and more importantly reconstructed) by self-aware creatures. If one talks about 'reality' in chemistry it is by way of describing elements and compounds and the relationship between them. More importantly they mostly rest on clearly defined physical laws. In the social world the relationship between individuals and society is contingent and laws of behaviour are notoriously difficult to establish.

At the risk of oversimplifying the problem, the inverted triangle analogy can also be said to represent ever-increasing complexity and contingency the further one moves from the apex. Whatever the relationship of the social world to the biological one, it must be the case that the social sciences would be in various positions close to the (upturned) base. The dream of physics has long been to describe the fundamental workings of the universe in a few very simple principles. This, as we have seen, was the dream of Laplace and remains the dream of physicists such as Hawking, Penrose, Weinberg or Witten (Horgan 1996: 3) who seek a 'theory of everything' (hence in the latter case superstrings). But there is an important difference between Laplace and the physicists of today. The former knew the world to be complex (and indeed made important contributions to probability theory; Mellor 1971: 128–38), whereas the latter know it to be complex *and* contingent. It is the awareness of contingency that has been the substantial hallmark of science in the twentieth century. The Laplacian deterministic world view was disturbed, as I have shown in Chapter 1, by the knowledge that the subatomic world did not behave deterministically and could only be known probabilistically. Just what is the nature of that contingency has remained controversial (see Rae 1986 for an account of the debate about quantum interpretations), but despite early optimism and later knowledge of the quantum world it has yet to yield insights into how the contingent behaviour of particles affects the non-quantum world. The second disturbance to determinism came rather later in the century with the 'discovery' of chaos by the meteorologist Edward Lorentz (Gleick 1987: 9–16). Chaos theory and its close conceptual relatives, complexity and emergence, have revolutionised thinking at a fundamental level in many areas of science. In short, the ideas of what might be termed 'new science' showed that future states of complex systems could not be known deterministically, but only probabilistically. Laplace believed that probabilities measure human ignorance. They are 'states of mind, not states of the world, the makeshift tools of intellects too feeble to penetrate immediately to the real nature of things' (Gigerenzer *et al.* 1989: 11), a principle violated by particle behaviour and shown to be the exceptional state of linear systems, rather than the non-linear ones predominating in nature.

In social science, what became known (often erroneously) as positivism was rarely overtly deterministic or anti-deterministic. John Stuart Mill, for example, though he talks of 'necessity' in human behaviour intended this to mean predictable regularity (Ayer 1987: 13), whilst Durkheim's holism might be said to prefigure later views of spontaneous self-organisation in systems. It was perhaps the use of the language of natural necessity in causation (Williams and May 1996: 53–7) that led to the view that naturalistic (positivistic) social science was determinist, but like a well-established rumour it is hard to say where it started. As a writer of a 1991 research methods textbook put it:

> The causal laws and the specific facts observed about social life are connected deductively by logic. Positivists believe that some day social science laws and theories will be symbolic systems similar to mathematics and to theories of the natural sciences.
>
> (Neuman 1994: 60)

This confuses a number of things. It is true that naturalistic social scientists (not just positivists!) would wish to derive deductive connections between empirical and theoretical statements in much the same way as is possible in natural science, but if by symbolic systems it is meant there will be axioms of behaviour that have the simplicity of classical laws of physics, then this would be demanding more of social science than has been demanded of natural science for some decades (Miller 1995: 127). In other words this is an archaic and simplistic view of what science is about. This is not to say that science no longer recognises any deterministic laws. Given certain initial conditions (the default state for the solar system for example) we can specify deterministically the effects of gravity, thermodynamics, etc. Rather it is that the social world resembles the complex systems studied in the life sciences, where the kind of 'positivism' described in the quote has been out of fashion for a long time.

The recognition of indeterminate nature of much of the natural world is important to social science for three reasons. First, if it is the case that complex systems in the social world behave similarly to ones in the natural world (and there is much evidence to suggest that this is so; see Khalil 1996), then it is possible that the same kinds of organising principles underlie these systems (I will expand on this below). Second, the techniques for studying complex systems are most likely to have similarities. Lastly the study of complex systems implies the study of the relationships between one system and another and so an interdisciplinary approach to the study of, for example, the interrelationship of social and biological systems is much more likely to yield results.

However, a revolution in ways of thinking about nature, and by implication the role of human social systems within it, is not enough. In addition such thinking must be operationalised into testable theories, and in this case such theories require more sophisticated equipment, particularly in the form of computers, than was hitherto available. Indeed it was through the building of simple deterministic computer models of weather that Lorentz discovered that weather systems were much more complex than had been believed (Gleick 1987: 14–15). Advances in chaos theory required more sophisticated computing and what is the final twist is that the development of this computing itself led to new insights about the nature of complexity, especially as the result of emergent properties in the computing environments themselves (Kelly 1994).

In this chapter I want to take a brief look at 'complexity' and 'emergence' in natural science and show how these concepts might open up the possibility of a new 'unity of science' that is non-positivistic. First I will turn to the related themes of chaos, complexity and emergence and show how new understandings in these areas will have implications for studying the social world. Second, I will look at how social scientists have responded to the new science, but also how statistical techniques have been imported from the natural sciences to useful effect. Finally I will look at the relationship between the social and the natural sciences, and in particular the implications of evolutionary thinking in biology on social science.

Chaos, complexity and emergence

When I was a schoolboy, in the late 1960s, it was an article of faith that the predictability of science had no limits. We were told confidently, for example, that by the turn of the century weather would be entirely predictable and would eventually be controllable. Whilst it is true that weather forecasting has become better, its techniques remain largely probabilistic. One of the first meteorologists to realise this was the aforementioned Edward Lorentz. He discovered that a small change in the initial conditions of a system can bring about enormously different effects later on. This is exemplified by what is known as the 'Butterfly effect', whereby the motion of the wings of a butterfly in the Amazon forest could lead to a tornado in Texas. Intriguingly, it might, or it might not. In other words, tiny perturbations can sometimes lead to major changes and sometimes they may not. What became known as 'chaos' was seen to be the characteristic of many systems in nature from the turbulence of a river flow (see my example of Pooh Sticks in Chapter 2), to plagues of locusts, even to crowd movements. The condition of certain systems at time *T1* cannot be known deterministically at time *T2*. Weather systems are chaotic systems.

Although Newton, as I have suggested, was not a determinist he is often described as such, possibly because Laplacian determinism can be argued to be the mathematical consequence of Newtonian mechanics. Laplace's belief was that, given the accurate position and velocity of all particles in the universe and sufficient computing power, we could determine all future states of those particles. That we could begin with the small in the here and now and project to a detailed future, must of course depend upon the principle that small causes produce small effects. Therefore a small error say in one's initial data should lead only to a small error in the final calculation. The belief was that the computing power required increases proportionally in relation to the number of particles and the time in the future for which prediction is made. However, the increase is not linear, but exponential. In order to precisely predict a complex system such as the weather, even only a few years ahead, would require a computer in which all possible external systems as well as all possible weather systems could be modelled. As Firth (1991: 1,565) notes, this would require the fabrication of the whole universe into a computer! Weather systems are referred to as computationally irreducible.

Newtonian mechanics is linear, that is, a given input to an equation will produce a given output. The operation of a linear system is entirely governed by its initial state and its environment. Nature, however, is mostly non-linear and it is enough for small changes in initial states, or later small divergences in a sequence, to lead to exponential numbers of different kinds of later interactions and consequently very different outcomes. To trace back a system in nature to its initial conditions is equally problematic, because each of those conditions would itself have an exponential number of earlier antecedent conditions.

Consider the interactions between some relatively simple objects, such as tiny ball bearings. Imagine further releasing several thousand ball bearings down a chute. Some ball bearings will hit each other hard, some less hard and some not at all. Consequently at different instances of releasing them, the distribution of the ball bearings at the bottom of the chute will vary. They are a non-linear system. The exact shape of the distribution of the ball bearings at the bottom of the chute could not have been known, the distribution can be said to have 'emerged'. Moreover, the slight changes in the initial conditions of the ball bearings' release would depend on a range of earlier states such as slight fluctuations in temperature, a bit of dirt on the chute, more or less wobble on releasing the chute etc.

Ball bearings, of course, are very simple objects and if we had only a few thousand of them then we could compute with some accuracy what the distribution would be. Biological systems and social systems are very much more complex. Let us first think about the former. Life is an emergent property of a complex system ultimately reducible to chemicals, but unlike its constituent chemicals life has the property of being able to reproduce itself. The whole is greater than the parts. As Stuart Kauffman (1995: 24) points out there is nothing mysterious in this, no vital force or extra substance is present. 'A set of molecules either does have the property that is able to catalyse its own formation and reproduction from some simple food molecules, or it does not' (*ibid.*). So it is in social life. Sapperstein's example of the diners (described in Chapter 3) was a representation of a very simple social system in which the emergent property of food poisoning for some diners could have only been predicted probabilistically. We know this is the case, but why? Well first of all even in such a very simple social system there are a number of interactions between systems. The initial diner who chose to have her wine glass to the left may have been left handed, or may have developed a habitual tendency to have her glass on the left, or she may have come from a culture, or a household where it was good manners to have the wine glass to the left. The antecedent systems could have been social, biological or a mix of the two. The presence of left-overs in the kitchen may have resulted from a management anxious to save money in order to keep the restaurant viable, or the chef might just have been lazy.

The terms 'chaos' and 'complexity' are used interchangeably, though some will insist there is a difference (see for example Sokal and Bricmont 1997: 123–31) but for present purposes the distinction between the terms will simply be to indicate the complexity of systems in a general sense from the chaotic nature of specific features (Lewin 1995: 12). Complex systems can be seen to exhibit different kinds of chaotic behaviour and this difference may well have implications for our knowledge of particular systems. 'Chaos' is something that arises within systems that may initially exhibit stability. Why and how this happens was for a long time something of an equivalent problem in physics to that of consciousness in studies of the social world. Mostly physicists regard problems, such as how parallel streams of smooth water become turbulent, or the disrupted patterns seen in the boundaries between liquid and solid states of substances, as insoluble and for the most part the problem was left to the mathematicians. In 1970 two mathematicians, David Ruelle and Floris Takens, demonstrated that this was indeed a mathematical problem where systems exhibiting certain cycles shifting from fixed points to whorls will then shift to what was termed quasiperiodic motion (see Casti 1991: 68–76 for a discussion of the mathematics of this). It is likely that the maths of what happens in a turbulence flow would hold for any non-linear system.

This leads to two important points. First, that it may be the case that despite the indeterminacy of complex systems a few simple mathematical rules may underlie complexity (see for example Cohen and Stuart 1994). How simple this may or may not turn out to be need not concern us, but what is of crucial importance is that the complexity of weather systems, turbulence flows or social organisation show enormous mathematical similarity. Specifically the onset of chaos, the shift to quasi-periodic motion, may be described similarly in all systems within which this occurs (Smith 1997: 62). The ontological and methodological implications of this for interdisciplinary work between natural and social scientists has begun to be demonstrated in, for example, work on the dynamics of children's friendships (Alisch *et al.* 1997).

Second, the onset of chaos does not mean predictability vanishes completely. Even turbulence has structure and this structure is exhibited in what are known as 'strange attractors'. Attractors are well known to physicists and mathematicians and are simply co-ordinates which may be points or trajectories in a dynamic system. Attractors exhibit periodic behaviour, and are predictable and measurable. Strange attractors arise in systems exhibiting quasi-periodic behaviour. Such systems may have passed through periods of apparently complete disorder before achieving the quasi-periodicity of strange attractors. Strange attractors can be visually represented as curves, which never cross themselves, but also which never close and although the specific co-ordinates cannot be predicted, order is present in patterns which display remarkable visual symmetry. Geometrically, as Firth (1991: 1,567) observes, they resemble *'millefeuille* pastry, which is made by repeatedly rolling out (stretching) and folding dough'. Some of the beautiful and complex forms these can take are illustrated in Gleick (1987).

Strange attractors are sometimes described as 'deterministic' chaos to distinguish them from 'stochastic' chaos (Smith 1997: 60–1). Whilst the former can demonstrate a virtually infinite number of trajectories, order nevertheless exists, whereas in the latter complexity increases exponentially in a system. Evolution can be cited as an example here (Price 1997: 9), where 'stochastic drift' towards more and more divergence is apparent. However, in complex systems it is not always apparent whether in the long term deterministic or stochastic chaos will prevail, or indeed whether equilibrium will be restored.

The strange attractor is an emergent property from chaos and can be seen as the generation of new information, which in many systems will be an important factor in future states of these and conjoined systems. For example stock markets operate stochastically, but the pattern of buying and selling of particular commodities may emerge at a specific point as a strange attractor, which in turn may influence the wider market.

Complexity and simulation in the social world

A social system might be defined as a patterned, or structured relationship between agents or the phenomena created or used by them. When the system takes on a character that does not depend on particular agents, then it can be said to have emergent properties. A conversation between two local councillors is not itself a social system, but the local council of which they are members is. Of course assuming their conversation was about council matters, then they are contributing to the continued existence of the council and may be creating other systemic (and therefore emergent) properties. The council, though it must have members who have been voted into office, exists as an entity that does not require any *particular* members or voters. Having come into existence the council can pass resolutions that lead to further emergent properties, such as the awarding of contracts, the building of roads etc. Explanations of the emergence of social structures and properties are a well-worn path in social theory (see, for example, Giddens 1984; Layder 1997; Archer 1998; Ruben 1998) and are certainly not new. However, can what we know of complexity have any relevance to understandings of the social world, and furthermore, if complex systems, such as weather, are computationally irreducible are we wasting our time trying to understand the social world, an even more complex system than the former?

What is known of complexity (and a great deal is not yet known) shows that complex systems exist throughout nature, from the development of galaxies to cell division (Kauffman 1995). Between the very large and the very small exist human social systems, the development of which can be seen to follow the same mathematical 'rules' as galaxies or cells. Further, although the problem of consciousness, specifically what philosophers call the mind–body problem, remains unresolved, there is evidence to suggest that individual cognitive activity and social interaction can be seen to be linked in the same complex system, whereby the second is functionally linked to the first (Smith and Stevens 1997: 197–214). This kind of finding should not be surprising if we consider that complexity exists not in discrete or isolated systems, but exists between systems. Whole systems, like Russian dolls, sit within each other and exhibit patterns of complexity at every level. Indeed some systems show close similarities at whatever level we intervene. This is particularly so in the case of fractals, geometric forms with the same structure at different scales of magnification. Objects such as coastlines and trees are irregular, but with the same kinds of irregularities at whichever level we look at them (Cohen and Stewart 1994: 23).

The above suggests only that there is evidence that the kinds of patterns of emergence in the physical and social world are both similar and conjoined. Some, for example Gunther Stent (Horgan 1996: 193), have been pessimistic about the possibilities for social science, post-complexity and specifically since Benoit Mandelbrot (1977) demonstrated the mathematical nature of fractal geometry. He believed that whilst it was possible to observe fractal patterns in nature, determining how they were created is quite another. We already know that the social world generates complexity as great, or greater than biological systems (itself being an outcome of, or conjoined with biological systems), so it would begin to seem that social systems are possibly computationally irreducible. Mathematically, of course, this is true, but it is also true of weather, or just about any other non-linear system. Stent may then be right in his pessimism, but the problem may be one of the degree of complexity, not the nature of the complexity. Nevertheless complexity does present us with a problem. In complexity the principal tool of investigation, and indeed the source of much of the knowledge so far, is the computer simulation. As David Byrne (1997: 1–2) points out the programming of computers depends on deductive logic, but the outcomes are contingent. Future system states are dependent on feedback in the system and such systems are sensitive to initial conditions. Byrne asks:

> ... if the world is chaotic and complex how can we ever set up the initial parameters of any simulation exercise with sufficient precision so that we can actually drive forward a simulation through time which has any correspondence to what might actually happen?
>
> (Byrne 1997: 1)

This problem is long known to social scientists, particularly in regard to specification errors in regression and path analysis, however these kind of analyses specify only a few variables. A realistic model of the social world requires more than that. Of course there are simulations of the social world. For example Doran *et al.*'s work on the development of hunter-gatherer societies in Paleolithic south-west France (Doran *et al.* 1993), or Epstein's work on the development of simple societies (Horgan 1996: 195–6). These societies are not real in the sense that they use data about real people that allow us to predict the likelihood of X or Y occurring in a given society. Instead they use techniques of artificial intelligence (AI) that simulate the characteristics of human intelligence. These computer 'agents' typically have a memory, a set of goals and a set of rules, but as Nigel Gilbert warns:

> ... each simulated individual is regarded as a 'black box'; that is, behaviour is modelled by probabilities and no attempt is made to justify these in terms of individual preferences, decisions or plans. Moreover, each simulated person is considered individually without regard to their interaction with others.
>
> (Gilbert 1993a: 3)

The problem faced in these simulations are similar to those Lorentz faced in producing laboratory models of weather: change the initial values slightly in a model and soon the outputs begin to diverge enormously (Gleick 1987: chapter 1). This is simulation, but the slight difference in initial values in the model that lead to radical divergence are probably less than measurement errors in real life – in weather forecasting as in survey sampling. Simulations that start from measuring variables in the 'real world' therefore may not even begin to approximate reality.

However, this does not mean that simulations of the social world are useless, though they are limited at present. Byrne holds, probably rightly, that prediction through simulation may not be attainable, but if instead we take an engineering model whereby we test certain situations to see what will happen if we do A or B, then we can know what might happen if we act a certain way. He concludes 'simulation is clearly a tool which helps us not know what will happen, but what can be made to happen' (Byrne 1997: 6).

Strange attractors, determinism and social prediction

The limitations of simulation do not mean that we cannot model the social world. Advocates of complexity approaches have ambitions that are altogether greater than those of most social scientists. Moreover the insights of complexity may well help us to understand why we don't understand! Some limited success, in specific disciplinary areas, has been achieved, in for example the aforementioned work on the biological foundations of social interaction (Smith and Stevens 1997). Other areas (reported in the same volume) include that on collective behaviour following disasters (Passerini and Bahr 1997) and the dynamics of children's friendships (Alisch *et al.* 1997). These studies use relatively simple models to predict very specific areas of social life. The Passerini and Bahr findings, for example, were that a simple model that makes few initial assumptions about social behaviour can accurately simulate 'well-accepted empirical knowledge about social behaviour after disasters' (Passerini and Bahr 1997: 227).

James Gleick, in recollecting Lorentz's thoughts about his weather models, observes that in the lines of print-out of his weather simulations winds and temperatures 'seemed to behave in a recognisably earthly way' (Gleick 1987: 15), indicating the existence of rules a forecaster could follow, but the repetitions were never exactly the same. 'There was a pattern, with disturbances. An orderly disorder' (Gleick *ibid.*) This 'orderly disorder' in the weather shows the existence of strange attractors. All systems contain islands of relative stability; in weather as in the social world these are recognisable. Chaos does not mean disorder and it is the characteristic of order which makes simple prediction within systems possible. The language of strange attractors is new, but such things have been visible to the naked eye, as it were, throughout human history. Almost any study of the social world will allow a certain number of initial conditions to exist as a 'black box', partly because these are taken for granted assumptions about the world, but partly because (as in the Sapperstein example) we couldn't specify them all anyway. In everyday life and in social science we probably do not need to, for strange attractors represent islands of stable probable behaviour. Even in Britain we consider it worthwhile showing up at the railway station for the advertised time of train departure, though we know that a few leaves on the line in Canterbury *could* lead to a major delay in Camborne. Train timetables are predictors of probable train departures and are right within a margin of error most of the time. As Raymond Eve suggests:

> The polychromatic images of the operation of strange attractors so often seen in books on the new science *are* probability statements. While one cannot say where the next point will appear on a strange attractor, it *will* appear somewhere on the strange attractor.
>
> (Eve *et al.* 1997: 279)

Looked at in this way we can think of the cultural consistency that allows *moderatum* generalisations (see Chapter 5) as strange attractors. The particular cultural stability does not necessarily arise in any particular form, nor can it be predicted in detail, but it can be regarded as a stability we can make modest and moderate generalisations about.

Prediction and determinism

The new insights in 'non-deterministic' approaches to science have not nullified most of the insights of early 'classical' science. As I have indicated Newtonian physics, though superseded by Einsteinian physics, still holds for the systems it describes. In other words the former can be best understood as a local subset of the latter. Planetary motion, tides etc. can still be described deterministically. Though deterministic systems in the social world are very rare, analogously, post-complexity early forms of analysis continue to have utility.

Nevertheless simpler models and analyses remain powerful tools in the social sciences as in the natural ones. The starting point for almost any further complex analysis will be the observation of an association between two variables. For example we may observe that there is an association between being a member of a non-manual social class and tendency to migrate. The claim would not be that class *caused* migration (class after all is an analysis category invented by the social scientist), but it will indicate an area for further investigation. Is it the case that all members of non-manual classes migrate? Well clearly not, so what do those who do (or do not) have in common? One strategy would be to 'control' for other variables one at a time and look for the strongest association. Over (say) ten years is it younger people that migrate (control for age), is it those who migrated before (control for previous move), or is it perhaps those who are at particular points in their 'lifecycle' (control for type of household composition)?

Simple analyses of contingency tables will often yield robust, if unsophisticated predictions and remain the mainstay of most quantitative analysis in social science. Moreover, they have their equivalents in many simple experiments in biology and chemistry where laboratory conditions are controlled in order to observe the relationship between just two or three variables. Although more sophisticated multivariate analyses can show relationships where there are more than two dependent or independent variables the implicit assumption from such models is that X causes Y. Though the causality assumed is Humean, the assumption is of a specific one to one relationship between variables (Gilbert 1993b: chapter 11).

That these relationships hold can be attributed to two things. First, in deriving variables such as class or migration we are subsuming a number of different kinds of behaviour or characteristic under one variable. That is not to say that they do not represent some real state of the world, but that they represent a number of states operationalised into a variable. The analyses then simply organise the hierarchy of relationships between the variables so derived. The relationship is purely mathematical and that it represents states of the world is a function of how well the variables were operationalised in the first place. Furthermore, in a model of migration ten variables may have been operationalised, but the explanation of migration may lie in what was not measured.

Critics of 'positivism' (for example Schutz 1965) have long criticised quantitative research for just this tendency. What is measured in the social world is a function of the theories of the researcher and may have little bearing on the lived experience of those it wishes to describe. Though this criticism has some substance, it does fail to explain the predictive and explanatory success of quantitative social science. So what is going on?

Multiple regression models depend upon two characteristics. First, that which is unstated, the 'black box' of what is not measured. By this I mean ethnicity so defined as E is actually made up of characteristics E ... N, which may be specified, but antecedent conditions which created them are not. Ethnicity is a good example in that the choice of ethnic categories to include/exclude is the decision of the researcher and which category chosen, that of the respondent. Second, that these variables, once defined, actually bear some resemblance to characteristics present in the 'real' world. That they do is attributable to two things. First, some variables will measure very stable categories. For example in an election where there are only three parties represented the number of behavioural options open to a respondent is four: a vote for one of the three parties or not voting/spoiling the ballot paper etc. A respondent is (usually) either male or female. In this case the maximum number of cells in a contingency table of voting by sex is eight. In other words a number of relationships are simple and can be at least treated deterministically. Second, much of what is operationalised successfully can be regarded as islands of stability in the social world, possibly strange attractors. These are visible not only to the researcher, but also in everyday life. We can, for example, observe the existence of particular ethnic communities exhibiting relative spatial stability, just as we can observe islands of relatively stable weather, or water flows. What is of course more difficult is the measurement and prediction of phase transition to other forms of stability.

A historical geography of the Spitalfields area of London serves as a useful example here. This quarter, adjacent to the business district of the City of London, has undergone almost continual change since the seventeenth century. Originally a haven for French Huguenot refugees, it later became the principal Jewish quarter of London. In the 1960s it was settled by Bengalis, who continue to live there in large numbers, though since the 1980s the western fringes (in particular) of the quarter have been encroached upon by the business district. Each of these periods, Huguenot, Jewish and Bengali, has been characterised by cultural and economic stability and would have exhibited properties amenable to measurement by researchers. Even some of the variables associated with the phase transitions would have been measurable, but to cite these as simple causal factors would be to oversimplify. For example the economic success of the Jewish community may have been an important factor, but this would not be uniform, moreover it would not explain why success itself motivated some to initially leave a culturally homogeneous district for somewhere culturally heterogeneous, or even quite alien.

Therein perhaps lie the present methodological limits of social science, that simulation models do not adequately explain the complexity of the real social world, because of the antecedent conditions that they cannot build into the model, and the sensitivity to change in initial conditions that can render the simple models useless as predictive devices. On the other hand the simpler 'deterministic' models favoured by many social scientists are limited to describing either simple relationships that can be treated deductively, or they depend on identifying relatively stable variables and specifying the probabilistic relationships between these.

Biology and social science

Gunther Stent may have been pessimistic for the wrong reasons. The social world is very complex, but simulating it and other complex systems is subject to the same kinds of constraint. Evolutionary prediction in biological systems faces similar difficulties. However, the biologist is at least in the position of being able to more clearly specify the vertical relationship between the phenomena she studies and the next level (chemistry) in the inverted triangle. The social scientist is mostly constrained to leave the relationship between the individual and the biological as a black box. For most there is quite enough trouble trying to understand the relationship between individual agency and social structure. Yet if we are to take a holistic approach to complex systems then there will be interactions across domains. Social systems will have physical antecedents (often biological) and many systems will be physio-social. Some systems will be co-ordinated intentionally to produce goals, whilst others will produce spontaneous order from unintentional actions (Khalil 1996: 11).

This, however, is disputed territory between some biologists who believe human social life can be biologically explained and (mainly) social scientists who insist on the necessity of explanations that are independent of the biological. The first (often described as biological determinist) position has been around, in various forms, since the nineteenth century and though not directly related to the causal determinism discussed above, nevertheless has some common philosophical antecedents. Some of its manifestations have been discredited as mistaken (as in the case of phrenology), or just bad science (see the example of the 'Bell Curve' in Chapter 6), whilst others, though controversial, remain influential, not just in biology, but also in the public mind. Such views have, however, been in public vogue since the late 1960s with popularisers such as Desmond Morris (1967), Edward Wilson (1975) and Richard Dawkins (1988, 1989) often considered as ambassadors for the public understanding of science. This popularity may stem from a common sense perspective of plausibility that the social world *is* biologically determined. We would, for example, not for a moment question the fact of a biological basis to the behaviour of other social animals, yet in the case of humans, many do. The basis for the counter argument is that culture, as a product of human consciousness, marks out humans as different. Furthermore that cultures so produced exhibit such diversity as to rule out the possibility of a biologically determined human nature.

I will examine 'biological determinism', and objections to it, in a little more detail.

The view mostly rests on a Darwinian view of natural selection. Natural selection can be summed up as: those individuals who are best adapted to their environment are the ones who survive and perpetuate their species. For example an animal that could run faster to avoid its prey would be more likely to survive and breed. Over a long period of time the slower runners would be gradually selected out, because they would not survive to breed. The characteristic which conferred advantage in the first place is simply a chance mutation and maybe just one of a number of mutations present in a species. In this way new species arise, flourish and diversify (Darwin [1859] 1998: 354), often bringing about the extinction or displacement of an earlier species. A recent example of this in Western Europe has been the success of the American grey squirrel in virtually completely displacing the native red squirrel.

That natural selection takes place is uncontroversial, though the mechanism over time is not yet well understood (see Horgan 1996: chapter 5). Nevertheless the natural selection argument in its simple form is elegant and on the face of it obviously applicable to humans. In human beings we find a very successful creature that has mutated from *Homo habilis* to *Homo sapiens* in about 1.5 million years. As a species *Homo sapiens* is able to survive in almost every climate and has shown a great deal of diversity in different habitats. Survival has been in competition with other species and within the species. It is these attributes that are the foundation of the biological determinist argument, or arguments. All of the arguments rest on the premise that human social arrangements represent the working through of the natural selection process, either successfully or unsuccessfully.

The transmitter of natural selection is the gene. Genes are units of heredity and the blueprints for cell construction, which in turn produce specific traits in species. Uncontroversially we can talk of genes for particular physical attributes, but this is carried further by sociobiologists such as Edward Wilson (1975, 1978) to suggest that social life is the direct outcome of our genetic inheritance. Indeed the success of particular behaviours and forms of social life can be linked to successful strategies for propagating our genes. Warfare, forms of social organisation and culture can all be seen in terms of a biological drive to reproduce our genes. The kin selection process, for example, is seen as a process in which individuals choose partners in order to maximise the propagation of their genes. This leap from biological replication to society as simply a mechanism for such replication has been controversial on political and scientific grounds. The former in that it is held that such determinism is simply an updated version of Social Darwinism which justified as 'natural' the economic individualism of the political right (Rose *et al.* 1984). Biological 'fitness' becomes translated into economic fitness, as John Kingdom put it the survival of the fittest becomes 'the survival of the richest' (Kingdom 1992: 16). Many, such as Dawkins, have denied political or ideological motivation and have pleaded that they have been misunderstood (Dawkins 1982: 10), but it nevertheless remains that sociobiological arguments have been succour to the political right (see Rose *et al.* 1984, for a discussion of this). Criticisms of ideological motivation for biological determinism (as opposed to naïveté) are hard to make, but other criticisms on the basis of the biological evidence for determinism are perhaps more telling.

The basis of the biological determinist claim is that certain social behaviours are universal and if they are universal, then they are genetically based. Consider three of these:

Child rearing

It is held, for example, that successful bonding between mother and child depends crucially on close contact in the few hours after birth (Lumsden and Wilson 1982: 80–2) and this occurs independently of any cultural context. But the evidence for this is experimental and replications of the experiments did not yield similar results, indeed some experimental findings have been quite opposite suggesting that cultural context is important (Dunn 1979). The difficulty for the sociobiologist is that she must show the universality of the connection and indeed show this outside of an experimental context, whereas the critic of this approach simply has to show that in a particular culture this is not the case.

Altruism

A difficulty for any Darwinian explanation of behaviour in animals as well as humans is that of altruism. Darwinian principles would seem to suggest that individual animals will compete with each other in order to maximise their chances of propagating their genes, yet it is well known that some animals will sacrifice themselves for the sake of others in their group and indeed such acts of altruism are often important in the survival or stability of the group, or society. How can this be? An explanation lies in kin selection. An altruistic act, though it may lead to the death of the animal that makes it, is nevertheless the best way to perpetuate that animal's genes (because these are shared with siblings, cousins etc.). In human societies (and in some animal ones) altruism extends beyond the gene group. Indeed in modern society, it may well be practised quite anonymously, through charities, or voluntary work. Sociobiologists invoke the concept of 'reciprocal altruism' here (Reynolds 1980: 42), the 'trading' of altruistic acts without immediate payoff, or, as Stephen Jay Gould describes it, 'if you scratch my back I'll scratch yours' (Gould 1980: 255). The behaviour is adaptive and successful. However, as Gould argues, the success of adaptive behaviour in producing stable human societies does not equate with direct genetic control. He offers the story of Eskimo altruism as an example of this. The social unit of traditional Eskimo society is the family group. In times of food shortage the group will migrate. When this happens elderly members of the family will remain to die, rather than risk the group's survival by slowing down the migration. The argument is that family groups with no altruistic genes succumb to natural selection, for these groups (who took the elderly with them) did not survive. The elderly with altruistic genes increased the chances of the propagation of their genes by remaining to die (Gould 1980: 256).

This explanation, Gould admits, is plausible but equally so is the one that the altruism is a cultural trait that has been adapted. It is successful because the families which did not adopt it did not survive. There is, he maintains, no evidence for a genetic link, but some for a cultural basis to the practice in the Eskimo customs which revere the elderly who make this sacrifice as heroes. As in the case of child rearing the biological determinist case cannot be proven.

Incest taboo

Incest taboo seems likely to be the best candidate for genetically based behaviour. Its avoidance and proscription are, and have been, commonplace in most cultures, according to the biological determinists, because genetic advantage accrues to those who do not mate with close relatives. This seems, on the face of it, a reasonable assumption, but worryingly for the biological determinist case is that, again, it is not universally true. In the last fifteen years or so attention in the West has been focused on the practice of child abuse (Ennew 1986). By no means all child abuse is incestual, but of recorded cases one of the commonest involve sexual relations between fathers and daughters. It is unclear whether the cases that have come to light in recent years are evidence of an increase in child sexual abuse and incest, or whether this has been commonplace, but hidden, for longer. If it is the former then biological determinists must show what has changed in the biological make up of males (particularly) in

Western society. If it is the latter then a social taboo existed, but was violated in practice.

Gould observes that criticism of biological determinism has often been construed by sociobiologists as a denial altogether of 'the relevance of biology to human behavior, of reviving an ancient superstition by placing ourselves outside the rest of "creation" '. He asks us, 'Are we pure "nurturists"? Do we permit a political vision of human perfectibility to blind us to evident constraints imposed by our biological nature?' (Gould 1980: 252).

His response to this is to deny that the issue is human biology versus human uniqueness, but biological *potentiality* versus biological determinism. The potentiality for a range of non-genetically based adaptive behaviour has, he suggests, its origins in the biological fact of larger human brain size, the development of which 'added enough neural connections to convert an inflexible and rather rigid programmed device into a labile organ, endowed with sufficient logic and memory to substitute non programmed learning for direct specification as the ground of social behaviour' (Gould 1980: 257). The development of consciousness through a larger brain can be seen as a translation mechanism from biological to the social.

But this view seems not to be so far from that of Gould's arch rival, ethologist Richard Dawkins. On the face of it the latter (author of *The Selfish Gene* [1976] 1989) is, or is described as, a committed biological determinist maintaining that genes have 'purpose', their only purpose, which is to survive and replicate. This does not imply consciousness intent, but can be more likened to the replicating behaviour of computer viruses. The information that genes carry gives rise to the characteristics in a species. In humans a defining characteristic is consciousness that arises from the genetic inheritance of a particularly complex brain. The brain, as we know, stores and transmits information, and according to Dawkins is the site of a non-genetic kind of replicator he calls a 'meme' (Dawkins 1982: 109). This in turn gives rise to a phenotype, which can be defined as the observed traits of an organism, arising from an interaction of hereditary material and the environment. 'The phenotypic effects of a meme may be in the form of words, music, visual images, styles of clothes, facial or hand gestures, skills such as opening milk bottles. ... ' (Dawkins 1982: 109).

The devil, of course, is in the detail, and the Gould–Dawkins debate continued into the late 1990s, but perhaps in the biological determinist–anti-determinist debate there is more rhetoric than substance? Anti-determinists do not doubt the existence at some point of biological antecedents, however far removed from social behaviour they may now be. Conversely biological determinists are not denying free will and Dawkins, at least, sees the link between genes and observed traits as probabilistic (Dawkins 1989: 12). The weakness of both arguments is that some translation mechanism between biology and social characteristics must be specified. For Gould this is the evolution of brain size, and for Dawkins the meme which gives rise to the phenotype.

Complexity, biology and social emergence

We have travelled a little way from the issues of complexity and the more general ones of mathematical modelling in the social sciences. Whilst I do not want to claim that complexity is either a methodological or ontological answer to the puzzle of the biological social interface, I would suggest that it may provide a new way of looking at matters, which in turn may solve some specific puzzles. One brief example of this comes from the work of Thomas Smith and Gregory Stevens (1997). They have used computational models to simulate anxiety modulation in humans, specifically in relation to the anxiety of separation (particularly between mothers and infants). The alleviation of stress is associated with the release of endogenous opioid peptides in the limbic structure of the brain (Smith and Stevens 1997: 199). Thus a number of social behaviours in humans (and other animals) can be shown to be associated with a specific biological phenomenon associated with the release of this substance, similar in some respects to opiates such as heroin. However, the relationship between the physiology of this process and environment is complex and non-linear. Briefly, it is this. Opioids released by the brain have a soothing effect, but when these are no longer released stress ensues, and in turn the stress stimulates the brain to release opioids. The factors in stress are often exogenous, but the brain seems able to respond to these external stimulants by releasing opioids, which in turn relieve the stress and thus produce environmental effects. This interaction is a complex system *par excellence*. One important finding was that an increase in the number of persons in an interacting system will produce stable, yet dynamic patterns of attachment and separation (Smith and Stevens 1997: 209). Such stability exists then on the rim of the physiological and the social. Indeed to talk of a physiological–social divide here is probably not meaningful, in so far as emergent properties that are physiological or social arise from a complex interaction between environment and biology.

Conclusion – the emergence of a unified science, or a science of emergence?

Ever since Comte there have been social scientists who have dreamed of a unified science that would unite study of the social world and the physical world under a few simple principles, or even laws. For the positivists this was allied to the traditional view of reduction in science, a view that remains important today. This view of reduction was, however, linked to a deterministic causality that would in principle allow the successful prediction of complex phenomena from simple initial conditions. However, even in the early years of this century the French mathematician Henri Poincaré (Poincaré 1913) had sounded a note of caution. The Poincaré Effect, which stipulates that a small difference in initial conditions produces very large ones in the final phenomena, prefigured later insights in chaos and complexity.

It may nevertheless be the case that the inverted triangle I described at the beginning of this chapter is a good metaphor for a reduction in principle of phenomena, but it does not follow that a reconstruction of a causal chain from the complex to the simple (even when this is possible) allows accurate prediction from the simple to the complex. Demonstrable reduction is a one way street and possibly a narrow one at that. Yet this does not mean the unification principle is dead. It is resurrected in two ways. First, methodologically, in that the complex systems of all kinds are amenable to the same kind of mathematical description. Water turbulence and crowd movements can, at an aggregate level, be similarly described. Second, the specific ontological problem for unification between natural and social science, that of the biological/social (or even mind/body) divide, might well simply be a hankering for Cartesian dualism. Nature presumably knows no such divide. This doesn't make the problem go away, of course, but the observable existence of emergent properties suggests that a new way of looking at the world might turn this into a non-problem.

This, Dave Byrne proposes, might lead us away from a science of what is, to a science of becoming. 'If we are dealing with a world characterised by emergent properties then what we want to be able to describe is the way in which those properties emerged' (Byrne 1997: 4). A science of emergence would undoubtedly require us to abandon the language of mechanistic causality and to stop thinking of the world as cogs, gears and chain drives. This does not mean that prediction is impossible. Some relationships are simple and straightforward and probabilistic prediction manifestly works (political polling for example), moreover the dynamic stability of strange attractors does allow aggregate prediction of the kind achieved in weather forecasting and economic trends (Eve 1997: 275). However, a consequence that Byrne suggests (citing Reed and Harvey) is an iconographic approach to science: 'In iconographic modelling the *gaze* is more important than deductive logic in grasping the evolution of a chaotic structure' (Reed and Harvey, cited in Byrne 1997: 5, original emphasis). Byrne concludes, 'At the farthest end of the mathematical programme the quantitative breaks down into the qualitative' (*ibid.*).

Byrne may well be right, but one gets the feeling that speculations about a new science of emergence shade into Horgan's 'ironic science' I referred to in the last chapter – they are fun and almost certainly necessary if we are not to slip into dogmatic complacency about our science. Indeed it has not been my intention in this chapter to propose a new dawn, but to give some indication of how new ways of looking at the world have synthesised with new methodological and technical possibilities. This synthesis does offer the promise of an eventual unity of science, but not one that is a unity of disciplines, but instead an interdisciplinary approach to knowing the world.

Suggested further reading

Byrne, D. (1998) *Complexity Theory and the Social Sciences: An Introduction*, London: Routledge.

Eve, R., Horsfall, S. and Lee, M. (eds) (1997) *Chaos, Complexity and Sociology*, Thousand Oaks, CA: Sage.

Horgan, J. (1996) *The End of Science*, London: Little, Brown.

Khalil, E. and Boulding, K. (eds) (1996) *Evolution, Order and Complexity*, London: Routledge.

8 Conclusion: the science of social science

In the preceding chapters I have described some key features of science and how these might relate to studies of the social world. In this final chapter I will review these and conclude that a 'moderate' science of the social world is both possible and desirable.

What is a moderate science?

The model of science I advocate for the study of the social world rests upon certain conclusions about what science is. One of the difficulties of defining science is that throughout its history it has taken on quite different forms. In Chapter 1 I showed how science developed as a result of complex relationships between social, metaphysical and cognitive factors. The relationship could perhaps be seen as a complex feedback mechanism, where external influences shaped and limited the science of the day, but the latter's success, particularly in the form of technological progress, impacted upon society. The more successful science became, the greater the impact. We can talk of progress in science, in particular cognitive progress in the ways the world is understood and the development of ways of elaborating relationships between concepts (through the development of deductive logic for example). Nevertheless despite evidential progress in method, knowledge and output, science must be seen as historically contingent. It is hard to say that its discoveries, or development, were necessary outcomes; it could have been otherwise.

Social constructionists take the view that such historical contingency demonstrates not a steady progress towards knowledge of nature, but the character of science as a purely social enterprise, a product of the political or ideological exigencies of the day. The conclusion being that science is simply what scientists do, or what they say they do. In some versions of social constructionism the scientists themselves are seen to come from dominant social groups and consequently science, from its topics of interest to its results, are cast in the image of that group. The difficulty with this view is its inability to explain the epistemological and technical success of science *contra* the other world views. By 'success' I do not imply that the outcomes are good, or bad, in the ethical sense, for one sector or for all of society, simply that as a result of science our ability to successfully predict, explain and manipulate the physical and social environment is manifestly greater than it was (say) in the fourteenth century.

However, the social constructionist argument cannot be lightly dismissed, for if we cannot look to the history of science and find a common philosophical or methodological thread then a universal model or even definition of science seems impossible. We could take the view that what counts now as science, perhaps in terms of its method, is science, but the problem is that we cannot be sure that it will be science in the future! Moreover, we have to account for success when science was not what it is now. Some philosophers of science, most famously Karl Popper, have tried to establish a demarcation criterion between science and non-science. Popper's demarcation, as I described in Chapter 2, that of falsification, rests on a logical objection to induction, namely that no amount of positive evidence can confirm a conjectural statement. Conversely it is held that negative evidence can refute the conjecture. This, as most now accept, was too harsh and took a logical hammer to crack a methodological nut. Only exceptionally are scientific theories abandoned as a result of 'refutations' made through the crucial experiments Popper advocated.

The Popperian programme has since been modified and moderated, notably by Imre Lakatos (1970). He took a longer term view of science proposing that whole research programmes were either progressive in terms of successful predictions, or degenerated and were sometimes abandoned. Lakatos described this in terms of a hard core of theories, which were rarely refuted or challenged, protected by a belt of auxiliary theories which often were. Of course occasionally the 'hard core' does come under successful attack. Lakatos' research programmes, or indeed other later sophisticated philosophies of science, allow for what might be termed a methodological falibilism (as opposed to a logical one). I would suggest that it is perhaps something like this, embodied as a critical attitude, that explains the growth of knowledge in science.

The application of critical attitude is an intersubjective and historical affair. Popper (1989: 244–7) allowed that the community of science is the arbiter of whether a theory is falsified or what counts as a test of that theory, but of course this begs the question of whether that community is influenced by extra scientific values, or indeed which scientific values (in terms of technique, or method for example) they hold. This internalist account, advanced by Popper, was challenged by historians and philosophers of science, in particular Thomas Kuhn ([1962] 1970) and Paul Feyerabend (1975). The former's 'paradigmatic' view of science, though not a denial of its progress (Kuhn 1977: 321–2), nevertheless claimed that psychological and social factors played an important part historically in determining which theoretical or methodological framework was adopted. Similarly Feyerabend claimed that an examination of the work of contemporary science suggested that there was no clear algorithm for method (and thus it follows decisions about which theory, or test, to reject or accept). Indeed the work of Kuhn and Feyerabend became a starting point for social constructionists, in particular the 'strong programmers' I described in Chapter 4. More recently social epistemologists such as Helen Longino have attempted to bridge the gap between internalist and externalist accounts. In Chapter 6 I discussed the latter's concept of 'transformative interrogation' in the scientific community, concluding that this programme, though valuable in that it proposes the widening of 'ownership' of scientific knowledge, nevertheless reduces objectivity to consensus in the scientific community. The problem with consensus is that it could just as easily be based upon social interests as a desire to get at the truth. Moreover it elides ethical and epistemological–methodological values, thus a view of science that locates epistemological authority in social values cannot readily distinguish between *types* of normative values, for example measurement values and political values.

The 'transformative interrogation' does nevertheless parallel Popper's 'scientific community' and indeed perhaps the 'ideal speech situation' of Jürgen Habermas in which an unconstrained dialogue allows all speakers equal access, thus (he claims) permitting the better argument to prevail (Habermas 1984). In each, albeit that they employ different theoretical and philosophical resources, a 'critical attitude' towards knowledge and the origins of that knowledge is advocated (see Stokes 1998 for a discussion of the similarities and differences in these programmes).

Historically something like a 'critical attitude' has been at work in science, in which there is a piecemeal elimination of error over a long period. The error that is eliminated may have arisen as the result of wrong methodological or theoretical assumptions, through charlatanism (as in the case of the Lysenko affair, for instance; see Medvedev 1969), or through a lack of rigour in method or technique (in for example the Herrnstein and Murray research discussed in Chapter 6). Of course we cannot know whether we have replaced error with error, only that new theories should be more productive in terms of explaining and predicting the world than old ones.

Though it is the case that what counts as truth or objectivity must be intersubjectively agreed, it does not follow that this precludes a value of an objective truth that can exist apart from any given scientist, or community of scientists. In the history of science error has often been uncovered through deviance from intersubjective agreement. The constructionist view – even the moderate kind espoused by Longino – would leave scientific discovery as merely accidental, if truth is given as socially constructed rather than agreement with reality. Whilst there is a great deal of serendipitous luck in science, of the kind I described in Chapter 2, much of science is purposeful. Perhaps, however, the key to explaining scientific progress is to see the pursuance of objective truth through a critical attitude as a value, either itself emerging as a happy accident, or one that is inevitable when people attempt to discover what the world is like. Objectivity (sometimes mistakenly construed as value freedom) has undoubtedly become a conscious value of science, but I would suggest that whilst it is a socially emergent value it is the only one that can produce epistemological progress.

A moderate science beyond this admits of contingency, but if the aim is objective truth, then science should embody the best possible means to that truth. These means will be manifested in different methodological and technical priorities at any given time, because objectivity must apply equally to method (or measurement) as it does to the assessment of knowledge claims. The realist can account for historical contingency in science by referring to an *historically* critical development, whereby better methods give rise to more reliable knowledge (and vice versa) and the elimination of error occurs in the long run.

Moderate science can be summarised, then, as the ensemble of knowledge and practices that best reflect and operationalise a critical attitude to the discovery of the world at that moment in time. Such a definition leaves open the character of specific sciences to be defined according to what is appropriate to them methodologically, or technically at any given time. The relative balance of deduction or induction may vary, some may rely on experimental method and others upon rigorous observation. Some may rest on well established laws, others may not. On this basis the social sciences are, at their best, scientific. In the second half of this chapter I will summarise the reasons why I believe this to be the case.

Social science as science

If one was to draw a much tighter definition of science, such as that proposed by the logical positivists (see Chapter 1), or even Popper, then the social sciences could not qualify. But of course neither would many of the natural sciences. However, for many opponents of science in social science, there are other reasons disqualifying investigations of the social world as science. I will briefly recapitulate these. They can be summarised as ontological and methodological.

Ontological

The ontological objection is a denial that the social world, as manifested, is of the same natural kind as the physical world. Rather, the social world is an intersubjective construction of meanings arising from self-interpreting animals. The categories of the social world, unlike the physical world, are free to vary in their characteristics as a result of how they are interpreted and then recreated by their participants. As I described in Chapter 5 this leads, it is claimed, to an inherent indeterminateness in the lifeworld.

Whilst I agree that this does give rise to methodological difference and limits, ontologically the case that the social world is of a different 'kind', as opposed to being more complex, is not proven. As I indicated in Chapter 7, in the last few years the inherent complexity of many systems in the physical world has become apparent. Determinacy seems to be both local and unusual, with most systems in nature defying predictability. That is not to say that probabilistic outcomes cannot be measured, but rather that we cannot determine the end point of a complex system from knowing its initial conditions. Weather systems, turbulence flows, even the development of whole galaxies seem to behave in such a way. Whilst it is possible that the complexity in these systems is less than in human social life, mathematically they behave with similar characteristics. I illustrated how this has been demonstrated using computer models. However, it might be argued that there is more than complexity in social life, that there are in addition feedback loops that arise from the subjective nature of consciousness. The awareness of particular features in the social world leads to orientations by agents which change or maintain those features (see Khalil 1996: 11–16). Individual agents assimilate and process information, and act upon it, in turn changing the nature of that information. This is quite different to the behaviour of a cold front in a weather system, which has no consciousness awareness of information, or 'things' acting upon it.

But is it different? Though a weather system is complex and might be thought of as a number of interacting smaller atmospheric systems, it does not take too many steps to 'reduce' those systems to simple components of water molecules etc. Human social systems are the outcomes of a number of other interacting contributory systems, psychological, biological and chemical. These are both within agents themselves and are part of other interacting non-human physical systems. The feedback mechanisms arising from consciousness are simply a more complex form of emergent property that exist through nature and indeed are as much part of nature as the aforementioned weather systems. This, however, is not to deny that such complexity may give rise to insurmountable methodological difficulties for social *science*.

Methodological

For many the foregoing would be irrelevant because it is said that whatever the underlying ontological properties and relations, human social life *manifests* itself as a web of intersubjectively understood meanings. Aggregate level prediction and explanation are about the manipulation of abstract concepts invented by the social scientist. These, it is said, are meaningless to individual agents. Thus a 'science' of the social world is superficial and cannot tell us what social life is really like. The only methodological strategy we can follow, to know the social world, is that of interpretivism. Many claim that the word 'know' is too strong anyway, that the best we can do is to produce interpretations in much the same way as a painter will interpret a landscape, or a novelist will interpret life through fiction.

I have not denied the value of the latter to our understanding of social life, to do so would be to deny the role of art in our humanity. However, this does not mean that we cannot have, or we do not need a science of social life. There are two points to be made in response to the methodological objections to social science: (1) that prediction and explanation are possible and (2) that interpretation can contribute to a science of the social.

1. *Prediction and explanation.* As in many of the natural sciences some explanations and predictions are harder to make than others. Just as we cannot predict which leaf will fall next from a tree, or explain why a particular leaf rather than another fell, we cannot predict or explain micro level interactions anywhere near as well as macro level ones. Our ability to do the latter arises from large scale regularities of the kind found in physical systems and whilst it is true our level of predictive accuracy is not as good as that found in some natural sciences it is better than that found in others. We are, for example, better at predicting local election results than meteorologists are in predicting local weather systems. The structure of explanation and prediction in the social world is logically no different to that in the natural world and in some cases the explanatory schema is about the interaction of the social and physical world. Likewise the difficulty of operationalising variables so that they reflect the 'real' character of the world is a problem for both social and natural scientists. Indeed, although it is the case that the social scientist must attempt to operationalise a construct that is 'meaningful' to those to whom it applies, at least she has the advantage (unlike the natural scientist) of being able to check that operationalisation against such meanings (Williams 1998: 16–17). This can be achieved through interpretation.

2 *Interpretation.* A social science cannot consist wholly of interpretation, but conversely I do not believe that there can be a social science without it. It represents both the start of any explanatory process in the social world and may also pose some limits to investigation. The theories that we test more generally will often originate in and be developed from the study of micro level interactions. The study of micro level interactions is tackled in two main ways: through the controlled conditions of the psychological experiment or through interpretation, employing a variant of folk psychology. Even those who advocate the former will admit of its limits, particularly that the action/meaning variability arising from human consciousness makes it hard to control for all variables and of course the experiment, in natural and in social science, is a deliberate manipulation of nature (see for example Bhaskar 1989: 15). The alternative of interpretation relies on our intersubjective understanding of the intentions and

actions of other agents, but this too will be limited by the problem of variability. Notwithstanding different levels of understanding, or different forms of meaning that might be interpreted by the investigator, there are also problems of validity and generalisation. How does the investigator know she has interpreted correctly and how widely can that interpretation be said to apply to other agents and situations? In Chapter 5 I argued that these things do indeed set limits to interpretivism, but do not make it impossible. Cultural continuity gives some conviction that what is interpreted will hold to other agents and similar situations beyond the site of investigation.

Moderate social science

Our need for knowledge of the social world, like that of the physical world, operates at different levels. On a day-to-day basis a 'folk psychological' knowledge suffices. This need only be fit for purpose. In other contexts we might require a deeper understanding of humanity that is expressed through art or literature. Great literature can tell us what we are 'like' because we can identify with characters or situations. However, we have need for knowledge at a third level; we need to *objectively* know what social life is like. In Chapter 3, quoting Harold Kincaid, I suggested that the evaluation of social programmes would be inane without being able to explain or predict the social world. Indeed if we believe in a better world – though differently construed by different people – we need universal, dispassionate, empirically testable knowledge. Only the objectivity of science can provide that. This is exemplified by Ismay Barwell in relation to the need for a criterion of objectivity in feminism when she writes:

> If an argument is needed for this I think that it is to be found in the fact that feminism in all its various varieties does understand itself to be a radical movement for social change. It aims at producing societies which are more than those it finds already in existence. Surely the rhetorical wing of feminism will require descriptions and analyses of the social arrangements about which the judgements about justice and injustice are being made, as well as explanations of how they come about and are sustained in existence.
>
> (Barwell 1994: 82)

A moderate social science is both possible and desirable. It is possible because our methods do lead to successful predictions and explanations in the social world. These in turn become actionable in terms of policy or the advocacy of particular courses of action. Of course it is true that what we ask and the way that we ask it will originate in earlier views and attitudes toward the world, but this is as much true in natural science as in social science. However, objective science in the moderate sense I employ above, takes a critical attitude towards not just results, but also the philosophical and methodological assumptions that underlay them.

It is desirable because human beings strive towards a better world and it is because there is disagreement as to what a better world is that we need science. A critical science is itself emancipatory because it is the tool with which we can examine our assumptions and prescriptions for the world. In this regard a social *science* is crucial because the prescriptions we hold for the world as citizens are about the *social* world. They rest on assumptions about that world. If they are not available to critical scrutiny then they are dogma and the acceptance of dogma is a licence to intolerance.

Glossary

The following philosophical and natural science terms are those used in the text with no, or minimal, explanation. The suggestions below, for further reading, are those I have found helpful and are not necessarily definitive writings on the subject. A number of very good dictionaries of science are published. Particularly recommended is that published by Penguin.

Algorithm A set of instructions to solve a particular problem, or achieve a particular task in a finite number of stages. Algorithms are particularly important in computer programming which requires precise instructions without any fuzziness or vagueness. (See Casti 1991.)

Atomism The belief that matter consists ultimately of discrete particles that have measurable properties, such as mass, size and position, similar to objects in the visible world. Since the discovery of the electron by J.J. Thomson in 1887, atomism gradually fell from favour as a doctrine in science, though it is often the intuitive view held by lay persons. Though modern physicists search for smaller and smaller particles, their properties are described in terms of energy and interaction with other particles. Particle classification is complex and over 200 elementary particles are known. (See Gribben 1984.)

Bayesian Probability/Inference Derives from Bayes' Theorem, a method for evaluating the conditional probability of an event. The method of inference involves working backwards from an effect to a cause by estimating the conditional probability of a cause given the occurrence of certain events. Though Bayes' Theorem itself is not controversial the method of inference derived from it is, in that it requires the scientist to assign degrees of belief to a proposition. These are then amended in light of new evidence. Bayesian probability is gaining in popularity in several areas, for example socio-medical research, and though open to philosophical and mathematical objection it has practical value. The Bayesian programme in the philosophy of science arose, in particular, from the post-Popperian school and can be seen as an attempt to resolve the problems posed by falsification and discussed here in Chapter 4. (See Howson and Urbach 1989.)

Determinism Determinism takes many forms, but generally can be seen as the view that all events, including human action, are determined. Determinism is neither inductively confirmable, or empirically refutable. An inability to establish a cause of X could always be held simply to be a gap in our knowledge of X, conversely any apparently 'determined' cause–effect relationship can be seen to be ultimately contingent. For example classical 'laws of nature' may not apply under certain circumstances, such as in the first microseconds after the 'big bang', or at the quantum level. However, in science, it is convenient to treat classical laws such as gravity, or thermodynamics as deterministic, though in recent years it has become apparent that much of nature (and here I include the social world) is contingent, though often regular, but only statistically so. Ultimately, of course, such contingency may turn out to be determined after all, or at least subject to some relatively simple underlying principles. (See Ruelle 1991.)

Entropy The second law of thermodynamics states that the entropy of the universe tends to a maximum. That is, disorder increases. Systems evolve from a state of order (and simplicity) to disorder and complexity. Locally there can be 'anti-entropic' systems – for example mechanical or electronic systems, etc., whereby order increases, but always this is at a price. Energy must be obtained from outside of the 'system'. A car engine produces energy allowing movement, but to do this it must burn petrol (which required energy for its production) and is dissipated into carbon monoxide, soot etc. (See Asimov 1966.)

Epistemology The branch of metaphysics concerned with how we know what we know and our authority for claims to knowledge. Compare with ontology. (See Dancy and Sosa 1993.)

Essentialism The term is used in different ways in philosophy, but is usually taken to mean that some objects can have essences, that is they have certain necessary properties without which they could not exist. Whether things have 'essences' or not, is held by some to be a function of our description of them and others as facts about the world independent of us. The question of 'essential' properties is somewhat different in the natural and the social sciences, because the phenomena so discussed have different ontological properties. (See Hospers 1973.)

Markov Chain The probability of an event occurring is conditional only upon an immediately preceding event in a series. A future system is then only effected by its immediate past. A useful concept in descriptions of complex systems. (See Hays 1988.)

Metaphysics The branch of philosophy concerned with matters beyond our existing knowledge. These may be fundamental questions of existence such as the question of the existence of God, or the nature of the beginning of the universe. They may, however, be simply to do with more mundane matters such as the nature of social (as opposed to physical) properties. Less grandiose philosophising, such as this, is usually referred to under its constituent branch of metaphysics, such as ontology or epistemology. Throughout the history of science investigation has begun from the basis of some metaphysical assumptions, but an implicit goal of science is to replace metaphysical speculation with scientific knowledge. (See Taylor 1983.)

Ontology   The branch of metaphysics concerned with the nature of existence. Ontological assumptions about what there is and is not, and the nature of existence itself, is at the heart of science, yet as in the case of metaphysical assumptions generally some kind of ontological assumption must underlie all investigation. Compare with epistemology. (See Hospers 1973.)

Parsimony   When choosing between theories or explanations scientists choose the simplest explanation, all things being equal. Such a test makes most sense when choosing between theories which are equally good in other respects. The principle is sometimes referred to as Occam's (or Ockham's) Razor. (See Newton Smith 1981.)

Probability   Probability is a controversial concept but can be summarised as the likelihood that a particular event or relationship will occur. Values for statistical probability range from 1.0 (always) to 0 (never). Thus in a toss of a coin the probability of heads is 0.5. Two important problems are: (a) where the possible range of outcomes is unknown (unlike a coin toss) odds cannot be fixed objectively beforehand; (b) in such cases, the ontological status or determinates of single cases that go to make up the frequency of events, cannot be known. These problems are especially important to scientists, particularly social scientists, who work with open systems. Some scientists and philosophers defend versions of subjective probability to overcome these kinds of problems (see Bayesian Probability/Inference above), whilst others, such as Popper (1985) have defended 'realist' theories of single case probabilities. (See Casti 1991.)

Quantum   Quantum physics and quantum mechanics are concerned with the characteristics and behaviour of the world at the subatomic level (see also Atomism). The word quantum is the Latin for unit and through this century has come to mean the indivisible unit of action that characterises both radiation and matter. However, to talk of matter at a subatomic level is somewhat misleading, for these particles have a character that can only be expressed in probabilistic, as opposed to the causal terms of classical physics. Though quantum physics is now well established it has so far proven impossible to reconcile this with the physics of relativity, though for many this is the 'Holy Grail' of science. Moreover though the quantum world is a probabilistic one and we know at the non-quantum level systems can often only be described probabilistically, the first has no known implications for the second. For most scientists then, including social scientists, the indeterminism of the quantum world is only of philosophical interest in

that it demonstrates the probabilistic character of nature at a fundamental level. (See Gribben 1984.)

Relativism Like so many other philosophical concepts relativism is used
in more than one way. Relativism stresses the diversity of social environment to determining what is, or ought to be the case. Moral relativists stress the differences in moral standards between societies and
points in time maintaining that a single standard of morality cannot be
applicable to all times and places. Epistemological relativists claim
much the same for knowledge and truth. Pascal's maxim that what is
true on one side of the Pyrenees is error on the other, sums up this
position. Postmodernists favour relativism in each of its forms, but the
problem with such assertions is that they must be subject to the same
relativistic standards as they espouse! Not to be confused with relativity discussed in Chapter 1. (See Harré and Krausz 1996.)

Superstrings Superstrings are in the realm of Horgan's 'ironic science'
(Chapter 6). Superstrings are considered by many physicists to be the
most likely candidate for a Grand Unified Theory (GUT) that will
unite the physics of the very small (quantum) with that of the very
large (relativity). The term 'superstring' refers to the claim that subatomic particles are better thought of as tiny vibrating strings, rather
than tiny points as was originally believed. (See Kaku 1994.)

Thermodynamics The first and second laws of thermodynamics are
amongst the most important in physics. The first law is simply that
energy is indestructible, that it can neither be created nor destroyed
and the universe will always contain the same amount of energy. In
'creating' energy we simply change from one form of energy to another, from say fuel to heat. Even an atomic explosion simply
'releases' the energy held in matter. The second law of thermodynamics is expressed by entropy, described in the entry above. (See Asimov
1966).

References

Advisory Council on Science and Technology (ACOST) (1989) *Defence R & D: A National Resource*, London: HMSO.

Ainley, P. (1991) *Young People Leaving Home*, London: Cassell.

Albrow, M. (1990) *Max Weber's Construction of Social Theory*, London: Macmillan.

Alisch, L.-M., Azizighanbari, S. and Bargfeldt, M. (1997) 'Dynamics of Children's Friendships' in R. Eve, S. Horsfall and M. Lee (eds) *Chaos, Complexity and Sociology*, Thousand Oaks, CA.: Sage.

Alvares, C. (1988) 'Science, Colonialism and Violence: A Luddite View' in A. Nandy (ed.) *Science, Hegemony and Violence: A Requiem for Modernity*, New Delhi: Oxford India.

Appleyard, B. (1992) *Understanding the Present: Science and the Soul of Modern Man*, London: Pan.

Archer, M. (1998) 'Social Theory and the Analysis of Society' in T. May and M. Williams (eds) *Knowing the Social World*, Buckingham: Open University Press.

Arendt, H. (1958) *The Origin of Totalitarianism*, London: George Allen & Unwin.

Ash, D., Knott, S. and Turner, G. (1996) 'A 4GYR Shock Age for a Martian Meteorite and Implications for the Cratering History of Mars', *Nature* 380: 57–9.

Ashall, F. (1994) *Remarkable Discoveries*, Cambridge: Cambridge University Press.

Ashford, S. (1991) 'A Statistical Afterword' in P. Ainley, *Young People Leaving Home*, London: Cassell.

Asimov, I. (1966) *Understanding Physics*, vol. 1, New York: Barnes & Noble.

—— (1995) 'Black Holes' in J. Carey (ed.) *The Faber Book of Science*, London: Faber & Faber.

Ayer, A. (1987) 'Introduction' in J. Mill *On the Logic of the Moral Science*, London: Duckworth.

Barber, W. (1967) *A History of Economic Thought*, Harmondsworth: Penguin.

Barnes, B. and Bloor, D. (1982) 'Relativism, Rationalism and the Sociology of Knowledge' in M. Hollis and S. Lukes (eds) *Rationality and Relativism*, Oxford: Oxford University Press.

Barnes, B. and Edge, D. (eds) (1982) *Science in Context: Readings in the Sociology of Science*, Buckingham: Open University Press.

Barwell, I. (1994) 'Toward a Defence of Objectivity', in K. Lennon, and M. Whitford (eds) *Knowing the Difference: Feminist Perspectives in Epistemology*, London: Routledge.

Bauman, Z. (1978) *Hermeneutics and Social Science*, London: Hutchinson.

Berry, B.J.L. (1976) 'The Counterurbanisation Process: Urban America since 1970', *Urbanisation and Counterurbanisation* (Urban Affairs Annual Review) 11, Thousand Oaks, CA: Sage.

Bhaskar, R. (1989) *Reclaiming Reality: A Critical Introduction to Contemporary Philosophy*, London: Verso.

Blackett, P. (1973) 'Big Science and Lesser Sciences' in E. Mendoza (ed.) *A Random Walk in Science*, Bristol: Institute of Physics Publishing.

Blaikie, N. (1993) *Approaches to Social Enquiry*, Cambridge: Polity.

Blake, J. (1979) 'The Intellectual Development and Social Context of the Study of Unidentified Flying Objects' in R. Wallis (ed.) *On the Margins of Science: The Social Construction of Rejected Knowledge*, Sociological Review Mongraph 27, Keele: University of Keele.

Block, N. (1980) *Readings in Philosophy of Psychology*, vol. 1, Cambridge, MA: Harvard University Press.

Bourdieu, P. (1977) *Outline of a Theory of Practice*, Cambridge: Cambridge University Press.

Bowser, B.P. and Seiber, J.E. (1993) 'AIDS Prevention Research: Old Problems and New Solutions' in C. Renzetti and R. Lee (eds) *Researching Sensitive Topics*, London: Sage.

Braybrooke, D. (ed.) (1965) *Philosophical Problems of the Social Sciences*, New York: Macmillan.

Brewer, J. and Hunter, A. (1989) *Multi-Method Research: A Synthesis of Styles*, London: Sage.

Bronowski, J. (1960) *The Common Sense of Science*, Harmondsworth: Penguin.

Brown, J. (ed.) (1984) *Scientific Rationality: The Sociological Turn*, Dordrecht: Reidel.

Bryant, L., Chandler, J. and Bunyard, T. (1995) *The Integration of Sea Service: A Report to the Royal Navy on the Integration of the WRNS into the Royal Navy*, Plymouth: Royal Navy/University of Plymouth.

Bryman, A. (1988) *Quantity and Quality in Social Research*, London: Routledge.

Bulmer, M. (ed.) (1982) *Social Research Ethics*, London: Macmillan.

Burt, S. and Code, L. (eds) (1995) *Changing Methods: Feminists Transforming Practice*, Peterborough, Ont.: Broadview.

Byrne, D. (1997) 'Simulation – A Way Forward?', *Sociological Research Online*, 2: 2; http://www.socresonline.org.uk.

—— (1998) *Complexity Theory and the Social Sciences: An Introduction*, London: Routledge.

Carey, J. (ed.) (1995) *The Faber Book of Science*, London: Faber & Faber.

Carnap, R. (1969) *The Logical Structure of the World and Pseudo-problems in Philosophy*, Berkerley, CA: University of California Press.

Casti, J. (1991) *Searching for Certainty: What Scientists Can Know about the Future*, London: Abacus.

Chalmers, A. (1982) *What is This Thing Called Science?*, 2nd edn, Buckingham: Open University Press.

—— (1990) *Science and its Fabrication*, Buckingham: Open University Press.

Cloke, P. (1985) 'Counterurbanisation: A Rural Perspective', *Geography* 70: 13–23.

Code, L. (1995) 'How Do We Know? Questions of Method in Feminist Practice' in S. Burt and L. Code (eds) *Changing Methods: Feminists Transforming Practice*, Peterborough, Ont.: Broadview.

Cohen, J. and Stewart, I. (1994) *The Collapse of Chaos: Discovering Simplicity in a Complex World*, Harmondsworth: Penguin.

Cohen, S. (1997) 'Ethics and Science' in A. Tauber (ed.) *Science and the Quest for Reality*, London: Macmillan.

Cole, S. (1992) *Making Science: Between Nature and Society*, Cambridge, MA: Harvard University Press.

Collins, H. (1975) 'The Seven Sexes: A Study in the Sociology of a Phenomenon, or the Replication Experiments in Physics', *Sociology* 9: 205–24.

—— (1981) 'Stages in the Empirical Programme of Relativism', *Social Studies of Science* 11: 3–10.

Coopey, R., Uttley, M. and Spinardi, G. (eds) (1993) *Defence, Science and Technology: Adjusting to Change*, Chur: Harwood.

Cotgrove, S. (1974) 'Objections to Science', *Nature* 250: 764–7.

Couvalis, G. (1997) *The Philosophy of Science: Science and Objectivity*, London: Sage.

Cox, M. (1995) *Life and Death in Spitalfields 1700–1850*, London: Council for British Archaeology.

Craib, I. (1997) *Classical Social Theory: An Introduction to the Thought of Marx, Weber, Durkheim and Simmel*, Oxford: Oxford University Press.

Dale, A., Arber, S. and Proctor, M. (1988) *Doing Secondary Analysis*, London: Unwin Hyman.

Dale, A. and Marsh, C. (eds) (1993) *The 1991 Census User's Guide*, London: HMSO.

Dale, A., Williams, M. and Dodgeon, B. (1996) *Housing Deprivation and Social Change*, London: HMSO.

Dampier, W. (1966) *A History of Science and Its Relations with Philosophy and Religion*, Cambridge: Cambridge University Press.

Dancy, J. and Sosa, E. (eds) (1993) *A Companion to Epistemology*, Oxford: Blackwell.

Darwin, C. ([1859] 1998) *The Origin of the Species*, Ware: Wordsworth.

Davies, P. (1989) 'Introduction' in W. Heisenberg, *Physics and Philosophy*, Harmondsworth: Penguin..

Davis, J. (1990) *Mapping the Code: The Human Genome Project and the Choices of Modern Science*, New York: John Wiley.

Dawkins, R. (1982) *The Extended Phenotype*, Oxford: Oxford University Press.

—— (1988) *The Blind Watchmaker*, Harmondsworth: Penguin.

—— (1989) *The Selfish Gene*, 2nd edn, Oxford: Oxford University Press.

Denton, F. (1925) *Relativity and Common Sense*, Cambridge, Cambridge University Press.

Denzin, N. (1983) 'Interpretive Interactionism' in G. Morgan (ed.) *Beyond Method: Strategies for Social Research*, Beverly Hills, CA: Sage.

Dickens, P. (1998) 'Don't Throw out the Baby with the Bathwater: A Response to Tom Shakespeare on Social Genetics', *Network* (January) 32.

Doran, J., Palmer, M., Gilbert, N. and Mellars, P. (1993) 'The EOS Project: Modelling Upper Paleolithic Change' in N. Gilbert and J. Doran (eds) *Simulating Societies: The Computer Simulation of Social Processes*, London: UCL Press.

Drew, D., Fosam, B. and Gilborn, D. (1995) 'Race, IQ and the Underclass: Don't Believe the Hype', *Radical Statistics* 60: 2–21.

Dunn, J. (1979) 'Understanding Human Development: Limitations and Possibilities in an Ethological Approach', in M. von Cranach (ed.) *Human Ethology*, Cambridge: Cambridge University Press.

Dunscombe, J. and Marsden, D. (1996) 'Can We Research the Private Sphere? Methodological and Ethical Problems in the Study of the Role of Intimate Emotion in Personal Relationships' in L. Morris and S. Lyon (eds) *Gender Relations in Public and Private: New Research Perspectives*, Basingstoke: Macmillan.

Durkheim, E. ([1896] 1952) *Suicide*, London: Routledge & Kegan Paul.

—— ([1912] 1961) *The Elementary Forms of Religious Life*, London: Allen & Unwin.

Einstein, A. (1956) *The Meaning of Relativity*, 5th edn, Princeton, NJ: Princeton University Press.

Elster, J. (1986) *Rational Choice Theory*, Oxford: Blackwell.

Ennew, J. (1986) *The Sexual Exploitation of Children*, Cambridge: Cambridge University Press.

Eysenck, H. (1981) 'Intelligence: The Battle for the Mind' in H.J. Eysenck, R. Eve, S. Horsfall, M. Lee (eds) (1997) *Chaos, Complexity and Sociology*, Thousand Oaks, CA: Sage.

Fay, B. (1996) *Contemporary Philosophy of Social Science*, Oxford: Blackwell.

Ferris, T. (ed.) (1991) *The World Treasury of Physics, Astronomy and Mathematics*, Boston, MA: Little, Brown.

Feyerabend, P. (1975) *Against Method*, London: New Left Books.

Feynmann, R. (1965) *The Character of Physical Law*, Cambridge, MA: MIT Press.

Fielding, N. (1981) *The National Front*, London: Routledge & Kegan Paul.

Firth, W. (1991) 'Chaos – Predicting the Unpredictable', *British Medical Journal* 303: 1,565–8.

Fodor, J. (1980) 'Special Sciences, or the Disunity of Science as a Working Hypothesis' in N. Block (ed.) *Readings in Philosophy of Psychology*, vol. 1, Cambridge, MA: Harvard University Press.

Foster, J. (1974) *Class Struggle and the Industrial Revolution: Early Industrial Capitalism in Three English Towns*, London: Weidenfeld & Nicolson.

Fox Keller, E. (1985) *Reflections on Gender and Science*, New Haven, CN: Yale University Press.

Fox Keller, E. and Longino, H. (eds) (1996) *Feminism and Science*, Oxford: Oxford University Press.

Fuller, S. (1988) *Social Epistemology*, Bloomington, IN: Indiana University Press.

—— (1997) *Science*, Buckingham: Open University Press.

Gauldie, E. (1974) *Cruel Habitations*, London: Allen & Unwin.

Geertz, C. (1979) 'Deep Play: Notes on the Balinese Cockfight' in P. Rabinow and M. Sullivan (eds) *Interpretive Social Science – A Reader*, Berkeley, CA: University of California Press.

—— (1994) 'Thick Description: Toward an Interpretive Theory of Culture' in M. Martin and L. McIntyre (eds) *Readings in the Philosophy of Social Science*, Cambridge, MA: MIT Press.

Gemes, K. (1989) 'A Refutation of Popperian Inductive Scepticism', *British Journal for the Philosophy of Science*, 40: 183–4.

Gerth, H. and Mills, C.W. (eds) ([1948] 1991) *From Max Weber: Essays in Sociology*, London: Routledge.

Giddens, A. (1984) *The Constitution of Society*, Cambridge: Polity.

—— (1993) *New Rules of Sociological Method*, 2nd edn, Cambridge: Polity.

Gigerenzer, G., Swijtink, Z., Porter, T., Daston, L., Beatty, J. and Krüger, L. (1989) *The Empire of Chance: How Probability Changed Science and Everyday Life*, Cambridge: Cambridge University Press.

Gilbert, N. (1993a) 'Computer Simulation of Social Processes', *Social Research Update* 6; http://www.soc.surrey.ac.uk/srv/srv6.html.

—— (1993b) *Analyzing Tabular Data*, London: UCL Press.

Gilbert, N. and Doran, J. (eds) (1993) *Simulating Societies: The Computer Simulation of Social Processes*, London: UCL Press.

Gillies, D. (1993) *Philosophy of Science in the Twentieth Century*, Oxford: Blackwell.

Gleick, J. (1987) *Chaos: Making a New Science*, Harmondsworth: Viking Penguin.

Glover, J. (1990) *Utilitarianism and its Critics*, New York: Macmillan.

Gould, S. (1980) *Ever Since Darwin: Reflections in Natural History*, Harmondsworth: Penguin.

Gower, B. (1997) *Scientific Method: An Historical and Philosophical Introduction*, London: Routledge.

Green, R. (1995) *Human Motivation*, Belmont, CA: Brooks Cole.

Gribben, J. (1996) *Companion to the Cosmos*, London: Weidenfeld & Nicholson.

Guba, E. and Lincoln, Y. (1982) 'Epistemological and Methodological Bases of Naturalistic Inquiry', *Education Communication and Technology Journal* 30: 233–52.

Habermas, J. (1984) *Theory of Communicative Action*, vol. 1, *Reason and the Rationalization of Society*, London: Heinemann.

—— (1987) *Theory of Communicative Action*, vol. 2, *Lifeworld and System: A Critique of Functionalist Reason*, Cambridge: Cambridge University Press.

—— ([1968] 1989) *Knowledge and Human Interests*, Cambridge: Polity.

Hage, J. and Foley-Meeker, B. (1988) *Social Causality*, London: Unwin Hyman.

Halberg, M. (1989) 'Feminist Epistemology: An Impossible Project', *Radical Philosophy* 53: 3–7.

Hammersley, M. (1989) *The Dilemma of Qualitative Method: Herbert Blumer and the Chicago School*, London: Routledge.

Hanson, N.R. (1965) *Patterns of Discovery*, Cambridge: Cambridge University Press.

Haraway, D. (1989) *Primate Visions: Gender, Race and Nature in the World of Modern Science*, New York: Routledge.

Harding, S. (1986) *The Science Question in Feminism*, Milton Keynes: Open University Press.

—— (1996) 'Rethinking Standpoint Epistemology: What is "Strong Objectivity"?' in E. Fox Keller and H. Longino (eds) *Feminism and Science*, Oxford: Oxford University Press.

Harding, S. and Hintikka, M. (eds) (1983) *Discovering Reality: Feminist Perspectives on Epistemology, Metaphysics, Methodology and the Philosophy of Science*, Dordrecht: Reidel.

Harper, P. and Morris, M. (1991) 'Family Screening for Genetic Disorders: Lessons from Huntington's Disease' in D. Roberts and R. Chester, *Molecular Genetics in Medicine*, Basingstoke: Macmillan.

Harré, R. (1986) *Varieties of Realism: A Rationale for the Natural Sciences*, Oxford: Blackwell.

—— (1998) 'When the Knower is also the Known' in T. May and M. Williams (eds) *Knowing the Social World*, Buckingham: Open University Press.

Harré, R. and Krausz, M. (1996) *Varieties of Relativism*, Oxford: Blackwell.

Harré, R. and Secord, P. (1972) *The Explanation of Social Behaviour*, Oxford: Blackwell.

Hartsock, N. (1983) 'The Feminist Standpoint: Developing the Ground for a Specifically Feminist Materialism' in S. Harding and M. Hintikka (eds) *Discovering Reality: Feminist Perspectives on Epistemology, Metaphysics, Methodology and the Philosophy of Science*, Dordrecht: Reidel.

Hawking, S. (1988) *A Brief History of Time*, New York: Bantam Books.

Hays, W. (1988) *Statistics*, 4th edn, Fort Worth, TX: Holt, Rinehart & Winston.

Heidegger, M. (1997) 'The Age of the World Picture' in A. Tauber (ed.) *Science and the Quest for Reality*, London: Macmillan.

Heilbron, J. (1995) *The Rise of Social Theory*, Cambridge: Polity.

Heisenberg, W. (1989) *Physics and Philosophy*, Harmondsworth: Penguin.

Hempel, C. (1965) *Aspects of Scientific Explanation*, New York: Free Press.

—— (1994) 'The Function of General Laws in History' in M. Martin and L. McIntyre (eds) *Readings in the Philosophy of Social Science*, Cambridge, MA: MIT Press.

Herrnstein, R. and Murray, C. (1994) *The Bell Curve: Intelligence and Class Structure in American Life*, New York: The Free Press.

Higgott, R. and Stone, D. (1994) 'The Limits of Influence: Foreign Policy Think Tanks in Britain and the USA', *Review of International Studies* 20: 15–34.

Hobbs, D. (1988) *Doing the Business: Entrepreneurship, Detectives and the Working Class in the East End of London*, Oxford: Clarendon.

—— (1995) *Bad Business*, Oxford: Oxford University Press.

Hobbs, D. and May, T. (eds) (1993) *Interpreting the Field: Accounts of Ethnography*, Oxford: Oxford University Press.

Hobsbawm, E. (1977) *The Age of Revolution 1789–1848*, London: Abacus.

Hoffman, B. (1963) *The Strange Story of the Quantum*, Harmondsworth: Penguin.

Holdaway, S. (1982) 'An Inside Job: A Case Study of Covert Research on the Police' in M. Bulmer (ed.) *Social Research Ethics*, London: Macmillan.

Hollis, M. and Lukes, S. (1982) *Rationality and Relativism*, Oxford: Oxford University Press.

Holton, G. (1993) *Science and Anti-Science*, Cambridge, MA: Harvard University Press.

Honderich, T. (ed.) (1979a) *Philosophy As It Is*, Harmondsworth: Penguin.

—— (1979b) 'One Determinism' in T. Honderich (ed.) *Philosophy As It Is*, Harmondsworth: Penguin.

Horgan, J. (1996) *The End of Science*, London: Little, Brown.

Hospers, J. (1973) *An Introduction to Philosophical Analysis*, London: Routledge.

Howson, C. and Urbach, P. (1989) *Scientific Reasoning: The Bayesian Approach*, La Salle, IL: Open Court.

Hughes, J. (1990) *The Philosophy of Social Research*, Harlow: Longman.

Hume, D. ([1739] 1911) *A Treatise of Human Nature*, Book 1, London: Dent.

—— ([1739] 1972) *A Treatise of Human Nature*, Book 2, London: Fontana.

Ikenberry, E. (1962) *Quantum Mechanics*, London: Oxford University Press.

Inglis, F. (1992) *The Cruel Peace: Living Through the Cold War*, London: Aurum.

Jackson, J. (1986) *Migration*, London: Longman.

James, W. (1949) *Pragmatism*, New York: Longman.

Jeffery, R. (1975) 'Probability and Falsification: Critique of the Popper Programme', *Synthese* 30: 95–117.

Jones, T. (1998) 'Interpretive Social Science and the "Native's" Point of View', *Philosophy of the Social Sciences* 28: 132–68.

Kaku, M. (1994) *Hyperspace*, Oxford: Oxford University Press.

Kamin, L. (1981) *Intelligence: The Battle of the Mind*, London: Pan Books.

Kauffman, S. (1995) *At Home in the Universe: The Search for the Laws of Complexity*, Harmondsworth: Penguin.

Kelly, K. (1995) *Out of Control: The New Biology of Machines*, London: Fourth Estate.

Khalil, E. (1996) 'Social Theory and Naturalism' in E. Khalil and K. Boulding (eds) *Evolution, Order and Complexity*, London: Routledge.

Khalil, E. and Boulding, K. (eds) (1996) *Evolution, Order and Complexity*, London: Routledge.

Kimmel, A. (1996) *Ethical Issues in Behavioral Research*, Cambridge, MA: Blackwell.

Kincaid, H. (1996) *Philosophical Foundations of the Social Sciences: Analyzing Controversies in Social Research*, Cambridge: Cambridge University Press.

Kingdom, J. (1992) *No Such Thing as Society?*, Buckingham: Open University Press.

Kolakowski, L. (1972) *Positivism: From Hume to the Vienna Circle*, Harmondsworth: Penguin.

Körner, S. (1955) *Kant*, Harmondsworth: Penguin.

Kuhn, T. (1970) *The Structure of Scientific Revolutions*, 2nd edn, Chicago, IL: Chicago Univesity Press.

—— (1977) *The Essential Tension*, Chicago, IL: Chicago University Press.

Lacey, R. (1994) *Mad Cow Disease: The History of BSE in Britain*, Jersey: Cypsela Publications.

Lakatos, I. (1970) 'Falsification and the Methodology of Scientific Research Programmes' in I. Lakatos and A. Musgrave (eds) *Criticism and the Growth of Knowledge*, Cambridge: Cambridge University Press.

Lakatos, I. and Musgrave, A. (eds) (1970) *Criticism and the Growth of Knowledge*, Cambridge: Cambridge University Press.

Langley, P., Simon, H.A., Bradshaw, G.L. and Zytkow, J.M. (1987) *Scientific Discovery: Computational Explorations of the Creative Processes*, Cambridge, MA: MIT Press.

Latour, B. (1987) *Science in Action*, Milton Keynes: Open University Press.

—— (1988) 'The Politics of Explanation: An Alternative', in S. Woolgar (ed.) *Knowledge and Reflexivity: New Frontiers in Sociology of Knowledge*, London: Sage.

—— (1998) 'Between the Siegfried and Maginot Lines', *LSE Magazine* 10 (1): 10–12.

Latour, B. and Woolgar, S. ([1979] 1986) *Laboratory Life: The Construction of Scientific Facts*, 2nd edn, Princeton, NJ: Princeton University Press.

Laudan, L. (1977) *Progress and its Problems: Towards a Theory of Scientific Growth*, London: Routledge & Kegan Paul.

—— (1984) 'The Pseudo Science of Science?' in · J. Brown (ed.) *Scientific Rationality: The Sociological Turn*, Dordrecht: Reidel.

—— (1997) 'Explaining the Success of Science: Beyond Epistemic Realism and Relativism' in A. Tauber (ed.) *Science and the Quest for Reality*, London: Macmillan.

Layder, D. (1997) *Modern Social Theory*, London: UCL Press.

Leakey, R. and Lewin, R. (1992) *Origins Reconsidered: In Search of What Makes us Human*, London: Little, Brown.

Lennon, K. and Whitford, M. (1994) *Knowing the Difference: Feminist Perspectives in Epistemology*, London: Routledge.

Levy, D. (1981) *Realism: An Essay in Interpretation and Social Reality*, Manchester: Carncanet.

Lewin, R. (1995) *Complexity: Life on the Edge of Chaos*, London: Phoenix.

Little, D. (1991) *Varieties of Social Explanation: An Introduction to the Philosophy of Social Science*, London: Westview.

Livingston, E. (1987) *Making Sense of Ethnomethodology*, London: Routledge.

Longino, H. (1990) *Science as Social Knowledge: Values and Objectivity in Scientific Enquiry*, Princeton, NJ: Princeton University Press.

Losee, J. (1980) *A Historical Introduction to the Philosophy of Science*, Oxford: Oxford University Press.

Lukes, S. (1981) *Emile Durkheim: His Life and Work: A Historical and Critical Study*, Harmondsworth: Penguin.

—— (1994) 'Some Problems about Rationality' in M. Martin and L. McIntyre (eds) *Readings in the Philosophy of Social Science*, Cambridge, MA: MIT Press.

Lumsden, C. and Wilson E. (1982) *Genes, Mind and Culture*, Cambridge, MA: Harvard University Press.

Lyotard, J. (1984) *The Postmodern Condition: A Report on Knowledge*, Minneapolis, MN: Minnesota University Press.

McCarl Neilsen, J. (1990) *Feminist Research Methods*, London: Westview.

Macfarlane, G. (1979) *Howard Florey: The Making of a Great Scientist*, Oxford: Oxford University Press.

McIntyre, L. (1994) 'Complexity and Social Scientific Laws' in M. Martin and L. McIntrye (eds) *Readings in the Philosophy of Social Science*, Cambridge, MA: MIT Press.

MacKenzie, D and Spinardi, G. (1993) 'The Technological Impact of a Defence Research Establishment' in R. Coopey, M. Uttley and G. Spinardi (eds) *Defence, Science and Technology: Adjusting to Change*, Chur: Harwood.

McKibben, W. (1990) *The End of Nature*, London: Viking.

McLellan, D. (1975) *Marx*, London: Fontana.

Maddox, J. (1972) *The Doomsday Syndrome*, New York.

Mandelbrot, B. (1977) *The Fractal Geometry of Nature*, San Francisco, CA: Freeman.

Manicas, P. (1987) *A History and Philosophy of the Social Sciences*, Oxford: Blackwell.

Marcuse, H. (1964) *One Dimensional Man: The Ideology of Industrial Society*, London: Routledge & Kegan Paul.

Marsh, C. (1982) *The Survey Method: The Contribution of Surveys to Sociological Explanation*, London: George Allen & Unwin.

Martin, M. and McIntyre, L. (eds) (1994) *Readings in the Philosophy of Social Science*, Cambridge, MA: MIT Press.

Marx, K. ([1887] 1954) *Capital*, vol. 1, London: Lawrence & Wishart.

May, T. (1996) *Situating Social Theory*, Buckingham: Open University Press.

May, T. and Williams, M. (eds) (1998) *Knowing the Social World*, Buckingham: Open University Press.

Maynard, M. (1998) 'Feminists' Knowledge and the Knowledge of Feminisms' in T. May and M. Williams (eds) *Knowing the Social World*, Buckingham: Open University Press.

Medvedev, Z. (1969) *The Rise and Fall of T.D. Lysenko*, New York: Columbia University Press.

Mellor, D. (1971) *The Matter of Chance*, Cambridge: Cambridge University Press.

Mendoza, E. (ed.) (1973) *A Random Walk in Science*, Bristol: Institute of Physics Publishing.

Mennell, S. (1974) *Sociological Theory: Uses and Utilities*, New York: Praeger.

Menzies, K. (1982) *Sociological Theory in Use*, London: Routledge & Kegan Paul.

Merton, R. (1968) *Social Theory and Social Structure*, New York: Free Press.

Mill, J. (1987) *On the Logic of the Moral Sciences*, London: Duckworth.

Miller, D. (1995) 'Propensities and Indeterminism', in A. O'Hear (ed.) *Karl Popper: Philosophy and Problems*, Cambridge: Cambridge University Press.

Mishra, R. (1981) *Society and Social Policy*, Basingstoke: Macmillan.

Moore, G. ([1903] 1959) *Principia Ethica*, Cambridge: Cambridge University Press.

Morgan, G. (ed.) (1983) *Beyond Method: Strategies for Social Research*, Beverly Hills, CA: Sage.

Morley, D. (ed.) (1978) *The Sensitive Scientist*, London: SCM.

Morris, D. (1967) *The Naked Ape*, New York: McGraw-Hill.

Morris, L. and Lyon, S. (eds) (1996) *Gender Relations in Public and Private: New Research Perspectives*, Basingstoke: Macmillan.

Mulkay, M. (1991) *Sociology of Science: A Sociological Pilgrimage*, Buckingham: Open University Press.

Murie, A. (1983) *Housing Inequality and Deprivation*, London: Heinemann.

Nagel, E. (1979) *The Structure of Science: Problems in the Logic of Scientific Explanation*, Indianapolis, IN: Hackett.

Nagel, T. (1986) *The View from Nowhere*, Oxford: Oxford University Press.

Nandy, A. (ed.) (1988) *Science, Hegemony and Violence: A Requiem for Modernity*, New Delhi: Oxford India.

Natanson, M. (ed.) (1963) *Philosophy of the Social Sciences*, New York: Random House.

Neuman, W. (1994) *Social Research Methods: Qualitative and Quantitative Approaches*, Boston, MA: Allyn & Bacon.

Newton-Smith, W. (1981) *The Rationality of Science*, London: Routledge & Kegan Paul.

Nisbet, R. (1970) *The Sociological Tradition*, London: Heinemann.

Nozick, R. (1974) *Anarchy, State and Utopia*, Oxford: Blackwell.

O'Hear, A. (1980) *Karl Popper*, London: Routledge & Kegan Paul.

—— (ed.) (1995) *Karl Popper: Philosophy and Problems*, Cambridge: Cambridge University Press.

Outhwaite, W. (1975) *Understanding Social Life: The Method Called Verstehen*, London: Allen & Unwin.

Papineau, D. (1978) *For Science in the Social Sciences*, London: Macmillan.

—— (1993) *Philosophical Naturalism*, Oxford: Blackwell.

Passerini, E. and Bahr, D. (1997) 'Collective Behavior Following Disasters: A Cellular Automaton Model' in R. Eve, S. Horsfall, M. Lee (eds) *Chaos, Complexity and Sociology*, Thousand Oaks, CA: Sage.

Passmore, J. (1978) *Science and its Critics*, London: Duckworth.

Pawson, R. (1989) *A Measure for Measures: A Manifesto for Empirical Sociology*, London: Routledge.

Perutz, M. (1991) *Is Science Necessary? Essays on Science and Scientists*, Oxford: Oxford University Press.

Pettigrew, T. (1996) *How to Think Like a Social Scientist*, New York: Harper Collins.

Pettit, P. (1993) 'Naturalism' in J. Dancy and E. Sosa (eds) *A Companion to Epistemology*, Oxford: Blackwell.

Philips, D. (1987) *Philosophy, Science and Social Inquiry: Contemporary Methodological Controversies in Social Science and Related Applied Fields of Research*, Oxford: Pergamon.

Poincaré, H. (1913) *The Foundations of Science*, Lancaster, PA: Science Press.

Popper, K. (1959) *The Logic of Scientific Discovery*, London: Routledge.

—— (1979) *Objective Knowledge: An Evolutionary Approach*, Oxford: Oxford University Press.

—— (1985) *Realism and the Aim of Science: Postscript to the Logic of Scientific Discovery*, London: Routledge.

—— (1986) *Unended Quest: An Intellectual Autobiography*, London: Fontana.

—— (1989) *Objective Knowledge: An Evolutionary Approach*, Oxford: Clarendon.

—— (1994) *Knowledge and the Body Mind Problem: In Defence of Interactionism*, edited by M.A. Notturno, London: Routledge.

Price, R. (1997) 'The Myth of Postmodern Science' in R. Eve, S. Horsfall and M. Lee (eds) *Chaos, Complexity and Sociology*, Thousand Oaks, CA: Sage.

Purkhardt, S. (1993) *Transforming Social Representations: A Social Psychology of Common Sense and Science*, London: Routledge.

Putnam, H. (1997) 'Beyond the Fact/Value Dichotomy' in A. Tauber (ed.) *Science and the Quest for Reality*, London: Macmillan.

Quine, W. ([1951] 1961) *From a Logical Point of View*, 2nd edn, New York: Harper.

Rabinow, P. and Sullivan, M. (eds) (1979) *Interpretive Social Science – A Reader*, Berkeley, CA: University of California Press.

Rae, A. (1986) *Quantum Physics: Illusion or Reality?*, Cambridge: Canto.

Randall, J. (1960) *Aristotle*, New York: Basic Books.

Rawls, J. (1971) *A Theory of Justice*, Oxford: Oxford University Press.

Reichenbach, H. (1978) *Selected Writings, 1909–53*, edited by H. Reichenbach and R. Cohen, Dordrecht: Reidel.

Renzetti, C.M. and Lee, R. (eds) (1993) *Researching Sensitive Topics*, London: Sage.

Rescher, N. (1993) 'Idealism' in J. Dancy and E. Sosa (eds) *Blackwell Companion to Epistemology*, Oxford: Blackwell.

Reynolds, V. (1980) *The Biology of Human Action*, Oxford: Freeman.

Richards, R. (1997) 'Theories of Scientific Change' in A. Tauber (ed.) *Science and the Quest for Reality*, London: Macmillan.

Riley, G. (ed.) (1974) *Values, Objectivity and the Social Sciences*, Reading, MA: Adison-Wesley.

Roberts, D. (1991) 'Introduction' in D. Roberts and R. Chester, *Molecular Genetics in Medicine*, Basingstoke: Macmillan.

Robins, D. and Cohen, P. (1978) *Knuckle Sandwich: Growing up in the Working-Class City*, Harmondsworth: Penguin.

Rose, H. (1983) 'Hand Brain and Heart: A Feminist Epistemology for the Natural Sciences', *Signs* 9: 73–90.

Rose, S., Lewontin, R. and Kamin, L. (1984) *Not Our Genes: Biology, Ideology and Human Nature*, Harmondsworth: Penguin.

Rosenau, P. (1992) *Post-Modernism and the Social Sciences: Insights, Inroads and Intrusions*, Princeton, NJ: Princeton University Press.

Rosenberg, A. (1988) *Philosophy of Social Science*, Oxford: Clarendon.

Roszak, T. ([1968] 1995) *The Making of a Counter Culture: Reflections on the Technocratic Society and Its Youthful Opposition*, Berkeley, CA: University of California Press.

Rouzé, M. (1965) *Robert Oppenheimer: The Man and his Theories*, New York: Paul Eriksson.

Ruben, D.-H. (1998) 'Social Properties and their Basis' in T. May and M. Williams (eds) *Knowing the Social World*, Buckingham: Open University Press.

Ruelle, D. (1991) *Chance and Chaos*, Harmonsworth: Penguin.

Runciman, W. (ed.) (1978) *Weber: Selections in Translation*, edited by E. Matthews, Cambridge: Cambridge University Press.

Russell, B. (1979) *A History of Western Philosophy*, London: Unwin Hyman.

—— (1991) 'Einstein's Law of Gravitation' in T. Ferris (ed.) *The World Treasury of Physics, Astronomy and Mathematics*: Boston, MA: Little, Brown.

Sagan, C. (1980) *Cosmos*, New York: Random House.

—— (1996) *The Demon Haunted World: Science as a Candle in the Dark*, London: Headline.

Sagan, C. and Druyan, A. (1996) 'House on Fire' in C. Sagan *The Demon Haunted World: Science as a Candle in the Dark*, London: Headline.

Sanitt, N. (1996) *Science as a Questioning Process*, Bristol: Institute of Physics.

Sapperstein, A. (1995) 'War and Chaos', *American Scientist* 83: 548–57.

Sarup, M. (1993) *An Introductory Guide to Post-Structuralism and Postmodernism*, Hemel Hempstead: Harvester Wheatsheaf.

Schumpeter, J. (1965) 'Is the History of Economics a History of Ideologies?' in D. Braybrooke (ed.) *Philosophical Problems of the Social Sciences*, New York: Macmillan.

Schutz, A. (1965) 'The Social World and the Theory of Social Action' in D. Braybrooke (ed.) *Philosophical Problems of the Social Sciences*, New York: Macmillan.

—— ([1932] 1967) *The Phenomenology of the Social World*, Chicago, IL: North Western University Press.

Scriven, M. (1964) 'Views of Human Nature' in T. Wann (ed.) *Behaviorism and Phenomenology: Contrasting Bases for Modern Psychology*, Chicago, IL: Chicago University Press.

Searle, J. (1984) *Minds, Brains and Behavior*, Cambridge, MA: Harvard University Press.

Shapin, S. (1979) 'The Politics of Observation: Cerebral Anatomy and Social Interests in the Edinburgh Phrenology Disputes' in R. Wallis (ed.) *On the Margins of Science: The Social Construction of Rejected Knowledge*, Sociological Review Mongraph 27, Keele: University of Keele.

Sharrock, W. and Anderson, R. (1986) *The Ethnomethodologists*, London: Tavistock.

Shiva, V. (1988) 'Reductionist Science as Epistemological Violence' in A. Nandy (ed.) *Science, Hegemony and Violence: A Requiem for Modernity*, New Delhi: Oxford India.

Skinner, Q. (ed.) (1985) *The Return of Grand Theory in the Human Sciences*, Cambridge: Canto.

Smart, J. (1984) *Ethics, Persuasion and Truth*, London: Routledge & Kegan Paul.

Smart, J. and Williams, B. (1973) *Utilitarianism: For and Against*, Cambridge: Cambridge University Press.

Smith, A. ([1776] 1970) *The Wealth of Nations*, Harmondsworth: Penguin.

Smith, T. (1997) 'Nonlinear Dynamics and the Micro-Macro Bridge' in R. Eve, S. Horsfall and M. Lee (eds) *Chaos, Complexity and Sociology*, Thousand Oaks, CA: Sage.

Smith, T. and Stevens, G. (1997) 'Biological Foundations of Social Interaction: Computational Explorations of Nonlinear Dynamics in Arousal-Modulation' in R. Eve, S. Horsfall and M. Lee (eds) *Chaos, Complexity and Sociology*, Thousand Oaks, CA: Sage.

Snow, C. (1959) *The New Men*, Penguin: Harmondsworth.

Sokal, A. and Bricmont, J. (1997) *Intellectual Impostures*, London: Profile.

Steiner, G. (1989) *Real Presences*, London: Faber & Faber.

Stokes, G. (1998) *Popper: Philosophy, Politics and Scientific Method*, Cambridge: Polity.

Strauss, L. (1963) 'Natural Right and the Distinction Between Facts and Values' in M. Natanson (ed.) *Philosophy of the Social Sciences*, New York: Random House.

Swingewood, A. (1991) *A Short History of Sociological Thought*, London: Macmillan.

Tacq, J. (1997) *Multivariate Analysis Techniques in Social Science Research*, London: Sage.

Tallis, R. (1995) *Newton's Sleep: Two Cultures and Two Kingdoms*, London: Macmillan.

Tarnas, R. (1991) *The Passion of the Western Mind: Understanding the Ideas that Have Shaped Our World View*, London: Pimlico.

Tauber, A. (ed.) (1997) *Science and the Quest for Reality*, London: Macmillan.

Taylor, C. (1994) 'Interpretation and the Sciences of Man' in M. Martin and L. McIntyre (eds) *Readings in the Philosophy of Social Science*, Cambridge, MA: MIT Press.

Taylor, K. (1994) 'Suspected Vertical Transfer of BSE', *Veterinary Record* 12 (February): 175.

Taylor, R. (1983) *Metaphysics* 3rd edn, Englewood Cliffs, CA: Prentice Hall.

Thomas, W. (1985)*Mill*, Oxford: Oxford University Press.

Thrift, N. (1996) *Spatial Formations*, London: Sage.

Tolstoy, I. (1990) *The Knowledge and the Power: Reflections on the History of Science*, Edinburgh: Canongate.

Trigg, R. (1993) *Rationality and Science: Can Science Explain Everything?*, Oxford: Blackwell.

Vertovek, S. (1994) 'Multi-Cultural, Multi-Asian, Multi-Muslim Leicester: Dimensions of Social Complexity, Ethnic Organisation and Local Government Interface', *Innovation* 7 (3): 259–76.

Visvanathan, S. (1988) 'On the Annals of the Laboratory State' in A. Nandy (ed.) *Science, Hegemony and Violence: A Requiem for Modernity*, New Delhi: Oxford India.

von Cranach, M. (ed.) (1979) *Human Ethology*, Cambridge: Cambridge University Press.

Wallis, R. (ed.) (1979) *On the Margins of Science: The Social Construction of Rejected Knowledge*, Sociological Review Monograph 27, Keele: University of Keele.

Wann, T. (ed.) (1964) *Behaviorism and Phenomenology: Contrasting Bases for Modern Psychology*, Chicago, IL: Chicago University Press.

Ward Schofield, J. (1993) 'Increasing the Generalizability of Quantitative Research' in M. Hammersley (ed.) *Social Research, Philosophy, Politics and Practice*, London: Sage.

Watson, J. (1968) *The Double Helix*, New York: Mentor Books.

Weber, M. ([1922] 1947) *The Theory of Social and Economic Organisation*, New York: Oxford University Press.

—— (1949) *The Methodology of the Social Sciences*, Glencoe, IL: Free Press.

—— ([1904] 1958) *The Protestant Ethic and the Spirit of Capitalism*, New York: Scribners.

—— (1974) ' "Objectivity" in Social Science and Social Policy' in G. Riley (ed.) *Values, Objectivity and the Social Sciences*, Reading, MA: Adison-Wesley.

—— ([1925] 1978a) *Economy and Society: An Outline of Interpretive Sociology*, New York: Bedminster.

—— (1978b) 'The Nature of Social Action' in W. Runciman (ed.) *Weber: Selections in Translation*, edited by E. Matthews, Cambridge: Cambridge University Press.

Weber, R.L. (1973) *A Random Walk in Science*, Bristol: Institute of Physics.

Wellings, K., Field, J., Johnson, A. and Wadsworth, J. (1994) *Sexual Behaviour in Britain*, Harmondsworth: Penguin.

Westfall, R. (1980) *Never at Rest: A Biography of Isaac Newton*, Cambridge: Cambridge University Press.

Weston, A. (1992) *A Rulebook for Arguments*, Indianapolis, IN: Hackett.

Whitehead, A. (1997) 'The Origins of Modern Science' in A. Tauber (ed.) *Science and the Quest for Reality*, London: Macmillan.

Whorf, B. (1956) *Language, Thought and Reality*, edited by J. Carroll, New York: Wiley.

Whyte, W. (1943) *Street Corner Society*, Chicago, IL: Chicago University Press.

Williams, M. (1998) 'The Social World as Knowable', in T. May and M. Williams (eds) *Knowing the Social World*, Buckingham: Open University Press.

Williams, M. and Champion, T. (1998) 'Cornwall, Poverty and In Migration', *Cornish Studies* (2nd Series) 6: 118–26.

Williams, M. and May, T. (1996) *Introduction to Philosophy of Social Research*, London: UCL Press.

Wilson, E . (1975) *Sociobiology*, Cambridge, MA: Harvard University Press.

—— (1978) *On Human Nature*, Cambridge, MA: Harvard University Press.

Winch, P. ([1958] 1990) *The Idea of a Social Science and its Relation to Philosophy*, London: Routledge.

Wolpert, L. (1992) *The Unnatural Nature of Science*, London: Faber.

Woolgar, S. (ed.) (1988) *Knowledge and Reflexivity: New Frontiers in Sociology of Knowledge*, London: Sage.

Worrall, J. and Currie, G. (eds) (1978) *Imre Lakatos, Philosophical Papers*, vol. 2, *Mathematics, Science and Epistemology*, Cambridge: Cambridge University Press.

Name Index

Subject Index